NATIONAL ISSUES IN EDUCATION

THE PAST IS PROLOGUE

John F. Jennings, Editor

Published by
Phi Delta Kappa International
Bloomington, Indiana
and
The Institute for Educational Leadership
Washington, D.C.

Cover design
by
Victoria Voelker

Library of Congress Catalog Card Number 93-83803
ISBN 0-87367-460-X
Copyright © 1993 by Phi Delta Kappa and
The Institute for Educational Leadership

Table of Contents

PART III. EDUCATION RESEARCH

PART IV. EDUCATION FUNDING

Preface

Phi Delta Kappa and the Institute for Educational Leadership are pleased to co-publish *National Issues in Education: The Past Is Prologue.* The purpose of this volume is to present diverse perspectives on current major education issues at the national level, particularly as these issues have played out and will play out in the legislative process in the U.S. Congress.

Too often, interesting and informative lessons are lost as institutional memories quickly fade and key participants flow in and out of the ever-fluid legislative scene in the nation's capital. Our hope and belief is that this publication on school reform, postsecondary education, education research, and education funding issues will be a timely and informative contribution that will not only illuminate the legislative process and the workings of interest groups but also increase understanding of some of the most salient problems confronting American education.

The issues on which this volume focuses reflect the continuity of the legislative and policy-making process. Although a new national administration has just assumed office and the winds of change are certainly blowing, impending legislative deliberations will in no small way be shaped by earlier discussions and debates on education issues in the U.S. Congress.

We would like to thank Jack Jennings, general counsel for education, Committee on Education and Labor, U.S. House of Representatives, for conceiving the idea for this joint venture and for his willingness to serve as editorial coordinator for the book.

We hope that this publication will be used in classrooms throughout the country, as well as for general discussion among educators, policy makers, business and political leaders, the general public, and others interested in the shaping and implementation of education policy at an exciting time of transition in the nation's capital.

Jack Kosoy
President, Phi Delta Kappa

Michael D. Usdan
President, The Institute for Educational Leadership

Introduction

When President Ronald Reagan received the *Nation at Risk* report at the White House in 1983, he in effect disclaimed any federal responsibility for school reform and instead urged the states to improve schooling. The states responded vigorously by toughening high school graduation requirements, raising teacher salaries, and demanding greater accountability for results.

By 1988, however, the American people had become so concerned about the condition of public schooling that a passive attitude about education on the part of the federal government was no longer acceptable to the electorate. Consequently, George Bush, Reagan's Vice-President, changed direction and campaigned for President pledging to make education a priority. Once elected, President Bush reversed Reagan's budget policy of asking for cutbacks or freezes in federal spending on education. He also proposed two different education reform initiatives, although neither was approved by Congress.

In 1992, Bill Clinton won the presidency, promising to improve America's long-term economic prospects and repeatedly asserting that new federal education and job-training programs were essential in that undertaking. Congress today is grappling with the Clinton program of education reform.

The last decade, therefore, has witnessed a sharp reversal in the federal government's attitude toward education. Reagan believed that the national government was part of the problem and ought to get out of the way of the states so that they could improve their schools. Bush, and much more so Clinton, believed that there is a role for the federal government in making schools better.

It is interesting that four of the governors who were most active in reforming education in their states in the 1980s then moved to the national level in the 1990s to seek ways for the federal government to help. Lamar Alexander, former governor of Tennessee, became Bush's second Secretary of Education. Clinton of Arkansas, of course, became President. Clinton chose another progressive southern governor, Dick Riley of South Carolina, to become his Secretary of Education; and Clinton chose Madeleine Kunin, former governor of Vermont, to become the Deputy Secretary of Education.

Clearly, the federal government is moving into a more active role in education; and the debate at the national level is affecting the way that states, school districts, and colleges approach the problems of education. Consequently, Phi Delta Kappa and the Institute for Educational Leadership felt the time was appropriate to bring the national debate more thoroughly into classrooms, homes, and meeting places. That is the purpose of this publication.

This volume will present four major education issues that were debated at the national level during 1991 and 1992 and will again be the subject of legislative attention in 1993 and 1994. The issues are school reform, postsecondary education, education research, and education funding.

For each issue, the usual format will be to have a writer representing the President, a writer representing Congress, and then representatives of national organizations or experts from the private sector. Since President Bush, a Republican, was in office in 1991 and 1992, the first presenters will represent the perspectives of high-ranking officials in his Administration. Since the other party, the Democrats, controlled both the Senate and House of Representatives in those years, the second presenters will be prominent committee or subcommittee chairmen or senior staff. The last two presenters, from outside government, were chosen to reflect other major points of view on each issue.

The writers were asked, if at all possible, to comment on these issues as they were considered in Washington in legislative form. The reason for that request is that ideas must be made more precise when written in legislative bills, and therefore the debate can be more concrete and instructive.

Some people may wonder why PDK and IEL are publishing this volume devoted to questions argued about during the last two years. Instead, why isn't there a publication based on the ideas of the new Clinton Administration and reactions to those concepts?

One reason is that, at the time this volume was being put together, most of Clinton's ideas for education were just being fleshed out. During a presidential campaign, the issues usually are phrased very generally; they have to be made more explicit once the new Administration takes the reins of power.

But more importantly, the nature of policy making must be understood. Washington, D.C. has been called a continuous debating society. That remark can be understood negatively to mean "all talk and no action."

To look at the comment more positively, however, is to understand that there are no abrupt starts and stops in discussions leading to the adoption of policies. Arguments based on ideas and politics are constantly being made in Congress, in the executive branch, among organizations, and very importantly in the different forums used to bring together the various actors from each of these arenas.

Thus many of President Clinton's ideas for education will grow out of the debates and experiences of the recent past. To fully understand those ideas, one must appreciate that history.

Another important point to bear in mind is that many of the characters who participated in these debates in 1991 and 1992 will remain involved in the future, even though their jobs may change. In other words, as the discussions continue, the debaters frequently change chairs. For instance, Congressman Leon Panetta was asked to contribute an article for this publication on federal budget policy as it affects education. Mr. Panetta wrote that piece as chairman of the Budget Committee of the U.S. House of Representatives. Mr. Panetta is now President Clinton's Director of the Office of Management and Budget, one of the most powerful positions in the executive branch of the federal government. So Mr. Panetta left Congress for the executive branch, but in his new position he certainly continues to be an important participant in the decision making that affects education.

All of the individuals who contributed to this publication have given freely and generously of their time and talents. I know they share with me the belief that it is important to document the history of the recent past while it is still fresh in our recollections. We hope that our efforts will better inform Americans about the national issues in education and to help us all find more effective ways to improve education.

John F. (Jack) Jennings
Editorial Coordinator
January 1993

PART I.
SCHOOL REFORM

What We Were Doing When We Were Interrupted

By Lamar Alexander

Lamar Alexander was nominated as U.S. Secretary of Education by President Bush in January of 1991 and was unanimously confirmed by the Senate in March. Immediately before taking office as ED Secretary, Alexander was president of the University of Tennessee, a position he had held since July 1988. He served as governor of Tennessee from 1979 to 1987. As chairman of the National Governors' Association, he led the 50-state education survey, Time for Results. *In 1988 the Education Commission of the States gave him the James B. Conant Award for "distinguished national leadership in education."*

Mr. Alexander is a Phi Beta Kappa graduate of Vanderbilt University and was a law review editor at New York University. He was born July 3, 1940. He and his wife, Honey, have four children: Drew, Leslee, Kathryn, and Will.

When the dust settles and the history books are written, President George Bush's leadership in education will be recognized as among his most significant and lasting contributions.

My definition of presidential leadership is the one George Reedy, Lyndon Johnson's press secretary, used in his book, *Twilight of the Presidency.* Reedy said that a President, aside from his responsibilities as commander in chief, should do three things: 1) see a few urgent needs, 2) develop a strategy to meet each of those needs, and 3) persuade at least half the people that he is right.

By this standard, President Bush did for education what a President can uniquely do: He helped to set a national agenda and make things happen. Because he did this for the most part in bipartisan partnership with the nation's governors, the agenda he has helped to set will be the American education agenda for the rest of this century.

More Was Going on Than You Thought

That agenda begins with the six National Education Goals, established in 1989 in Charlottesville by the President and all of the governors. Next, in April 1991, came the America 2000 strategy to mobilize the country, community by community, toward meeting those goals. By December 1992, more than 2,700 communities in every state were working together on the goals in the monthly America 2000 Satellite TV Town Meetings.

In addition to the America 2000 community effort, the President's agenda included a series of truly radical initiatives designed to create a framework within which parents, business leaders, teachers, and others within the community can more easily change the schools to help them fit today's families. These initiatives were: 1) a new set of national standards in core curriculum subjects, including science, history, English, geography, arts, civics, and foreign languages (math already was done); 2) a voluntary national examination system geared to those new standards; 3) a new generation of thousands of start-from-scratch, "break-the-mold," or charter schools; 4) giving teachers more autonomy and flexibility in their classrooms by waiving federal rules and regulations; and 5) a GI Bill for Children to give middle- and low-income families $1,000 scholarships to spend at any lawfully operated school of their choice, giving those parents more of the same choices wealthy parents already have.

An Agenda for the Rest of the Century

This agenda will not disappear with the arrival of a new Administration. President-elect Clinton helped write the National Education Goals. A bipartisan National Education Goals Panel of governors, members of Congress, and Administration officials has been created to monitor progress toward the goals until the year 2000. Forty-four states, including Arkansas, have created their own America 2000 state efforts. The goals panel will continue the monthly America 2000 Satellite Town Meetings. The America 2000 Coalition of more than 80 nonprofit organizations and business groups from bankers to nurses to the Boy and Girl Scouts has been formed to help communities succeed.

Seven task forces, created to develop the new national academic standards, are funded and are scheduled to complete their work by 1994-95. States and the private sector, stimulated by the goals panel, already are working on new performance-based achievement tests geared to the standards. The New American Schools Development Corporation has raised

4

$50 million to fund 11 design teams who will help communities create break-the-mold schools; more than 200 more design teams that were not funded have announced their intention to continue their work. California and Minnesota have passed charter schools legislation. Charter school initiatives have been or will be introduced in Arizona, Colorado, Connecticut, Florida, Massachusetts, Michigan, New Jersey, and Tennessee.

Congress did not approve the President's proposal to relieve the inflexibility of federal rules on classroom teachers, but it almost certainly will do so in 1993. In the meantime, states such as Ohio and Texas have moved ahead of the federal government in getting government off the backs of teachers. Neither did Congress approve the President's GI Bill for Children, but the idea remains powerful, even inevitable, for it commands 70% support in public opinion surveys. Giving tax dollars to parents instead of to schools as a way to change schools and help pay for the changes will be hard to suppress permanently.

Finally, federal spending and program priorities have been rearranged to focus on the National Education Goals and the President's larger agenda for change. For example, Head Start is one of the most powerful aids to Goal One, that all children should arrive at school ready to learn. As a result, during the four Bush years, funding for Head Start more than doubled, making the program available to all eligible 4-year-olds whose parents want them to participate. Two billion dollars in federal funding were refocused on math and science, especially teacher training, a critical element in helping reach the higher standards envisioned by Goals 3 and 4. A new $100 billion, five-year Higher Education Act increased to record levels the number of grants and loans available to college students and the funding for them. These grants and loans help support Goal 5 workforce training objectives.

Congress did not approve the President's proposal for large new increases in federal spending that would have supported his agenda for change. The President had recommended spending more than a half-billion dollars during the next three years to help communities retool the first 535 "break-the-mold" schools. He also proposed a half-billion dollars to begin giving federal scholarships to parents under the GI Bill for Children. Ironically, those two programs — for "break-the-mold schools" and the GI Bill for Children — were the largest new proposals for federal spending to help local schools since 1965, when the Chapter 1 program began. This could have been the beginning of two entirely new long-term methods of using federal funds to help pay for

The New Congress

In 1993 Congress will be considering the five-year renewal of the Elementary and Secondary Education Act. In plain English, this means that Congress will be setting federal rules that will govern 110,000 local schools until the end of the century.

In order to do that wisely, here is what I believe a member of Congress should vote for:

• Support for a new generation of American schools. School reform has been piecemeal. Communities need to begin comprehensive reforms in education, including the development and implementation of thousands of "break-the-mold" or charter schools.

• World-class standards and voluntary national tests. Setting goals for performance in education is essential to the reform of education. Developing world-class standards of achievement in core subject areas, and encouraging voluntary national examinations to determine progress in reaching these standards, will be essential to reaching the National Goals for Education.

• Cutting red tape — getting government off the backs of teachers and principals. This includes developing a broad waiver authority for the U.S. Secretary of Education, as well as providing flexibility in federal rules and regulations to states and localities in exchange for high program performance and accountability.

• New options for teacher training and certification. Educational reform will not happen without the outstanding teaching, leadership, and support of our nation's teachers. Retraining should be available to teachers and school leaders to update subject knowledge to meet the highest standards, as well as to increase administrative expertise in facilitating reform.

• Giving families more choices of all schools. Choice is a key component of educational reform. Every parent and child in the United States should have more educational options open to them. The GI Bill for Children would provide additional funds to give middle- and low-income families more of the same choices of all schools that wealthier families already have.

• Encouraging the private sector to help improve schools. The rich, creative, American private sector is constantly at work helping to create the best colleges and universities in the world. It should be just as hard at work for our schools.

local schools, namely, funds to help redesign and retool thousands of New American Schools and funds to give hundreds of thousands of families dollars to spend at schools that serve the children who need help the most. Yet, ironically, these two proposals (which were supported in Congress by conservatives) were defeated by those who insist that what schools mainly need is more money from the federal government! The problem seemed to be that the new federal money threatened to bring with it more change than those in charge of our schools could stomach. Even without enactment of these two proposals, federal spending for education during the Bush presidency increased more rapidly than state and local spending. And in 1992, President Bush advocated more new federal discretionary dollars to go into the relatively tiny Education Department than into any other department.

More Change Than Those in Charge Could Stomach

Whether this much change really is necessary is still — 10 years after *A Nation at Risk* — the central issue before us. On one side are those who believe that polite changes in the existing structure plus a lot more money will do most of what needs to be done in education. The view of President Bush, most governors of both political parties, and a growing number of Americans is that we must construct an entirely new and radically different education system over time — as well as rethink community and family responsibilities toward children — if those children are to be able to learn enough to live, work, and compete in the world the way it is today and will be tomorrow.

That difference of opinion crystallizes the issue that is at the core of most of the school debate: Who shall have control? For example, creating break-the-mold schools transfers more control of school structure, standards, and policy to the community at large. So does the process of setting national academic standards and examinations geared to those standards. The 541 organizations in Washington with "education" in their names have thus far persuaded Congress not to transfer to classroom teachers more control over the spending of federal dollars. To be more precise, the president of the National Education Association in a National Public Radio debate refused to go with me to ask Congress to give his own teacher-members more freedom to spend federal dollars in the way they think best helps children in their classrooms.

The biggest control arguments of all are whether to involve private companies in the management of some schools or school functions, and whether to transfer to parents more control of the school their child attends. All of these efforts would restrict the control now enjoyed by unions, government bureaucracies, local education monopolies, Congress, Congressional staff aides, and the 541 lobbying groups in Washington. The proposed shifts of control would generally give more power to parents, classroom teachers, community groups, the private sector, and citizens at large. Today's school debate is primarily about who should have control of an enterprise that now spends more than the nation does on defense, and that most Americans believe has more to do with our future than any other enterprise: the education of our children.

These proposed changes of control would produce truly wrenching changes in the American system of education. That is why the prospect of these changes produced enormous resistance within the education community, especially during the 1992 presidential elections. It had become obvious that if the President were re-elected, he would have insisted on his agenda during the 1993 reauthorization of the Elementary and Secondary Education Act. Because of the respect Americans generally have for their educators, this resistance within the education community created widespread skepticism about the President's policies within the community at large. So, despite the fact that rhetoric for "real change" was a dominant theme in the 1992 elections, the specific education changes advocated by the President turned out to be more change than most Americans were comfortable with. About the only thing all those arguing seemed to agree upon was that these changes, if they were enacted, would produce schools that by the end of the decade would only faintly resemble the schools we have today.

To understand more fully why we still believe such radical changes are necessary, how and where the movement to cause these changes began, and where it had advanced when the voters interrupted the President in November 1992, it is useful to step back to the early 1980s and to the publication of *A Nation At Risk*.

A Nation at Risk: 1983

In 1980 I was governor of Tennessee. I recall the Democratic legislative leaders coming to my office to talk about their resolution creating a commission to look at our state's education system.

I asked them, "Will this be just another resolution and commission, or will we take this seriously and appoint the best people and do what they say we need done?"

8

We agreed that it was time for a serious look at education. Together we appointed a bipartisan commission of the state's most outstanding citizens and legislators. One year later, this commission produced a sweeping blueprint for change. Based upon that work, in January 1983 I proposed a 10-point "Better Schools Program."

It was into this environment that the U.S. Education Department's report, *A Nation At Risk*, appeared in March 1983. The report triggered a national alarm about what our children knew and were able to do. I know that in our state the report helped galvanize support for more change in our schools, as well as our attitudes, than most observers had thought was possible.

The elements of Tennessee's "Better Schools Program" were like those that began to appear in state after state: a focus on basic skills and the core curriculum, new kinds of assessments so we could know what children were learning, computers in the schools, alternative schools for disruptive children, Governor's Schools in the summer for gifted children, across-the-board teacher pay raises as well as a new career ladder to pay teachers more for teaching well, higher admissions standards at universities, centers and chairs of excellence at the universities, expansion of community colleges and new focus on workforce skills, and tax increases to pay the bill for the new initiatives.

The National Education Association fiercely opposed the career ladder (although the American Federation of Teachers was open to it). I vetoed all teacher pay raises one year and promised to veto such raises every year in order to force passage of the career ladder. For two years, I spent more than half my time working to enact these legislative reforms. It was my first lesson in how real change in the education system can be difficult even for a single-minded governor.

The Governors' Year of Education: "Time for Results"

Governors in almost every state were learning the same lessons. By 1985-86, interest in school reform had grown so that the nation's governors did something they never had done before: They devoted an entire year to a single subject — education. I was chairman of the National Governors' Association that year. Bill Clinton of Arkansas was vice-chairman. All of us had become convinced that, in the midst of a world of change, American education seemed to be stepping forward briskly in the same old ruts. So we sought to change the agenda.

The agenda of the Seventies had been mostly desegregation and more money. The agenda that the governors sought to make the national education agenda of the future is reflected in the following seven questions that we asked:

1. Why not pay teachers more for teaching well?
2. What can be done to attract, train, and reward excellent school leaders?
3. Why not let parents choose the schools their children attend?
4. Aren't there ways to help poor children with weak preparation to succeed in school?
5. Why are expensive school buildings closed half the year when children are behind in their studies and many classrooms are overcrowded?
6. Why shouldn't schools use the newest technologies for learning?
7. How much are college students really learning?

The governors divided into seven task forces to consider these questions. We issued our answers and recommendations in 1986, calling it "Time for Results: The 1991 Report," because we pledged to follow the progress on answering those seven questions for five years. I said at the time, and the major premise of the report was, "The Governors are ready for some old-fashioned horse trading. We'll regulate less if schools and school districts will produce better results."

Leadership: Setting the Agenda, Making Things Happen

Governors began to discover that if they set a limited education agenda, presented their arguments in a compelling way, and leaned into it with everything they had for as long as they were in office, they could wear everyone else out. They also found that governors, with the exception of a few business people like Ross Perot in Texas, were really the only individuals with sufficient authority to build coalitions powerful enough to challenge the education establishment, which was at first surprised by and then generally resistant to many of the changes that the governors and business leaders proposed.

By the time of the 1988 presidential election, almost every governor was describing himself or herself as an "education governor." State spending for elementary and secondary education had nearly doubled during the previous decade. George Bush announced in the midst of his campaign that he intended to be the "Education President."

In 1988 George Bush was elected President. (I had become president of the University of Tennessee.) Shortly after his election, during a meeting of university presidents, I remember the President asking,

10

"If we have the best colleges, why not the best schools?" In that meeting we discussed the possibility of an education summit. I suggested keeping the summit small, limiting it to the chief executives of our nation: the President and the governors. I also reminded the President of George Reedy's advice about seeing a few urgent needs, developing strategies to reach them, and working hard to persuade at least half the people that he is right.

Reedy's formula was the kind of agenda-setting leadership the governors had been practicing during the 1980s as they worked through state-by-state solutions to the seven questions we had asked ourselves in "Time for Results." It would become the basis for the same kind of leadership when in October 1989 the governors and the President committed themselves to six ambitious National Education Goals and to trying to move the country toward them by the year 2000.

The Summit and the National Education Goals

The summit at the University of Virginia in Charlottesville went remarkably well. Terry Branstad of Iowa, the Chairman of the Governors' Council that year, appointed Governor Clinton of Arkansas and Governor Carroll Campbell of South Carolina to lead the effort. Working with the President's representatives, they came up with the first National Education Goals. The goals were bipartisan, comprehensive, and direct. They spoke to students of all ages and to issues inside and outside the classroom. The governors pledged to go home and go to work moving their states toward the goals.

The goals declared that, by the year 2000:

1. All children in America will start school ready to learn.
2. The high school graduation rate will increase to at least 90%.
3. American students will leave grades 4, 8, and 12 having demonstrated competency in challenging subject matter, including English, mathematics, science, history, and geography; and every school in America will ensure that all students learn to use their minds well, so that they may be prepared for responsible citizenship, further learning, and productive employment in our modern economy.
4. U.S. students will be first in the world in science and mathematics achievement.
5. Every adult American will be literate and will possess the knowledge and skills necessary to compete in a global economy and exercise the rights and responsibilities of citizenship.

11

6. Every school in America will be free of drugs and violence and will offer a disciplined environment conducive to learning.

It could be said that, after a decade of unprecedented school reform, America backed into its goals for the reforms. At the beginning of the 1980s we would have done well to consider guitarist Chet Atkins' advice, "In this life you have to be mighty careful where you aim because you're likely to get there." We finally took the advice, but only after going in circles for a while.

America 2000

I was president of the University of Tennessee in December 1990 when the President telephoned to ask me to be U.S. Education Secretary. To be specific, I was chairing a fairly arcane session on assessment (all sessions on assessment are, to put it charitably, arcane) at Alex Haley's farm when the phone started ringing. First it was John Sununu. Then it was Howard Baker, to whom Sununu had talked. Then the President was on the line asking if I would take the job.

Having had a few hours to collect my thoughts, I asked the President two questions: "First, may I develop a strategy to help the country reach the six National Education Goals and would you then either change or approve the strategy, but at least give me my marching orders? Second, may I then, subject to your OK, recruit a team of men and women capable of carrying out such an ambitious undertaking?" The President said yes to both questions.

So on January 16, 1991, the same night the United States began bombing Baghdad, a few of us met in the Tennessee mountains to consider how the federal government could, in partnership with the governors, accelerate America's effort to reach the National Education Goals by the year 2000. The group included, among others, former Xerox Chairman David Kearns, Vanderbilt Professor Chester (Checker) Finn, former New Jersey Education Commissioner Saul Cooperman, Denis Doyle, and University of Tennessee vice-presidents Michael Nettles and John Rudley.

That process continued during the next several weeks and involved dozens of others — for example, Columbia University Professor Diane Ravitch, ALCOA Chief Executive Officer Paul O'Neill — until March 18, when the U.S. Senate confirmed my nomination. On March 19 our proposal for an America 2000 strategy was at the White House. On March 21 we met with President Bush, and on April 18 he presented his strategy to the nation at a special East Room ceremony.

12

Not only did the President keep his promise to approve a strategy quickly, he allowed me to recruit a really first-class "President's education team" to carry out the strategy, and in some cases he participated in the recruiting. David Kearns' willingness to come to the Education Department as deputy secretary signaled a seriousness of purpose that helped to attract others, such as Diane Ravitch to head research, Carolynn Reid-Wallace from City University of New York to head postsecondary activities, and IBM executive Don Laidlaw for human resources and management. Washington, D.C., attorney Jeff Martin became general counsel; White House Director of Cabinet Affairs Steven Danzansky came as chief of staff; and Vanderbilt University Associate Vice-Chancellor for News and Public Affairs Leslye Arsht became director of communications. Former Labor Secretary Ann McLaughlin was elected president of the private New American Schools Development Corporation. Former U.S. Chamber of Commerce President Ed Donley founded and chaired the nonprofit America 2000 Coalition.

In addition, we found a large number of talented men and women already working at ED who liked the boldness of what we were planning and who especially liked all the presidential attention. Once the President mistakenly referred to the Education Department as "the Department of Energy." He wasn't that wrong. Lights at the department were burning most nights until 10 p.m. as we focused on how to mobilize such a huge, diverse country toward such ambitious goals.

Community by Community

The America 2000 strategy, precisely defined, is a partnership between the President and the governors to help America move community-by-community toward the six National Education Goals by the year 2000. The President was determined that the strategy would be as bipartisan as the formulation of the goals themselves had been. Democratic Governor Donald Schaefer of Maryland endorsed America 2000 the day it was announced. The President and Mrs. Bush traveled to Grand Junction, Colorado, in June 1991 to help Roy Romer, the chairman of the Democratic Governors Association, kick off Colorado 2000, the first of 44 such state efforts. I recall Democratic Governor Ben Nelson of Nebraska, an enthusiastic architect of Omaha and Nebraska 2000, rising at the governors' meeting with the President at the White House in February 1991 and saying, "Mr. President, when you talk about America 2000 please remember to refer to it as a partnership with all the governors, not just as your program."

The President asked every community to become an America 2000 community by doing four things:

1. Adopt the six National Education Goals.
2. Develop a communitywide strategy to achieve them.
3. Design a report card to measure results.
4. Plan for and support a New American School

By December 1991 more than 2,300 communities were working on this challenge. More than 2,700 communities were meeting monthly in the America 2000 Satellite TV Town Meeting.

Some of the President's other proposals for change — notably giving families more choices of all schools, including private schools — proved to be controversial but did not interfere with the America 2000 community efforts. Teachers were involved in every community effort. For example, the Minnesota Education Association joined the Minnesota Business Council and Governor Arne Carlson in launching Minnesota 2000. "We'll all get on the train and have these arguments while we're moving down the tracks," I would tell people. "It won't help the children if we stand around in the train station arguing." For the most part, most people got on the train; and the trains began to move slowly down several tracks at once.

There are four broad tracks to America 2000:

1. For today's students: better and more accountable schools.
2. For tomorrow's students: a new generation of break-the-mold New American Schools.
3. For the rest of us (yesterday's students/today's work force): a nation of students.
4. Communities where learning can happen.

I recall a discussion in the fall of 1991 with one school board member in New Hampshire who said, "I'm disappointed in America 2000. There are not enough details about what to do."

A Concord principal to whom I told this story later in the day said, "That's exactly why America 2000 will work. It leaves to the communities and the teachers the opportunity to fill in the details. It creates a framework within which we all can operate; sometimes that is the hardest thing to do for ourselves."

More Consensus Than Meets the Eye

The acrimony from teachers unions and others over proposals for school choice and private-sector involvement tended to obscure the fact that there had developed a strikingly broad consensus about many of the underlying issues on school reform. At least, this consensus existed outside Washington, D.C.

There was consensus about Problem Number One: Too many people still believed, "The nation's at risk, but I'm OK." There also was growing consensus among those who participated in the reforms of the Eighties that, in retrospect, the reforms looked too timid, too slow, and very expensive given the (lack of) results.

There seemed also to be consensus about why schools needed to change. First, standards were higher. Today's auto workers have to know and be able to do more than yesterday's. Governor Romer often spoke of Americans prepared to pole vault 15 feet with bamboo poles at a time when the rest of the world is jumping 19 feet with fiberglass poles. Second, children are growing up differently. It is harder today to be a teacher, a student, or a parent. Families and communities and schools are unprepared for this and are literally overwhelmed. Third, the schools themselves are designed for our great-grandparents' times — out-of-date, literally in a time warp, too often stymieing teachers and boring children. In inner cities, where parents work until 6 p.m., we still send children home at 3 p.m. to empty houses and give teachers summer vacations to bring in the crops. And fourth, all of us of all ages need to go back to school. Most of us cannot do a child's seventh-grade math homework.

In the 101 communities I visited during my last 18 months in office, I found some other generally held working assumptions:

1. *Made in Washington is not the solution.* Federal recipe books just don't help children in distant classrooms. Congress itself is so dominated by Washington interest groups and so removed from classrooms that its solutions are not much help and sometimes get in the way.

2. *"It takes an entire community to educate one child."* This African proverb is the favorite motto for America 2000 community efforts. I never visited a classroom that was more dangerous than the community in which it existed.

3. *All children can reach reasonably high learning standards.* Most Americans, deep down, don't really believe this; but the most inspiring efforts in American education today are teachers trying to prove that it is true.

4. *Changes in technology will drive many other needed changes.* One hundred years after the invention of the telephone, most teachers do not have easy access to one. At countless schools, I have been inspired

by dedicated teachers; but I often left feeling they had been issued a Model T Ford to compete in the Indianapolis 500.

5. *We are wasting assets and hurting children when we close school buildings.* Almost all break-the-mold school designs have schools open all day, all week, all year. Families choose the times and places and schools their children will attend; the school fits the needs of the family.

Trains Moving Down the Track

The short report card about progress along the new education agenda would say:

1. *The National Education Goals.* Don't underestimate them. As Arianne Williams, a fourth-grader at the Cog Hill Elementary School, said at the kickoff of New Orleans 2000, "These are not the President's goals, these are not the governor's goals, they are the nation's goals."

2. *The America 2000 community effort.* Forty-four states, 2,300 communities working to reach the goals; 2,700 communities meeting monthly in the Satellite TV Town Meeting.

3. *New National Standards by 1994-95.* The task forces are organized and funded. The National Goals Panel now includes members of Congress in its consensus about the need for standards. This will be the most comprehensive rethinking ever of what we teach.

4. *A Voluntary National Examination System.* We've not made as much progress here; but, nevertheless, the system is inevitable. No test maker who wants to stay in business will ignore the new standards; and the Goals Panel will let teachers, school boards, and parents know whether the new tests are really geared to the new higher standards.

5. *Break-the-Mold Schools.* Hold your reins tightly. Nothing will be more powerful in the 1990s than state laws and school boards deciding to give teachers and others the opportunity to start from scratch to design completely new schools and academic programs. Watch California, Minnesota, Pennsylvania, North Carolina, New Jersey. The New American Schools Corporation's design teams are working with hundreds of school districts. The private Edison Project is planning 1,000 new schools. "Break-the mold schools" are not a few experimental schools; this is renewing the entire system over time by starting over, thousands of different times.

6. *Getting government off teachers' backs.* States are loosening the rules so teachers can teach. The federal government will catch up soon.

7. *Giving families more choices of all schools.* My prediction: Choice won't even be an issue at the end of the 1990s. Once America designs

16

thousands of very different new schools and academic programs, we won't *assign* children to them, will we? The schools will *attract* the child. And to make it fair for all families, the federal and state government will have to begin to give scholarships to middle- and low-income families so their children will have more of the same choices wealthy parents do. This new consumer power will help change the schools and pay for the changes.

8. *Involving the private sector in education.* If you are dubious about this, my suggestion is to go to Baltimore, where a courageous superintendent, Walter Amphrey, has hired a private company to help operate nine inner-city public schools. For the same amount of money spent in other Baltimore schools, this public/private partnership is putting two teachers in every classroom, new computer equipment in every school, an individualized education program for every child, and telephones on teachers' desks. And the schools are clean. Why do we use our most creative private-sector minds only when we want to put missiles down smokestacks?

My Education in Public

During the last 18 months I have visited more than 101 communities, in virtually every state. I was in California 20 times. I have received more of an education in this job than I had expected. I am not a professional educator. I became interested in my own education because my parents, who were teachers, and my community valued education. As governor of Tennessee I found that if I wanted to move my state, nothing was more important than improving the schools, colleges, and universities. I next found myself as president of our state university because I did not think Tennessee would succeed without continuing to develop a first-class public university. I felt privileged to be invited by President Bush to be Education Secretary because I agreed with him: If we want to change America, we must change our schools and our attitudes about education.

Most of my time in this job was spent not with politicians but in the schools. You can learn about a community in this way. You can learn a lot about America's future by getting to know its children. I had not expected to find myself at 3 p.m. on a street corner in East Los Angeles with Evelyn Lucero, the principal of Hollenbeck Middle School, watching to discourage gangs from forming as children left school. I did not really know much about the lives of those children until I met them and read their book of poems, "*Adios a La Manana*" ("Farewell to the

17

Morning"). Every American should have the experience I had watching teachers in P.S. 25 in the Bronx helping children from South America learn about George Washington by reminding them about Simon Bolivar. You should have a chance, as I did, to work with Octavio Visiedo, the Dade County (Miami) superintendent, as he developed his "Project Phoenix" after Hurricane Andrew to create 50 new schools that are the best in the world, including high schools open 20 hours a day, elementary schools in hospitals, schools managed by the private sector — any school with high standards that shows promise of helping children the way children are growing up today.

Education has become America's national worry. Creating the best schools in the world for our children is becoming the movement of the 1990s as civil rights became the movement for the 1960s. Gallup surveys show that Americans rate having the best education system far and away first in importance to our country's next 25 years. Response to this concern is coming from all quarters. The Business Roundtable executives have committed to 10 years of priority for our schools. The U.S. Chamber of Commerce is involved in at least 1,000 communities with America 2000 community efforts. The nation's math teachers have taught the country how to create higher standards in essential subjects. The President of the United States invited the New American Schools Development Corporation Board to Camp David for its first meeting. The Advertising Council has launched a campaign to remind us to "Keep the Promise." Ohio jelly maker Tim Smucker told me, "Not one person turned me down when I asked them to be part of Orrville 2000, and I have asked 400 different people."

Each day since the opening of school this fall, I have presented an "A-Plus for Breaking the Mold" award to some school or community that is taking risks to help children. I have done this because I am convinced that by the time our fifth-graders, the Class of 2000, are seniors, our schools should be as different as the children themselves will be. If we want to paint a picture of what America itself will look like in the year 2000, the most accurate picture will be a picture of those schools and those children.

The Nation Is at Even Greater Risk Now

By Senator Edward M. Kennedy

Edward M. Kennedy has represented the Commonwealth of Massachusetts in the United States Senate since 1962. He was educated at Harvard University, the International Law School at The Hague, and the University of Virginia Law School. Senator Kennedy is currently chairman of the Senate Labor and Human Resources Committee. He also serves as a member of the Judiciary, Armed Services, and Joint Economic Committees. He is the recipient of numerous awards for his efforts to reform America's education and health-care systems, strengthen civil rights legislation, and promote nuclear disarmament. Mr. Kennedy is the father of three children and lives in both Boston and Washington with his wife, Vicki.

Thirty years ago, in 1963, in the shadow of the Lincoln Monument, Martin Luther King spoke to the conscience of the country. He talked of the "fierce urgency of *Now*," and urged America to open the doors of opportunity to all children. Twenty years later, in its 1983 report, *A Nation At Risk*, the Commission on Excellence in Education urged the people of America to act quickly on reforming the public schools. On April 26, 1993, as President Clinton completes his first 100 days in office, America will mark the tenth anniversary of that landmark report. The report's famous finding — "The educational foundations of our society are presently being eroded by a rising tide of mediocrity that threatens our very future as a nation and a people" — was part of an open letter to the nation. The commission was confident that the "American people, properly informed, will do what is right for their children and for the generations to come."

Thirty years after Dr. King's passionate plea, ten years after the commission's warning, that confidence is shaken. The "rising tide of mediocrity" has risen higher. *The nation is at even greater risk.* Education remains among the great unsolved national problems facing the new Administration and the new Congress.

We know how to educate children well. Many public schools across the country are succeeding; they make progress with each child, regardless of background or economic status. But the overall goal set out ten years ago — to educate *every* child to a high standard — is still a distant dream. Each year of delay in directing adequate attention to this challenge means the loss of thousands more children, further weakening our society.

Though there have been promising steps forward, the response to *A Nation at Risk* has not resulted in any significant systemic changes in education. In the years following the report, states and local districts across the country added new tests and requirements, mandated more hours of study, and strengthened graduation rules. For the most part, the approach was to achieve change through government regulations, with solutions imposed from the top down. Few reforms were based on emerging research about effective education. The federal response was similarly groundless, lacking a well-conceived plan to attack the problem comprehensively. Not surprisingly, the reforms have done little to change what goes on in the average classroom and thus have produced few results.

Twenty-three million Americans are illiterate. Twenty percent of white and 40% of black male high school graduates do not earn enough to support a family of four above the poverty line. Reading scores for white students remained essentially unchanged during the past 10 years; scores for black students had been going up during the decade, but now have begun to decline again. The gap between advantaged and disadvantaged students had been closing, but is now widening. Twenty-four percent of all college mathematics courses are still remedial. Even the most elite colleges are concerned about the high school preparation their entering students have received. Sixty percent of all those who go to college fail to receive a degree. Only 30% of American employers questioned in a recent survey thought their newest employees could comprehend written instructions. If international comparisons in science and math are accurate, Americans are falling behind other countries.

The collective efforts of the past decade have yielded little noticeable change in the education system. In spite of good intentions, the practices of teachers are largely unchanged; and the average classroom remains essentially as it was 10 years ago — and to a large extent as it was 50 years ago or even 100 years ago.

Those who look with nostalgia at their own schooling and see the answer as a simple matter of restoring traditional education ignore today's realities. An education system designed for an agrarian or manufacturing-based society in which most women were not in the workforce and in which minorities were systematically excluded from most jobs cannot effectively meet the nation's needs in today's diverse, global, high-tech, information-based economy.

Nationally, the last 10 years have been characterized by too many false starts and unfounded claims. The Reagan Administration approach was to absolve the federal government of responsibility and cut the education budget. Pouring new money into a failing system will not produce better results, but neither will drastic cuts in funding lead to improvement. Since *A Nation At Risk*, federal funding for education has dropped 40%; and the federal share of education spending for elementary and secondary schools has dropped from almost 10% to 6%.

In more recent years, the Bush Administration, too, turned away from public schools and toward the private sector for the answer — first with a proposal to fund vouchers for parents to send children to private schools, then with a plan to fund a single model school in each Congressional district. The voucher proposal would have helped only 1% of the nation's children while diverting scarce federal dollars to help private schools. The so-called "New American Schools Development Corporation" asked Congress to spend $535 million for one model school in each of 535 districts, in spite of long-standing experience that public schools cannot and will not reform themselves by emulating private education or a few model schools. Not surprisingly, Congress debated and decisively rejected both of the proposals. Our goal is to create conditions for permanent improvement and reform, not in a few schools but in all schools, not for a few students but for all students in every school in America.

Congress recognized the need to encourage the development of a new system of education and knew that system can be created through a combination of top-down and bottom-up approaches. Innovative and successful schools need encouragement, but states and districts have to take steps to work them into an effective system. We sponsored the Neighborhood Schools Improvement Act, which, had it passed, would have been a significant move in that direction. Unfortunately, politics intervened; and the bill died before the end of our last session.

We need a new educational vision that looks not just at school reform but at overall *education reform* in the context of modern society. The common school of Horace Mann can no longer be set on automatic pilot. In other major industrial nations, the elementary and secondary school systems prepare students for successful and productive lives. America must do the same.

The first step is to change attitudes about schools and about the role of the federal government. In the words of Theodore Sizer of Brown University, "We need to change the way we think about our schools: what they are and what they must do." Responsibility to educate children does not begin in the first grade and end in the twelfth. Nor does it last only from 9:00 a.m. to 2:30 p.m. for 180 days a year. Whatever we can do to strengthen families and make sure that children are ready to learn when they start school and keep on learning once they are in school — whatever we can do to give children real options when they leave school, whether through school-to-work programs or through student aid for higher education — are aspects of education that demand federal leadership. The same is true of health care and other services that function as safety nets for all children, and without which no child can succeed. Universal public education set America apart from the rest of the world a century ago. It remains at the heart of the American experience, but it needs to be reinvented for the modern world.

Last spring I visited the Mason School in Roxbury, a poor, inner-city neighborhood in Massachusetts. Three years ago it was threatened with closing because of low attendance. No one wanted to go there. Today it is oversubscribed and one of the best schools in Boston. The principal, teachers, and parents have transformed their school. Sound, proven ideas form the basis of a common vision throughout the Mason School, a vision that governs all aspects of the children's and the teachers' school day. Part of a nationwide network of schools, called Accelerated Schools and based on the work of Dr. Henry Levin of Stanford University, all children at Mason learn together, whatever their disabilities. Learning is accelerated, not remedial. Students have a full-day program, from 8:00 a.m. to 5:00 p.m., and have mentors from the City of Boston Parks Department. Volunteers from Boston's City Year, an urban peace corps, staff the after-school program. Affiliation with Harvard helps teachers continually review their teaching strategies and work on assessment of children's progress.

There are hundreds of such schools across America. One by one, they are making progress — struggling against great odds, without vast infusions of new money, making radical changes in their classrooms, breaking the mold in responsible, effective, and replicable ways. They usually have help from local universities, businesses, or skilled administrators who view their roles not as telling teachers and principals what to do but as making sure that the schools have what they need. These schools are devising new ways to improve teaching and learning. Their activities are the heart of education reform, and our challenge is to build these kinds of schools into a system.

There are no silver bullets that will magically solve all the problems. But a series of essential steps, taken together and implemented simultaneously and nationwide by federal, state, and local governments, can form the basis for a coordinated and comprehensive education system in America. I see these steps as falling into eight categories:

1. Invest in children early, *before* they fail, not after it is too late.
2. Adopt voluntary national content standards and model assessments as guidelines for states and local districts to use in setting goals, planning improvements, and measuring progress.
3. Reaffirm the commitment to disadvantaged and underserved students, but realign existing federal programs to support system reform and restructuring at the state and local levels.
4. Invest in the professionalization and preparation of teachers and administrators; place them at the center of these reforms and give them sufficient authority.
5. Revitalize traditional high schools to integrate them better with the workplace and higher education.
6. Improve financial aid and its management so that student aid funds reach all students who can benefit from college.
7. Bring education technology to the same high level as military, space, and industrial technology.
8. Finally, connect the schools with the health and social services that are safety nets for poor children.

Let me elaborate on each of these eight categories in the remainder of this paper.

1. Invest in children before they fail, not after.

The first national goal adopted by President Bush and the Council of State Governors in 1990 was the most important one: *Every child will start school ready to learn.* Students who do not will never catch up to their better-prepared peers. When it comes to supporting healthy early-childhood development, we know what to do. Programs such as Head Start and Women, Infants, and Children (WIC) are proven, cost-effective ways to enhance children's lives while saving millions of dollars in later costs. These programs are underfunded and fall far short of serving all eligible recipients.

Head Start has been identified by experts and commissions as the key to meeting the first education goal. Despite 25 years of proven effectiveness, it still reaches only a quarter of eligible 3-, 4-, and 5-year-old children.

We must begin adding funds to Head Start each year until it is fully funded — and we must also be vigilant in ensuring program quality. We cannot serve more families with less money; our goal cannot be just a greater number of "slots." Increased access is needed to the comprehensive, high quality services that are the hallmark of Head Start.

Once children reach school, we must make sure that the schools are ready for them, regardless of the children's economic or ethnic background. In too many American schools, first-graders are quickly sorted and arranged by degrees of readiness; and those least ready are relegated to the lowest tracks, which they never leave. We must expand and revise early childhood programs to encourage schools to make innovative efforts; in Kentucky, for example, all children are in ungraded rooms until fourth grade. Other such arrangements may be even better suited to the developmental needs of young children.

2. Adopt voluntary national standards.

Standards — an agreement about what all students should know and be able to do — are central to the vision of school reform. One of the most perplexing phenomena in education is the high degree of satisfaction that parents have with their own children's schools. In a Phi Delta Kappa/Gallup poll last summer, 73% of the respondents with children in school were satisfied with the school that their oldest child attended last year. In the face of large dropout rates for high schools, a 60% non-completion rate for those who start college, and widespread dissatisfaction among employers about the skills of high school graduates, the 73% satisfaction figure is a wake-up call that parents have no adequate standards to measure how well their children are learning.

Devising standards in core subjects is a necessary step, and it makes sense for the federal government to oversee that process and pay the expense. In a remarkable initiative, the National Council of Teachers of Mathematics has created widely acclaimed new standards for math; but we should not underestimate the difficulty involved in fashioning and certifying adequate standards for other subjects. Especially at the elementary grades, it will be difficult to integrate the standards, because good instruction at the beginning levels is by its nature interdisciplinary.

Standards alone, however, will have little effect. Once they are completed and available to states and local districts, the federal government will have a further responsibility to help schools and teachers prepare students to meet them. It is easy to assert that all children can reach high standards, but it will never happen unless all levels of government — federal, state, and local — work in a coordinated way.

A further important question involves assessing how much students are learning. Adequate techniques need to be developed to measure what is taught. In too many schools, one standardized test drives much of the instruction. This current practice of depending solely on such standardized measures cannot accurately gauge the learning required by the new standards. We must find ways to measure student progress that are valid, reliable, and fair. Again, the federal government should offer support to develop models for others to use.

3. Renew the commitment to disadvantaged and underserved students, but realign existing federal programs to support system reform and restructuring at the state and local levels.

Education is still primarily a state responsibility and a local function. The federal role is small, and federal funds account for only 6% of total spending on elementary and secondary education. Because of the way federal funds are dispensed, however, they have a multiplier effect far greater than the dollars themselves. But they also contribute to the bureaucratic and highly fragmented school organization that characterizes many of our school districts.

Historically, federal education policy has been designed to target specific student populations with special needs, such as economically disadvantaged students, pupils with disabilities, and those with low proficiency in English. It has also targeted priority disciplines, such as science and math, anti-drug education, and vocational education. When problems are identified, the federal government comes up with programs to address them. The approach has been programmatic rather than systemic.

Almost 30 years ago, the federal government committed itself to special support for the nation's poorest children, adding later support for limited-English-speaking children and special needs children. We cannot renege on those commitments. But this ad hoc approach reinforces the status quo, rather than promoting change and better schools for these children. Categorical programs tend to have a fragmenting effect on efforts to create coherent approaches to student needs. Requirements and regulations, while often useful and necessary, can also inhibit coherent school planning and the creativity of teachers in the classroom. The best teachers spend too much energy finding ways around poorly thought-out rules and requirements.

In 1993 Congress will extend the core law that contains most of these programs, the Elementary and Secondary Education Act. In that review, we will examine whether the current array of separate categorical programs is the best way to help specific populations, or whether schools and teachers need more flexibility to fashion comprehensive and individualized solutions to the challenges facing their students.

Federal legislation in 1988 allowed schools to undertake "schoolwide projects" and use Chapter I funds as part of an overall plan. The response by the schools provides an intriguing glimpse into the way a small amount of federal or other funds can be a catalyst for change.

A related major issue at the heart of new thinking about schools is the way they are organized. Concerned about disadvantaged and underserved children, the federal government has set up many rules to help ensure that all children are helped. Often, there is so much monitoring that the goals of the program are lost. We cannot ignore the negative effects on children of isolating them and labeling them. The emphasis on remediation and basic skills in many special classes is not enough to prepare students, especially disadvantaged students, for work or college. To teach reading, it is not sufficient to drill students in reading skills. We must also teach them to like to read and to become lifelong learners.

In addition, much has been written about the design of school buildings, class schedules, labor relations, and administration. School restructuring is an essential part of school reform. Major regulatory changes are needed to make it easier for schools to organize themselves around students' needs, to see that accountability is based on real educational results, not mindless paperwork.

4. Invest in the professionalization and preparation of teachers and administrators; place them at the center of these reforms, with increased authority.

It is teachers who educate children, not schools, school systems, federal laws, or Congress. As Deborah Meier, the MacArthur Award-winning educator from Harlem, has said, "Today, it is clear that since we need a new kind of school to do a new kind of job, we need a new kind of teacher, too." Few issues are more complex. Congress appropriated funds in 1991 to enable the National Board for Professional Teaching Standards to set up a certification process for teachers similar to that for doctors, and the work is well under way. As in the case of standards for students, identifying high and rigorous standards for what teachers should know and be able to do is an essential part of teaching reform and school reform. "Board certification" of teachers could be the first step in redefining good teaching and in creating models for outstanding teachers. Then teachers, in turn, can lead school-based efforts to collaborate with colleges and universities to bring all teachers to a high standard.

None of this will happen if schools are not reorganized to give teachers and students more time — time to acquire the skills and knowledge they need, time to help each other and work together, time to plan and share effective strategies, time to draw parents into the education of their children, and most of all, time to develop personal relationships with their students. It may be that we need to lengthen the day and the year to accomplish this goal. Congress has created a National Commission on Time and Learning, and we look forward to their report.

The important work by Harold Stevenson and his colleagues comparing Asian and American schools highlights one important reason the average proficiency of Asian students is superior to our own; teachers are present in the school building longer than American teachers each day, but they teach only three or four hours.

The federal government can help meet this challenge by supporting increased professional development set-asides in programs such as Chapter I and Chapter II. At first glance, this may seem to be taking funds from children to give to teachers; but few things will help children more than well-prepared, engaged, and energetic teachers.

To overcome the inertia of familiar and ingrained teaching methods, we must not resort to more of the same tired techniques of sending teachers back to school themselves or imposing new requirements. The changes that teachers need to make must be worked out by the teachers themselves in the course of their own teaching. To quote Deborah Meier again:

> The habits of schooling are deep, powerful, and hard to budge.
> No public institution is more deeply entrenched in habitual behavior
> than schools. . . . Such changes cannot be "taught" in the best
> designed retraining program and then imported into classroom prac-

27

tice. What is entailed is changing the daily experiences of teachers, substituting experiences that will require them to engage in new practices and supporting them in doing so.

The federal government has provided grants to support the preparation and the renewal of teachers, beginning with the National Defense Education Act grants to grants from the Fund for the Innovation and Reform of Schools and Teaching (FIRST) today. But these programs have too often been focused on helping individual teachers, not on improving the nature of teaching. The "central problem of all education," philosopher Alfred North Whitehead once said, is the "problem of keeping knowledge alive, of preventing it from becoming inert. . . . The evocation of curiosity, of judgment, of the power of mastering a complicated tangle of circumstances, the use of theory in giving foresight in special cases — all these powers are not to be imparted by a set rule embodied in one schedule of examination subjects." Such powers can only be awakened in students by teachers who find learning an adventure, and who seek to share that adventure by making students active participants in the enterprise of education. But if teachers are to be successful in this task, we must give them the time and support they need to keep the learning experience fresh for both themselves and their students.

5. Revitalize traditional high schools to integrate them better with the workplace and higher education.

After *A Nation at Risk* was published, American high schools were singled out for special attention in later reports. The problems identified were low expectations for students; a proliferation of watered-down courses; teachers unprepared to teach difficult or higher-level courses; rigid tracking that sorts students into college preparation, general education, or special education tracks; little academic rigor in courses for non-college-bound or vocational-track students; lack of motivation or willingness by students to work hard; awarding diplomas to students for just showing up for four years; lack of relationship between skills taught in school and those required by employers; and excessive reliance by teachers on lectures and individual work that fails to engage today's technologically assaulted teenagers.

As these reports made clear, high schools are sending too many unprepared students to college and doing too little to help young men and women who do not enroll in postsecondary education. Employers wring their hands, and colleges readily admit that most students' first year is largely remedial.

Despite these reports, high schools have been resistant to change. Major restructuring is needed so that all students, college-bound or work-bound, emerge with stronger basic and academic skills.

An important place to begin is with new federal attention to vocational education and school-to-work programs. The bipartisan Commission on the Skills of the American Workforce put it best in its 1990 report:

> America invests little in its front-line workforce. We do not expect much from them in school. We give them few job skills and training. And we let them sink or swim when they are the people we must count on to lead the way to a competitive and productive economy.

The comparison with other nations is striking. Starting at age 12, occupational information is integrated with school lessons in Sweden, Denmark, and Germany. These nations provide a wide range of occupational training for students and simultaneously reinforce their continuous acquisition of basic skills. These European systems are cooperative efforts that involve schools, businesses, labor unions, and local communities. Coupled with strong basic and problem-solving skills, these programs produce a highly trained, productive workforce and give those nations a major advantage in international competition.

Any reform we put in place here must start with local high schools and build on their strengths. But equally important in implementing these changes are postsecondary institutions, businesses, labor, and local communities. The federal government must play a leadership role by forming goals, helping to set standards, offering incentives, and improving the coordination of existing programs.

6. Improve financial aid and its management so that student aid funds reach all students who can benefit from college.

The federal government is the single most important source of financing for higher education. For the 1990-91 academic year, the federal government made more than $21 billion available to help students and their families — nearly double the $11 billion available in 1981-82.

The federal government must pursue a two-pronged agenda to improve its higher education programs. First, programs to help students meet the cost of tuition must be funded more adequately.

Additional funding for Pell Grants is a prerequisite if access to higher education is to be more than an empty slogan. In the last decade, the maximum Pell Grant has grown 33%, far less than the 110% increase in the cost of higher education.

For 20 years, Pell Grants have been designed to ensure that the financially neediest students receive grant assistance before they are forced to borrow money. The federal government must place a higher priority on such grants, and it should move to fully fund the program.

Increased funding also is needed for the campus-based programs — Supplemental Grants, College Work Study, and Perkins Loans. These funds are provided directly to the colleges and then made available to financially needy students. The programs are effective, but over the last decade appropriations have failed to keep pace with inflation. Funding for the Supplemental Grants has fallen 12% in real terms, while money for the Work-Study program is down 32% and funds for the Perkins Loans have dropped 67%.

Student loans have become the dominant form of financing for higher education. In 1992, 4½ million college students and their families borrowed $13 billion in funds under the Guaranteed Student Loan program. Despite its importance, the program has a number of shortcomings: it is expensive and relies on costly subsidies to lenders to make the loans; it is, needlessly, terribly complex for students and institutions; and it is plagued by high default rates.

These problems with Guaranteed Student Loans underscore the failure of the Department of Education to administer student aid programs effectively. Addressing these severe management problems is a major challenge that the federal government has ignored for too long.

The Department of Education has historically been a thinly staffed, low-prestige agency with dubious administrative capabilities. In the 1980s, the department suffered because of the Reagan Administration's overt hostility. The Reagan Administration tried and failed to eliminate the agency, but it emasculated it by cutting its staff and other administrative resources. In the 1980s, the department's oversight activities fell sharply. Not surprisingly, the number and cost of student loan defaults increased dramatically — from $239 million in 1980 to $3.4 billion in 1992.

The problem of skyrocketing defaults has been attributed in large part to the dismal record of the department in administering the program. A year-long investigation by the Senate Committee on Governmental Affairs, chaired by Senator Sam Nunn, concluded:

> . . . the Department of Education has failed to effectively or efficiently carry out its Guaranteed Student Loan responsibilities. Virtually every witness described instances of gross mismanagement, ineptitude, and/or neglect in the department's performance of its regulatory and oversight functions.

30

Effective operation of the student loan program must be a high priority. This result can be achieved only if the President makes it clear that efficient operation is a major goal. Poor quality schools should be eliminated from the program, and schools in the program must be more effectively regulated.

"Ending waste and abuse" is often given lip service by government, but few areas offer greater opportunity to deliver substantial budget savings at a time of scarce federal resources.

7. Bring education technology to the same high level as military, space, and industrial technology.

In fashioning the schools of tomorrow, we must provide teachers and students with the tools and skills of modern technology. In few other institutions do the professionals have such limited access to modern telecommunications as do teachers and schools. Most teachers lack easy access to tools as commonplace as telephones. Many of the obstacles to widespread, effective use of technology in education remain the same as they were a decade ago, when *A Nation at Risk* pointed out the "high costs of purchasing, maintaining, and upgrading equipment; the lack of adequate software that dovetails with teachers' curricular needs; the absence of assessments that reflect the complex thinking skills encouraged in technology-rich environments, and the dearth of teacher training."

Every classroom in America should have a telephone, a television receiver, access to cable television, a networked computer, and a teacher who is trained and familiar with such technology. Numerous federal programs enable schools to purchase computers; but there is no national plan to improve the use of technology, provide training for the teachers, and develop needed standards and programming.

Technology in schools is by its very nature a national issue, since its effectiveness derives largely from the capacity for national networking. The urgency of this issue is heightened by the fact that if the government does not assume responsibility for a comprehensive, national technology plan, the private profit-making sector will. As the success of Channel One proves, profits can be made by putting technology in schools. But leaving such a challenge to the private sector will create endless conflicts between private profit and public education. Channel One puts shareholders first; schools must put children first.

31

8. Connect the schools with the health and social services that are safety nets for poor children.

As Harold Howe II, former U.S. Commissioner of Education, has wisely pointed out, education can blunt the effects of poverty, but schools cannot do the job alone. They must have more help from others in the community and from all levels of government — local, state, and federal. Too often, teachers and education professionals are forced to perform the role of health and social service professionals for needy children. Too many children come to school hungry, sick, neglected, abused, or homeless and therefore unable to learn. Too many families fail to get the services they need because they are unable to untangle the complex web of state and federal bureaucracies that are supposed to be serving them.

Simplifying existing programs is one answer — making it easier to serve all the child's needs through a "one-stop-shopping" process. The federal government can provide incentives to states and localities to encourage coordination of services to children and families. The objective should be to maximize access and minimize red tape. Families should be able to obtain a full range of services — health care, child care, parenting training, job training — at a single location either in the school or linked directly to the school in the community. Either way, we need to take the burden off teachers.

Conclusion

Public education in America is in trouble. A system that has served this country well for so long needs far-reaching reform. All of us in public life — Democrat, Republican, Independent, Congress, the Administration, states, and local districts — must work together to achieve it. The challenge is complex and difficult, with no easy answers. We must summon the same dedication and resources we have used to put a man on the moon, or defeat Saddam Hussein, or feed Somalia. We must recognize "the fierce urgency of *Now*."

If the challenge is enormous, so are the stakes. If we fail in this task, we shall fail in many others, too; and America itself may fail. The gridlock of the past 12 years is ending. Education has suffered heavily, but a new day is finally at hand.

Federal Action Essential for Education Reform

By Gordon M. Ambach

Gordon Ambach has served as executive director of the Council of Chief State School Officers (CCSSO) since 1987. As executive director, Ambach represents all of the state commissioners and superintendents of education as the advocate for their state and national education policy positions and in leadership of their council offices. Ambach's service with CCSSO follows 10 years as the New York State Commissioner of Education and president of the University of the State of New York. His experience with federal education programs and policies began with summer assignments in the United States Office of Education in 1956, 1959, and 1969. He served from 1961 through 1964 as program planning and legislative specialist to Commissioner Frank Keppel during the time the major federal education acts of the 1960s were formulated. He appears before Congress often and has initiated several national projects directed toward shaping federal legislation.

Americans were optimistic as the year began that education will improve in 1993 and that we will "move ahead under Bill Clinton." Furthermore, the Louis Harris poll of December 1992 found that Americans believe "making sure our public schools are second to no other nation" is more important than reducing the national debt (71% to 26%). Public sentiment, the calendar for federal education legislation, and the interests of the Clinton Administration and Congressional leadership seemed to be aligned. Many of us hoped that the most significant surge of federal action in education since the Kennedy/Johnson mid-1960s was in the making. Certainly American education was in desperate need of national action to bring localities, states, and the federal government together to achieve the National Education Goals enunciated by the President and Council of Governors in 1990.

Americans are deeply concerned about the quality of elementary and secondary education. They know their children must prepare for a global job marketplace, for preserving international security, and for their part in family and civic responsibility in a global community where travel to the Persian Gulf takes as long as the journey to grandmother's house during their childhood.

We have embraced national education goals, standards, and assessments within the past three years; and, although the traditions of local and state education control are deeply imbedded, Americans are looking more and more at nationwide actions on education problems. Among the chief factors contributing to this changed outlook are the new reliance on education to deal with the environment, to maintain security through extraordinarily complex technologies, and to ensure better health and reduce the cost of coverage. All lead to national education solutions and federal actions.

But what should the federal government do? Can the partner who now provides only 6% of total revenues for elementary and secondary education really make a major difference? What will work best, in view of the slim likelihood of substantial dollar increases in FY 1994?

The Federal Education Agenda for 1993

In my view, President Clinton and Congress can make a significant difference by promoting both education excellence and equity in education opportunity this year. The agenda must combine fast action on the Congressional initiatives built up (but not enacted) in 1992, funding new authority passed in 1992, and completing the major reauthorizations scheduled for this year. Six actions are needed:

1. *Establish national education goals and policies to achieve them; develop national standards and assessments to measure student progress.* This effort is essential to set high performance expectations for all students and schools throughout the nation.
2. *Support school, school district, and state activities to restructure and improve the entire education system.* It takes an extra bubble of funding to change a school, or any institution, while it continues operating. Federal funding for the "change strategy" is essential. The effort must penetrate 100,000 schools!
3. *Promote youth apprenticeships and other pathways for preparation for employment.* The high school graduate headed directly for work needs as much help to perform effectively as the federal government offers the college enrollee.

34

4. *Funding staff development for elementary and secondary teachers as authorized in the Higher Education Act, Title V.*
5. *Support learning technology infrastructure throughout all 100,000 schools and colleges as part of an economic stimulus package.* This support should include school construction, telecommunications, and learning technologies.
6. *Reauthorize the 45 Hawkins/Stafford elementary and secondary programs to provide a cohesive and powerful wedge to improve total system quality, lift the performance of special-needs populations, and set standards for all.*

To carry out an effective mission requires shaping the strategy in a new way to raise total system performance through systemic change at the same time identified populations which are poor get the extra federal dollar. But this does not require starting from scratch. The federal government now funds education research and development, teacher training, learning technologies, curriculum development, assessments, and school improvement projects. The trouble is that they are not up to scale; we lack the long-term comprehensive vision required for strong impact on our overall education system of 100,000 schools and 45 million students.

The federal role needs reshaping to meet the national challenge. This paper recommends how that should be done in 1993, with special reflection on the experience of the past two years and what has been learned about the best way to use federal power to restructure and improve the schools.

The National Stake in Education Performance

For more than two centuries the orientation of education policy-making in the United States has been primarily at the state and local level. There have been several occasions for specific federal initiatives to be taken in association with a particular national need, but authority and funding have been essentially state and local. Within the past 15 years, however, there has been a rapid growth of concern about the "national interest" in education and the need for strategies to strengthen education throughout the nation. This has come about for several reasons, including a growing need to prepare students for international economic competition, for national security and international peace-keeping, for furthering education continuity in a mobile population traveling across states, and for using pooled nationwide resources to strengthen education through R&D and new test development.

These factors have led the nation within just the past three years to the unprecedented establishment of National Education Goals by the President and the state governors. They have led to the current debate about national testing, shot through with the issues of how to improve the quality of educational results through the use of testing and how to determine which jurisdiction (local, state, or federal) ought to be in charge of reform.

A History of Bold National Initiatives

An important federal mission needs to be launched now. This mission would connect the kinds of major initiatives the federal government has used from time to time through the last two centuries in order to achieve our new National Education Goals. The federal government has never had direct responsibility for education, but recall what has happened when special needs arose. Two centuries ago, when a major activity was expansion of the nation to the West, the federal government established the concept of land grants to ensure that common schools were available in all communities, particularly through the model of the Northwest Ordinance. In the latter part of the 19th century, when reconstruction of the nation and the development of our mechanized agricultural and industrial capacity was so important, the federal government established the land grant colleges and universities. Over the past century and a third, these institutions have been powerhouses of research and development and have educated a technical and professional workforce unmatched in the world. The universities transformed this nation's technological capacity in a way not available in other countries.

In the early 20th century, at the onset of mass production and at the time of World War I, the federal government enacted vocational education and vocational rehabilitation programs in order to ensure that workers were trained in the necessary skills. During the Depression years of the Thirties, several federal initiatives in child care, early childhood education, school construction under WPA, and other education support programs were enacted as part of economic recovery.

After World War II, the G.I. Bill was the major federal initiative of this type. It had an extraordinary impact on opportunities for higher education, more than any other single action ever taken by any of the states or the federal government. In the latter 1950s the National Defense Education Act, enacted in response to Sputnik, focused on mathematics, science, and foreign languages. There were programs to attract and retain teachers in these areas.

In the 1960s, the Elementary and Secondary Education Act, the Higher Education Act, Library Services and Construction Act, Manpower Development and Training Act, and other initiatives were started especially to provide equity and opportunity in elementary, secondary, and postsecondary education. The mid-1960s also brought Head Start, which represented a federal commitment to ensure that poor children would be at the starting gate of school, ready to succeed alongside their more affluent peers. The 1970s saw enactment of the Education of All Handicapped Children Act, a further expansion of equity and opportunity for the disabled. During the past two decades these various acts have been reshaped through reauthorizations, but their basic directions and purposes have been kept intact.

Federal legislation on the books today is extensive. One major problem is that the promise of these acts — whether Chapter 1, Head Start, the education of Handicapped Children Act, or the Pell Grants — has never been fulfilled because they are underfunded. The target populations are not completely reached or not fully served. If the National Education Goals are to be achieved — for example, the goal of a 90% high school graduation rate with a program of high standards — economically disadvantaged or disabled student populations, together constituting 28% to 30% of all students, must be served so well that a much larger portion of them graduate.

The Federal Role in System Restructuring

The challenge of the 1990s is much too great to be met through existing federal programs, even if they are fully funded. The task is not only to lift performance of identified populations to current standards but to raise the performance for the entire system and for all students. New federal initiatives must reshape the rigor and quality of education in *all* states and localities for *all* students to meet standards that prepare them for worldwide competition. Federal programs must provide for long-term, systemic, schoolwide change throughout the nation. They must ensure that educational content demands higher-order thinking and helps students develop the capacity for creativity, analysis, questioning, and judgment. These are the abilities that will enable them to deal with ever-changing circumstances and fashion informed solutions for new situations.

The federal role in the past has been to target for improvement a particular subject area, such as vocational education, or a particular population group, such as migrant children or economically disadvantaged children. In the Nineties, in addition to such targeting, the federal government must help states and localities to transform the institutions themselves. While the federal government cannot do it all, it can provide important incentives. And it can provide resources that enable states and localities to design plans for reform and test new practices.

Strategies for Change: R&D, Staff Development, Technologies, and Accountability

The Congress and President Clinton have a unique opportunity to reshape the education of American students for the 21st Century by turning federal programs in a new direction. The context is right for a federal strategy that will be as significant for the 1990s as was enactment of the Elementary and Secondary Education Act in 1965.

The National Education Goals have been accepted with great speed and with an urgency for national action to achieve them. Agreement on strategies for implementation and, particularly, the specific federal role in education, has not yet been achieved. To reach the national goals requires that the major types of federal intervention currently used — support for student access and equal opportunity; research, development, and demonstration of innovative programs; staff development; and support for materials and learning technologies — must be used much more extensively than in the past. In addition, the strategy must be built around coordinated use of federally funded activities systemically connected with state and local initiatives. Recommendations for reshaping and expanding support for student access and equal opportunity will be presented later as part of the proposals for reauthorization of the Hawkins/Stafford Amendments of 1988.

Before that, let's examine the types of activities that can be a driving force for major system change in education. These concepts are established in restructuring business, the military, and other large-scale enterprises.

1. *Strategic Design.* There must be a thorough design of strategies by those responsible for education performance to integrate actions step-by-step to achieve high-performance schools. This design work must be done by the authorities who control the resources of education systems, assisted by the best advice available. They must have time and the extra resources to do it.

The lesson of federal, state, and privately supported education reform efforts over the past 25 years is that piecemeal programs that address parts of the system do not yield lasting aggregate results. When R&D

38

is done through one jurisdiction, staff development through another, and learning technologies through yet another, these separate efforts — while they may produce isolated positive gains — do not generate sustained improvement. When federal programs are implemented in local districts, sometimes through the states and sometimes directly from the Department of Education, there is no cohesive multiplier impact.

Federal funds intended to effect change in public elementary and secondary schools (currently totaling 6% of expenditures in these schools) must be linked with state and local education funds if comprehensive change is to occur. This fact requires careful strategic design closely linking federal programs to state and local administrative responsibility under federally approved plans.

2. *Research and Development.* The strategy of federal programs to support education research and development and to establish new high-performance schools must be reshaped to develop an entire system of high-performing schools. During 1993 action on federal proposals to promote high-performance schools, reauthorization of the Office of Educational Research and Improvement will be considered. The approach must differ significantly from the Bush Administration's America 2000 attempt at R&D.

The America 2000 program strategy banked heavily on business funding of education R&D completely apart from government. The strategy had three major flaws. First, the privately supported R&D program had little, if any, connection with the institutions that operate schools — that is, the institutions that would presumably use the results — or with state and local education agencies. Second, the effort was not matched with any increase in federally funded R&D or linked with use of the $75 million in federal money currently funding education R&D. The effort missed its own target of $200 million by a large margin. Only about $15 million has actually been spent. And, third, the R&D effort was out of sync with the Administration's attempt to support New American Schools. The R&D results were not due until after all the new schools were to be selected and each given $1 million of federal support.

It is hard to comprehend why the Administration relied solely on a privately funded and managed research effort as the centerpiece of its design for change in education. Private enterprise can help, but it was not sound to assign education R&D to the private sector any more than the nation would turn to the private sector to fund and control R&D for health, defense, transportation, or other public services. Education R&D has long been a major function of the federal government. The

Administration gave up on its own department's capacity to provide leadership in education R&D. The Education Department's capacity for R&D has been devastated, and Congress has very little confidence in the Office of Education Research and Improvement. American schools will pay a price for this.

Congress should establish within ED a major R&D institute, with counterpart activity incorporated in the states. Private matching contributions to this institute should be encouraged. They would then be incorporated in the institute's total program. This program should be linked directly with state and local R&D, giving a multiplier effect in doing the research and using it to change school practice.

We need to be periodically reminded of the magnitude of the task of reforming American education, a system with 100,000 schools spending $230 billion a year. Schools must change one by one; but they cannot be reformed unless local and state systems provide the leadership, assistance, and support for reform. Neither can the system be reformed without a structured pattern to connect R&D with start-up money for demonstration schools and then to use the experience of demonstration schools to help all other schools. There must be a plan for effective multiplier effects from early models to universal practice. The task may start with 500 schools, but it will not start sensibly unless the design leads rapidly to reach 1,000 to 10,000 and then 100,000 schools in this decade.

To transform a mediocre existing school into a high-performance school requires expenditure beyond regular operating costs for planning and design. It requires building consensus on new direction, staff training, purchasing new materials or equipment, restructuring facilities, and establishing new ways of operation for schools and school districts. Federal funds are essential for this to occur.

3. *Staff Development.* Restructuring of business and the military has occurred only where personnel have been trained extensively and continuously to change the way they work. Restructuring requires personnel to work "smarter."

The change in strategy to achieve national education goals must put highest priority on staff development, both preservice and on-the-job. Teacher training was at the heart of the National Defense Education Act. It has been a part of federal programming in various other acts, such as the Higher Education Act. But funds for this purpose are far below the need if education practice is to be changed systemically. The reauthorization of the Higher Education Act, Title V, provides essen-

40

tial new authority for staff development. Early action in 1993 for a supplemental budget appropriation would enable teacher training programs to start this summer.

4. *Using Technologies*. The driving force for restructuring business, the military, and other services has been technological change. The impact of developments in computation, automation, robotics, and telecommunications in enterprises other than schools is abundant. Yet learning technologies are at the margin in most of education. They will stay there unless strategies for change incorporate requirements for use of learning technology at the core of education restructuring. Separate categorical programs for learning technology will not change the system. Use of learning technologies must be required in start-up funds for high-performance schools and in staff-development programs. The cost of providing the nationwide infrastructure for learning technologies throughout all schools should be part of a federal economic stimulus program. Training teachers to use the technology should be a required provision of federal systemic change legislation.

5. *Improving Student Assessment and Information for Accountability*. The characteristics of achievement tests and the use of such tests can have a profound impact on what and how students learn. Across the nation we are having an important debate about the ways tests are constructed and the use of tests at local, state, and federal levels. The debate on testing is critical to the task of stimulating effort to set new standards for higher-order learning to achieve national goals, as it also is to monitoring progress on the goals.

Those serving at the state level have debated the role of national testing. We have concluded that a nationwide testing system with federal, state, and local components should be authorized formally through federal legislation. This nationwide testing system should include both program assessment, such as the current National Assessment of Educational Progress (NAEP), and a system of individual student examinations. Both sets of tests would be developed from common standards.

The component of the system for individual examinations requires extremely careful design work and pilot demonstration of different forms of exams and patterns of their administration among states, localities, and the federal government. The primary use of such individual exams is to improve teaching and learning in elementary and secondary education, rather than to monitor performance. The system of individual examinations should be related to curriculum and instruction. It should emphasize testing of subject mastery when students achieve it, rather

41

than follow a fixed grade schedule. It should encourage development of a variety of types of testing, including performance assessments, but its principal use should be to challenge students, teachers, and schools to achieve a higher level of performance.

A key federal investment must be made in expansion of education assessment and information systems. The NAEP was begun in the 1960s. It has provided important trend data about education in this country. It must be expanded to assess more subject areas to increase the use of assessment data on a state-by-state basis. The nation has already had the first experiences of assessing mathematics state-by-state. Authority for NAEP state-by-state testing stops in 1992 unless there is action to expand it in 1993, which is essential.

There should also be an increase in the resources available for collection of information on other education indicators. In the Departments of Labor, Agriculture, and Health and Human Services, the federal government spends from five to six times as much to keep accurate indicators of progress as it does in education. In labor, health, and agriculture these costs range from $240 million to $300 million. In education, the figure is closer to $55 million today. We will not have progress reports on national goals; we will not have data to tell us whether the federal investment is effective; we will not have information about good practices in the states or localities — none of this unless we invest approximately six times more on assessment and data collection for education at the federal level. Keep in mind that this would be a cost of $250 million out of federal expenditures of $230 billion annually.

These are the key ingredients of federal support for system change. How can they be incorporated in legislation?

Creating Legislation for Education Reform:
The Lessons of 1990-1992

In 1989 the governors and President Bush agreed at Charlottesville, Virginia, to establish national goals for education. The goals were stated by the President in January 1990 and were formally approved by the Council of Governors in February 1990. The Administration advanced no federal legislative proposals related to the goals during 1990. During the same year, the Congress developed a major education reform act, H.R.5932, the Education Equity and Excellence Act of 1990. After passage by the House and the Senate, an agreed-upon bill was passed by voice vote in the House on the last day of the 101st Congress. The bill was blocked in the Senate on procedural grounds by conservative

Republicans that last evening. The National Education Goals had been in place one year, but no program or strategy was enacted to achieve them.

In 1991 the Administration advocated a legislative program for America 2000, including endorsement of the national goals for education and the National Education Goals Panel, establishment of a process for developing standards and assessments of education, providing flexibility and deregulation in the administration of federal education programs, supporting 535 new American schools over a four-year period at $1 million each (first year appropriation, $180 million), and a proposal for using Chapter 1 and Chapter 2 funds (Elementary and Secondary Education Act) to provide certificates for disadvantaged students to use in private schools.

As a major alternative, Democrats in both the House and Senate, using H.R.5932 of 1990 as a basis, developed the early versions of the Neighborhood Schools Improvement Act (NSIA), H.R.3320. Because most attention of the 102nd Congress was on reauthorization of the Higher Education Act in 1991, the NSIA was not advanced for floor action in either the House or Senate. By the end of 1991, two years had passed since the proclamation of the National Education Goals without any enacted strategy or program to achieve them.

On January 28, 1992, the Senate, as its first order of business, passed the Neighborhood Schools Improvement Act by a vote of 92-6. The final vote was taken after the Senate, with bipartisan support, rejected use of federal funds under this act for private schools.

The House passed its version of the Neighborhood Schools Improvement Act on August 12, 1992, by a 279 to 124 vote. During the debate, Rep. Richard Armey (R-Texas) introduced an amendment on behalf of the Administration earmarking 25% of local funding for private school choice programs, reducing the total authorization by $100 million, and substituting formula grants to states with competitive grants among states to be determined by the U.S. Secretary of Education. The Armey amendment lost by a vote of 80-328. The bipartisan vote demolished the Administration's America 2000 legislative strategy. The House version authorized no use of federal funds in private schools.

Provisions of the Neighborhood Schools Improvement Act, S.2

On September 25, 1992, following several days of difficult conferencing complicated by the election campaign, House and Senate conferees approved a conference report for the bill. Republican conferees refused to sign. Democratic conferees unanimously approved the following:

• A Neighborhood Schools Improvement Act that supported school-wide restructuring, not a piecemeal or categorical approach ($800 million in the first year). Federal legislation had never done that before. The act provided that governors, state legislators, business leaders, mayors, and community leaders would have key roles in developing state and local education reform plans. Federal legislation had never done that before either.

• 1) Distribution of funds on a formula basis among all of the states; 2) state education agency responsibility for the state's application to the Secretary of Education; 3) local school districts and schools competitive grants to be used by districts and schools for comprehensive education restructuring; and 4) program authorization for ten years, with the first state application for five years and the second five-year period covered by re-application.

• Codification of the National Education Goals and authorization for development of voluntary national education content standards for students and voluntary national school delivery standards. It provided funds for developing model assessments in mathematics and science. These were all breakthroughs in federal legislation.

• The Neighborhood Schools Improvement Act, providing for demonstration of deregulation by giving flexibility to 10 states and 75 school districts in each of the states in administering federal programs. Such flexibility was brand new in federal education legislation.

• Fundamental changes proposed by the President and members of both parties in the use of federal authority to promote educational change and excellence. This too was a remarkable federal initiative for the 1990s, crafted from concepts advanced by both parties.

The House approved the conference report by voice vote on Wednesday, September 30, 1992, following a vote to recommit the bill that was defeated by a 254 to 166 vote. On October 2, 1992, just prior to the session's close, Senate Republicans blocked passage of the act by rejecting a cloture motion. The vote was 59-40. All 57 Democrats and two Republicans voted yes. Sixty votes were needed for cloture.

Three years had now passed since proclamation of the National Education Goals and still not one program or strategy had been enacted to achieve them. Indeed, at the close of 1992, after 1,000 days, the goals had neither been endorsed by the Congress nor signed into law.

Understanding the Political Attack on S.2

The House/Senate conference report on the Neighborhood Schools Improvement Act came under vigorous attack by the Bush Administration, particularly Secretary Lamar Alexander. As noted, the report was ultimately blocked in the Senate by lack of one vote on a cloture motion. Had the cloture motion passed, the report would have sailed through the Senate. Whether President Bush would have signed it is not known. Certainly it would have been awkward for the President, just one month before the election, to veto a bill that codified his national education goals, embraced his advocacy of national standards and assessments, authorized his call for regulatory flexibility, and committed federal funds to support school-by-school restructuring.

At the end of the 102nd session of Congress, the political rhetoric on this issue was thick and often deliberately obscured the report's provisions. The provision of S.2 will be before the Congress and Administration in 1993. Because of their importance as part of the federal role in education reform, it is necessary for the record to summarize here the arguments made against the reported bill, primarily by Secretary Alexander, and the responses based on the actual content of the bill.

1. *Attack:* The bill does not include $500 million for private school choice, as the President requested.

Response: Both the House and Senate, in bipartisan action, rejected the use of public funds under this bill for private school vouchers. In January the Senate voted 92-6 for the bill with no funds for private schools. In August the House rejected by a 80-328 vote a proposed amendment to earmark funds for private school vouchers. The President's proposed GI bill was never even advanced as an amendment to this legislation in either the House or the Senate. Since the Senate and House both passed bills that included no funds for private schools, the conference report could not have included such a provision. The vote on the Neighborhood Schools Improvement Act was not a vote for or against federal funds for private schools. It was a vote *for or against federal initiatives for public school reform.*

2. *Attack:* The Neighborhood Schools Improvement Act creates a new state and local bureaucracy instead of getting funds to schools.

Response: This act sets up a ten-year program for reform for *all* schools through state and local education agencies. School districts and states must have plans and strategies to reach all schools in addition to making specific grants for individual school restructuring. The bill supports this work. In the first year, if states and local school districts have

45

plans and strategies in place, funds may flow directly to schools. Most important, in this bill decisions are made at state and local levels by education agencies with the participation of governors, state legislators, mayors, the business community, and the public working together with local and state education agencies through special panels and committees.

The objection that this bill sets up a new state and local bureaucracy needs to be considered in light of the President's proposal for a New American Schools program that would establish a federal bureaucracy to assist the Secretary of Education in deciding on each and every one of the 535 schools to be selected for reform. Local and state school authorities and the National Alliance of Business strongly supported the Neighborhood Schools Improvement Act. They would not have done so if it would add bureaucratic impedances.

3. *Attack:* The act would provide for development of national school delivery standards, thereby establishing a "national school board" that would control inputs like class size and teacher/pupil ratios in schools.

Response: The President and the state governors have agreed on the need for standards for students and standards for schools. If the nation is to expect higher performance from students, it must expect schools to provide the opportunity for that performance. The conference report, based on provisions in S.2 and advocated by the National Council on Education Standards and Testing, had the President's blessing, provided development of *voluntary* national standards. Providing authority to the National Education Goals Panel to develop voluntary content standards (what students should know and be able to do), which the President advocated, is no more or less to establish a "national school board" than having the panel develop voluntary school delivery standards. Opponents cannot argue that developing school standards creates a national school board of the "panel" but developing student standards does not. It must be noted that the panel that develops the voluntary standards has 12 of 18 members who are state governors or state legislators. This bill ensures that the standards for both students and schools would be established with strong control by state representatives.

4. *Attack:* The act does not include funds for New American Schools, "break the mold schools," or public school choice.

Response: The act provides broad authority to local school districts and states in using funds. If they wish to use the funds for public school choice programs, they may do so. If they wish to have individual school restructuring efforts, such as New American Schools, "break the mold schools," "essential schools," "accelerated schools," "charter schools," or any other type of schools, they may do so. The money moves to local school districts by competition and within school districts to schools by competition. They have wide latitude for innovation and could fund any of these projects.

5. *Attack:* The act is "business as usual" with the "education establishment" in control.

Response: A lead advocate for this act is the National Alliance for Business, representing major businesses and industries across the country. The National Alliance for Business is not the "education establishment." This act, for the first time in federal legislation, provides a significant role for governors, state legislators, business leaders, and public representatives in developing reform plans and actions. The act provides competitive local grants. The act is not business as usual.

6. *Attack:* The funds go to state and local bureaucracy and not to schools. All the funds in the first year are used for state planning and administration.

Response: The first year authorization focuses on developing state restructuring plans with participation by governors, state legislators, business leaders, and the education community. If a state already has its restructuring plan, the state may request the Secretary of Education for approval to move funds immediately to local school districts and schools in the first year. In subsequent years, 80% of the funds automatically move to school districts and schools; 20% are used for statewide projects that include support to school districts or consortia of school districts for direct services. Because the heart of this program is competitive grants for school districts and schools, not all districts and schools will receive direct aid. It is essential for statewide programs to spread innovative practices to those districts and schools not receiving direct grants through technical assistance, staff development, and curriculum and materials development. This is necessary for widespread impact to all schools.

Enacting the Provisions of S.2 Early in 1993

The provisions of the Neighborhood Schools Improvement Act, S.2, are essential for the nation's education restructuring agenda. They are essential to guiding federal, state, and local efforts in a coherent and coordinated campaign to achieve the National Education Goals. A successor bill must be enacted as early as possible in 1993 to authorize local and state action beginning before the 1993-94 school year. The authorization must be accompanied by a timely FY 1993 supplemental appropriation to launch the program.

One-third of the decade, starting with the promise of ambitious National Education Goals, has gone with no significant federal action. If action on an S.2 successor bill is not taken fast, federal impact will not be felt until the school year 1994-95, when the reauthorized Hawkins/Stafford Amendments take hold. We cannot lose another year. The S.2 successor must lay down the basis in policies and framework for reauthorization of Hawkins/Stafford, including reauthorization of the Office of Education Research and Improvement. It must provide the foundation for the use of staff-development funds under the Higher Education Act, Title V.

There is an exceptional opportunity to pull the several federal interventions together now. The first step is with S.2. The second is a supplemental appropriation for S.2 and HEA, Title V. The third is reauthorization of Hawkins/Stafford. This paper concludes with recommendations on how this reauthorization builds out the federal role in education reform.

Building Out the Federal Role in Education Reform

Reauthorization of the Hawkins/Stafford Amendments of 1988 provides President Clinton's administration and the 103rd Congress with an extraordinarily important opportunity to restructure the major federal elementary and secondary education programs. The reauthorization should build on review of the experience and strength of nearly three decades of these federal programs and on analysis of the greatest potential for federal influence in developing high-performance learning. The reauthorization should be designed around two central purposes of federal action in education, cast in a comprehensive program to achieve the National Education Goals.

The first purpose of federal action is to increase academic success among groups of identified students who will not reach high standards without extra assistance. The second is to change the capacity of the entire elementary and secondary education system to achieve high-performance learning for all students.

The origins of the program under the Hawkins/Stafford Amendments go back to the early 1960s. From the beginning, the Elementary and Secondary Education Act was a comprehensive bill with the largest program providing extra services to economically disadvantaged children. Although some parts of the original act focused on strengthening the entire educational system, the principal program provided opportunity to raise the level of performance of the economically disadvantaged students to that of all students. Over three decades of legislation has expanded to include more than 45 different programs. Some have been targeted on children in need of special assistance, such as those with limited English proficiency, children of migrant families, recent immigrants, and homeless children. Other programs have been added to strengthen particular aspects of the educational system, such as learning mathematics and science or using learning technologies. Although individual programs have had significant success, the aggregate effect of all of the programs is not sufficient to meet current challenges.

These challenges must be addressed in the reauthorization:

1. The student populations identified as needing special federal assistance under current programs have not been fully served. In many cases students eligible for service have not been served at all because of underfunding. In other cases, students eligible for service under several different federal programs have not been provided integrated and coordinated service among the federal programs and among federal, state, and locally funded programs. The aggregate impact of these programs must be stronger.

2. The entire elementary and secondary education system in our nation is not achieving at the necessary high-performance level. Our nation must simultaneously raise the capacity of the entire system as it assists identified populations to reach the higher standards expected of all students.

3. Federal support for elementary and secondary education from a variety of sources must be more effectively coordinated for better student performance. This requires better coordination of programs under the Hawkins/Stafford Amendments; the Higher Education Act/Title V, staff development; the Office of Educational Research and Improvement (OERI); programs of the National Science Foundation and National Endowments of the Arts and Humanities; programs for early childhood development, including Head Start; for school-to-work transition; and for comprehensive services among health, social, and education services.

The key challenge in this reauthorization is to restructure the programs to gain greater aggregate student results and to ensure that all eligible populations are served. The reauthorization of Hawkins/Stafford should

49

provide for a continuing, identified federal impact on elementary and secondary learning while providing state and localities with greater opportunity to implement the federal programs flexibly and in better coordination with state and local efforts.

The organizing concept for reauthorization of these 45 programs should be "federal program clustering with state and local options to consolidate." The concept maintains the "categorical" characteristics of key federal programs such as targeting toward identified population groups and to particular uses of funds. Separate line-item appropriations would be continued for each of the categorical programs, thereby enabling the Administration and Congress to make determinations on budget priorities among programs and adjust appropriations to changing conditions. By clustering programs that have similar characteristics under the several titles of a new bill, the legislation will enable states and localities at their option to consolidate federal programs in ways that most effectively serve the intended populations and uses.

Reauthorization of the largest program, Chapter 1, should open greater opportunities for schoolwide projects where there is high concentration of eligible identified populations. The potential for overall school improvement is stressed because it is increasingly clear that separate programs have limited impact if they are in a school that does not have good quality schoolwide. A change in the assessment and accountability systems is needed also to permit evaluation of the aggregate effect of the federal efforts rather than project-by-project assessments. The restructured federal programs will stimulate student performance-based education to a much greater degree.

The Hawkins/Stafford programs should be clustered under four titles. The first title, "Opportunity for All to Learn," should include those programs that serve identified student populations with additional assistance to ensure learning at the same level expected of all students under standards established by the states. The programs in this cluster would include Chapter 1 basic and concentration grants, the Chapter 1 program for migratory children, bilingual education, immigrant education, and the Adult Education Act.

The second title, "High-Performance Schools for All," should include those programs that have the objective of raising the quality of the entire education system. Programs such as Chapter 2, magnet schools, the Eisenhower Math and Science Program, foreign languages programs, FIRST, and programs for gifted and talented students should be included. The option to consolidate programs under this title would strengthen the capacity of schools, school districts, and states to make systemic changes through establishment of standards and assessments; research, development, and dissemination; development of curriculum frameworks; professional development; and use of learning technologies. This title would provide the resources that enable the system to change while continuing to operate. The experience of businesses, military systems, health enterprises, and other large institutions has demonstrated the necessity of having resources above and beyond regular operating budgets to effect change and improve the system. This is an essential federal role in education during the 1990s.

Title III, "Healthy Students/Safe Schools," should include the cluster of programs that link education with health, social service, and community activities. Clustered under this title should be the Drug-Free Schools and Communities Act, a program of AIDS education grants from the Centers for Disease Control, the Child Care Development Bloc Grant, the Medicaid Early Periodic Screening Diagnosis and Treatment Program (EPSDT), and the National Community Service Act as it pertains to elementary and secondary level students. Also included in this title should be a new initiative that provides the support to connect major federal funding programs, such as Medicaid, with education programs so that together they further good-quality, comprehensive services for children and their families on school sites or in appropriate community locations.

Title IV, "R&D, Learning Technology, and Education Indicators," should include the cluster of programs administered directly by the U.S. Education Department in support of education research and development, nationwide innovative projects, multi-state learning technology initiatives, and education data systems. This title, linked with reauthorization of OERI, would further better alignment of nationwide education support activities.

For each of the first three clusters, states and localities would be required to have plans indicating strategies for consolidation. States and localities would be encouraged to have single plans across clusters and to link those plans with their use of funds under the HEA, Title V.

The concept of clustering programs with local and state options to consolidate them offers a unique solution to the issues of sustaining an identified, targeted, and supplemental federal presence in education while enhancing local and state capacity to gain more powerful effect from federal resources. In using this concept, the 1993 reauthorization would capture and strengthen the best of federal program experience and shape

51

a new solution to the challenge of better integrated local, state, and federal support to achieve excellence and equity in the 1990s.

The Hawkins/Stafford Amendments include the largest portion, but are not the sole source of federal programs that have an impact on elementary and secondary education. Other acts, such as the recently reauthorized Higher Education Act, Title V, on staff development; the pending reauthorization of the Office of Education Research and Improvement; pending provisions of the Neighborhood Schools Improvement Act; school-to-work transition proposals; and early childhood development proposals must also be considered in the 103rd Congress. The Hawkins/Stafford reauthorization must be completed in that broader context with direct ties to each of the other federal programs.

The federal initiative *America 21* will require a significant additional investment over the decade, not a popular thought in light of budget problems. The crisis in savings and loan associations has required billions of dollars for a federal bail-out. The crisis in the Persian Gulf required billions as well. The crisis in reshaping American education demands federal action that should be considered against the following perspective on federal expenditures for elementary and secondary schools: In 1965-66, federal funds were 7.9% of total federal, state, and local expenditures for elementary and secondary education. The percentage increased to 9.8% in 1979-80. By 1988-89, the figure had dropped to 5.6%.

According to the Department of Education's own reports, between FY 1980 and FY 1990, after adjusting for inflation, federal program funds for elementary and secondary education declined by 15%. In constant FY 1990 dollars, federal expenditures in 1990 are back to where they were in FY 1970. The use of federal funding to have an impact on elementary and secondary education has gained no ground in 20 years. The decade of the 1970s showed significant increases in our commitment to federal funding of education. Those increases have all been wiped out in the past decade. The challenge is twofold: 1) to regain the momentum of the 1970s in providing funding for programs of equity and opportunity, such as Chapter 1 and support for disabled students, so that full service is provided; 2) to build a new initiative — on the scale of an NDEA, or ESEA, or the initial Land Grant College program — that will establish a vision and a strategy for systemic reform of our schools to serve students for the 21st century.

Concluding Note

To realize the potential of the federal role in education reform will require consensus on a shared vision of how this nation must revitalize its schools and a disciplined agreement among the Administration, Congress, and education powers to act together to achieve the National Goals. The direction must be established for the nation as a whole. National resources must be focused on the unique interventions of the federal government that support localities and states in their responsibilities. The 1990s' equivalent of the Land Grant College Act or the Elementary and Secondary Education Act of 1965 can be enacted. Education reform for the 21st century can be realized nationwide if a federal education agenda for 1993 is approved.

From the Business Roundtable: A Business Perspective on Education

By Christopher T. Cross

Christopher T. Cross is executive director of the education initiative of the Business Roundtable. He is a former assistant secretary for educational research and improvement, U.S. Department of Education, and a former Republican staff director of the Committee on Education and Labor of the U.S. House of Representatives.

An article on the front page of *The Wall Street Journal* for November 11, 1992, said it all. The headline read, "Construction companies face a worsening skills gap."

The text of the article quoted the president of a Houston construction company as saying that job applicants have fewer skills than in the past although "There's more complex instruction, new materials." Computer and math skills are especially needed.

While the business community has for decades supported public schools in those areas where there are manufacturing plants or other major facilities, it was not until 1989 that the role of business as a change agent began to emerge.

The change can be traced to the annual meeting of the Business Roundtable in June of 1989 when, for the first time in its history, we devoted the entire annual meeting to the single topic of K-12 education. The program that day included governors (Bill Clinton), education leaders (Albert Shanker), and national political leaders (George Bush).

At that meeting the business community (specifically the Roundtable) was challenged to become actively involved in reform and to stop playing

55

the role of a professional critic who comes without a constructive solution. In fact, then-President Bush asked Roundtable leaders to come to the White House in September to let him know what level of commitment they were willing to make and how they proposed to carry out that commitment.

As fate would have it, that September meeting took place the evening before the nation's governors met with the President in Charlottesville, Virginia, for the first non-economic summit of national and state leaders in the history of the nation. In fact, the Charlottesville meeting was the first such meeting on any topic since the Great Depression.

While the Business Roundtable had not yet developed the details of its technical agenda at that time, it did commit to at least a ten-year program of systemic reform, led by chief executive officers, that would concentrate on the states in recognition of their constitutional and financial status as the level of government charged with the provision of public education.

During the next six months the leaders of the Roundtable, under the chairmanship of IBM CEO John Akers, consulted with the best educational policy makers and practitioners in the country. They were determined that whatever they did must be directed at changing the system for all children, not just improving it for some.

The motivation for this basic tenet of their strategy lies in the fact that unless we radically improve the system for all of our children we will not be able to sustain our economy, not to mention our democratic institutions. What I see gives me great concern about the future viability of our democratic society. For, as Thomas Jefferson noted, an educated populace is essential to the maintenance of freedom and democracy.

As recently as the 1940s, fewer than half of all 18-year-olds graduated from high school. As a society, we simply accepted the fact that we would only utilize fully the minds of a fraction of our population. For the rest, they either became blue-collar workers, held service-sector jobs in small retail establishments, or remained at home.

Today, even the most basic blue-collar jobs require skills that were needed only by white-collar/college-graduate types in earlier decades. As my opening lines suggest, construction workers are simply one group of blue-collar workers among many that today require high levels of education and conceptual skill.

Indeed, despite the infamous pictures of hamburgers and french fries on the cash register keys at McDonalds, the majority of service-sector jobs are also growing more complex and technologically demanding.

56

Notice, for example, the steps that a clerk goes through the next time you use your credit card to make a purchase at a department or clothing store. Or, better yet, walk into the back shop at a car dealer and see what is required of a mechanic who is trying to repair a car manufactured in the last eight to ten years.

Therefore, as a society we can no longer afford to allow a significant segment of our young people to enter adult life without the skills to hold worthwhile jobs and the capacity to become productive citizens who can learn new skills several times in the course of their adult lives. For the vast majority of us will hold many different jobs and will probably work for many different employers in the course of our lifetimes.

As a consequence of our understanding of the issues, the Roundtable created a nine-part public policy agenda that defines the characteristics of a successful school system. Because the agenda calls for systemic change, it represents an integrated whole. Each component is built upon the others, and it is the adoption of all taken together — even if over a period of a few years — that will bring about systemic change. It is not a menu or shopping list from which one could select one or two or even five items and then believe that the job is done. To achieve the systemic change that is required, all of these recommended changes must be adopted in a way that calls for redefinition of the school system. It is the Roundtable's belief that if every state recreates its school system in a way that reflects all nine components of the agenda, then we will, as a nation, raise a generation capable of re-establishing our leadership in the international marketplace.

While the Roundtable's public policy agenda consists of nine points, the first of those nine points consists of four operating assumptions that every school system should subscribe to as the core of its basic commitment to children, their parents, and the community.

The four operating assumptions for the new system are:

1a. *Every child can learn at significantly higher levels*. As noted above, this is a fundamental change in our expectations for both schools and students. It is, however, a key component if we are to educate those whom we have historically failed.

In particular, this means that we should not track students, thereby implying that some significant percentage of students is incapable of learning. It also means that we must strive to bring out the very best in every student and not simply settle for the lowest common denominator of performance.

While the reform movement that followed the release of *A Nation at Risk* in 1983 was significant, what it taught many of us was that if we set minimal expectations for students, they will, indeed, meet our expectations. If we expect a certain proportion of our young people either to fail or perform poorly, the first student we encounter who has difficulty will be identified as one of those who cannot measure up. That student will then be either literally abandoned or figuratively abandoned when consigned to classes with low expectations, few stimulating resources, and a curriculum that too often is boring.

1b. *Every student can be taught successfully.* There is a tremendous body of knowledge out there about what succeeds in reaching kids and teaching them. Hence the challenge is not to invent new ways to teach, it is to identify successful practices and then to train the professionals in those skills. We have example after example of places in the United States where we are reaching all students: rich and poor, majority, minority and immigrant, native-English speakers, and those who come with no English language skills.

Unfortunately, we do little to learn from one another. Each school, each district, even each state, believes that it is so unique that it must invent (reinvent!) ways of solving the myriad problems that they face. If we took even a fraction of the resources devoted to reinvention and invested that money in replication, we could achieve some amazing results.

However, at the same time that we reaffirm what we know works, I am not suggesting that we possess all knowledge in this area and need not invest further. We must continue to push back the frontiers of knowledge. We do know much more than we practice about how to teach students at a much higher level. The challenge is to put that knowledge into practice. For many, it is a bit like buying a home computer. We keep delaying the decision because the technology keeps changing and prices keep falling. All of a sudden, however, we realize that a great deal of time has passed and we have done nothing and achieved none of the personal goals related to that purchase.

1c. *High expectations for every student are reflected in curriculum content, though instructional strategies may vary.* We should focus student time and energies on thinking, problem solving, and the integration of knowledge — the same skills that we look for in our employees. We also need to be certain that all students are offered a rigorous curriculum, not a watered-down version that would result in some students not being challenged, stimulated, or motivated.

We must also recognize that how, when, and where teaching/learning occurs may vary widely. The differences should be based upon what works for each child.

We also must move away from the practice in education of holding time as the constant and achievement as the variable. In almost every other part of our lives we take the time to do a job right. We do not, as occurs so often in education, say that we accept whatever learning takes place in 180 days out of each year and that this time constraint becomes a driving force. If a dentist needs five extra minutes to do the job right, he takes it. If a product takes an extra month to come to market, we make that investment and commitment.

1d. *Every student and every preschool child needs an advocate — preferably a parent.* For each of us, no matter what age, there are times and circumstances where we need an advocate. Anyone who has been in a hospital probably feels this most vividly.

But the same is true for children. Once they enter a school, children are subject to having to cope with the school culture, including the bureaucracy. And few are able to really cope with that. Everyone who succeeds in our society (indeed, in any society) does so, in part, because they have had help — often a mentor.

Children need to be read to and talked to, nurtured and cared for. All children need both to be secure and to feel secure. Each and every child must know that education is valued by those with whom that child has some association.

The parent is the advocate of choice and the best source of this assistance and support. However, data from the 1990 census tell us that in some urban areas fewer than 75% of children are living with one or both parents. While we must strongly support efforts to strengthen the American family, because a strong family will increase a child's chance of success, where parental support is not feasible an advocate must be found who can work with that child.

These are the four basic assumptions that guide the Roundtable's public policy agenda. From here we must venture forth with the substance of an agenda that will provide specific direction to the program and operation of the schools. We at the Roundtable have avoided imposing ourselves in discussions of such matters as what courses should be taught, in what order, or in what way. We believe that decisions of this sort must be left to subject matter experts and to those closest to the delivery of services. (I will discuss this later.)

2. *A successful system is performance or outcome based.* The second major component of our agenda, and one which is a natural outgrowth of the four basic assumptions, is that we must discontinue determining school success by measurement of such inputs as the number of stu-

59

dents per teacher, the number of volumes in the library, or the square feet of space available. Instead, we must ask, "What have we accomplished in educating our children?"

Perhaps because we have had so many varying interpretations of the goals of our schools, we have been reluctant to set a single specific objective and use it in measuring school success. While many have felt that education was the first objective, for instance, others have argued for socialization goals and others for such objectives as integration.

While these latter objectives are laudable, we now have remarkable agreement in this country that, important as they are, none of them count unless students are getting a first-rate education — and we don't know they are unless we can demonstrate that they have learned what the schools have tried to teach.

3. *A successful system uses assessment strategies as strong and rich as the outcomes.* A majority of the testing programs used today are not consistent with the concept of an outcome-based system, since they are norm-referenced, not designed to measure whether a child has learned a specific skill.

While there is a place for standardized testing, we must invest in assessment programs that determine what a child actually knows or can do as determined by objective criteria.

I have heard many, many arguments that testing influences what is taught. I do not consider that to be wrong so long as what we are testing is what we agree children should know and be able to do. Much has been invested in devising new modes of assessment. Some of these assessments are known as authentic assessment, performance-based assessment, and portfolios. Whatever they are called, we must make the investment to be certain that assessments are developed that will reflect emphasis on higher expectations, critical thinking, integration of knowledge, understanding of ideas, and problem solving. We must put in perspective those assessment systems that emphasize the ability to recall or to recognize the "right" answer in multiple-choice questions. Data from these assessments must become publicly available at the state, district, and school level. Data on the performance of individual students must be available to assist teachers and parents in meeting the needs of individual children.

Concurrent with all of this, we must also move in international organizations to be certain that we are cooperating with other nations so that we may have reliable and frequent data on the performance of the U.S. system in comparison with those in other nations. The children of today who will become the work force of the first half of the 21st century will succeed only if they do well internationally. That is the reality of our global society.

4. *A successful system rewards schools for success, helps schools in trouble, and penalizes schools for persistent or dramatic failure.* Like it or not, it is a human characteristic that both people and organizations respond best when there are consequences for performance.

Somehow in education, as in almost every public-sector enterprise, we seem to be adverse to the idea of motivating people with the same methods that work well in the private sector. Recently that tradition has come under scrutiny. (An interesting assessment of this phenomenon comes in a book published in early 1992 titled *Reinventing Government*, by Osborne and Gaebler.)

When schools succeed today, the most that the staff can expect is a pat on the head, a plaque, or some mention by political or education leaders. When a school fails, it is almost inevitable that nothing happens — except that the children in that school have been the real losers. For it is the children who may suffer every day for the rest of their lives, in ways too countless to recite.

If we are to have a system that is based on performance or outcomes, then a system of consequence is inevitable. Those consequences should flow to the school team, not to individual teachers and not to the child. The objective is to use the concept of consequences to create a real team effort at the school, so that it is in everyone's interest that every teacher succeed with every child. And the unit of measurement should be at the school level.

Performance should be defined by the progress a school makes in having all of its students succeed. Success should be measured by how well that school does against its own past performance. We should not take a school that has a majority of at-risk children and compare it with a school where parents are high-income professionals. What is vital is value added, that is, value that the school contributes to the education of each and every child.

Also important in this context is that schools that are not doing well receive assistance. This assistance might be in the form of expert consulting, additional staff, or an innovative program that will meet the needs of the children in that school. If such assistance is not successful, then sanctions might need to be applied. A number of approaches are worth considering. For example, the school team might be given a lump sum of dollars equivalent to, let us say, 10% to 20% of salaries.

It would be up to the school team to determine the use of those dollars, including bonuses to the staff. On the other end of the scale, a school that fails might be taken over and a new team put in place, or staff might be denied merit increases. Whatever they are, it is important to have a range of sanctions and rewards, so that flexibility exists and rewards, assistance, and sanctions can be tailored to circumstances.

5. A successful system gives school-based staff a major role in instructional decisions. If we are to have an outcomes-based system, then we must be certain that those we hold accountable have control over significant elements of their environment. It is a basic principle of motivation that people who have such control "own" the consequences of their actions; for this reason they make decisions in a thoughtful way.

By providing school-based accountability for outcomes, linked to school-based authority to decide how to achieve those outcomes, we achieve delegation to the level of the organization with the greatest knowledge of the child. This authority should include real involvement in the selection of school staff, both certified and non-certified, and significant control over the budget, curriculum, school calendar, instructional practices, disciplinary measures, and the assignment of teachers and students.

6. A successful system emphasizes staff development. The contrast between the public and private sector is most striking on this one point. The most successful companies, over time, are those which recognize that their staff is their most important resource, then invest in them accordingly. Major companies typically invest from 1% to 3% of payroll in training and development. Schools, by contrast, will cut staff development first when money gets tight. Staff development among teachers is also most often linked to advancement on a salary scale; usually missing is a strategic vision of how staff development can be used to advance systemic reform.

There are several components to staff development, beginning with preservice training programs offered at the undergraduate level. These programs must place greater emphasis on mastery of subject matter, provide field experience for prospective teachers, and train them in the effective use of technology.

Provision must also be made for alternative certification opportunities for well-qualified education majors and those who desire to make a mid-career change. I recall a U.S. Senate hearing in which Senator Barbara Mikulski of Maryland reported that in her state she would be ineligible to teach civics and Sally Ride, the astronaut, could not teach science!

Investment in staff development also requires that adequate time be provided to enable staff to participate, with compensation, so long as that training is directed toward the systemic reform agenda of the system. Non-instructional staff also should participate, so that everyone in the school setting can make a positive contribution to reform.

Finally, an effective staff development program should include a research and development strategy to identify those practices that work with children in that district and then teaches those skills to all staff.

7. *A successful system provides high-quality prekindergarten programs, at least for every disadvantaged child.* The evidence is strong that an investment at this early age can significantly reduce the price that society will pay at a later age for such things as dropout prevention programs, special education classes, teenage pregnancy, and criminal behavior. If a child is turned off on education by age 6, in many cases we will have lost him or her. A child who has not learned to read will become progressively more alienated. That alienation can take many forms, none apt to be viewed as socially acceptable.

8. *A successful system provides health and other social services sufficient to reduce significant barriers to learning.* This is an item that many find surprising in an agenda for education reform. First, it should be made clear that we are not proposing that the schools *provide* these services. Schools have more than enough to do without having their essential mission fragmented by non-education requirements.

At the same time, however, the school is the logical site for the coordination and often the provision of these other services. Unfortunately, for all too many children, simply raising our expectations for educational performance will not make it happen if there are other significant barriers — for example, poor health, chaotic families, criminal activity in or near the school and home, and inadequate nutrition.

We expect our employees to come to work healthy and ready to work, and we help that happen by providing health insurance, exercise programs, and other forms of assistance. We need to make similar provisions for the school children of the nation.

Often, the biggest barrier is the simple lack of coordination and cooperation among schools and other social service agencies — even among primary social service agencies. If we merely achieved coordination, facilitating delivery of help, we would have accomplished a great deal.

Effective collaboration will require an unprecedented realignment of governance responsibilities among the various agencies involved, but collaboration is essential.

9. *A successful system uses technology to raise student and teacher productivity and expand access to learning.* Children today are barraged by technology; yet when they enter the school building, they are virtually cut off from that experience. Most classrooms in the nation lack even a phone, so that teachers are isolated from parents and from outside resources for most of the day. In fact, teachers are often made to feel like supplicants when they even ask for access to a phone in the school office.

Many schools either cannot attract or cannot afford specialized teachers in subjects like advanced math, foreign languages, and higher-level science. But through technology we can provide students with the best teachers and the best courses available.

Let me hasten to add that I do not see technology as a replacement for the teacher in the classroom. Technology is not a stalking horse to reduce the teaching staff. At its best, technology should be used to stimulate, supplement, and elaborate on what can be done in the classroom by the staff at the school.

Appropriate technology (computers, interactive videodiscs) permit students to work at their own pace and explore in depth areas that might not be of interest to everyone.

Disabled students and students at risk can often benefit from the extra attention that can be provided through a mix of technology and teaching.

Finally, schools benefit when technology is used for improved management, for student information systems, and for staff development. The portability of software is especially attractive. A videotape or computer software program can be carried home and previewed by the teacher there. Or it can be taken into another classroom to use with other students.

While these nine components form the basis of a systemic reform agenda that can and should be installed in every state, it does not set limits. There are many other possibilities for improvement. For example, the Virginia State Board of Education has added a school-to-work transition objective. The intent is to provide students who are not college-bound with marketable skills and a developed path to carry them into the workplace. Other states have included objectives related to values or ethical education, so that children will be taught what is right and wrong.

The key essential is that whatever is done be systemic. State leadership should create a vision of education for the 21st century and convince the citizenry that the vision is worth the investment of time and resources to make it a reality.

While it may take a state several years to implement all elements of a successful strategy, it is critical that there be an up-front agreement on the vision behind the strategy and a commitment to achieve it. It should be recognized that certain strategic elements naturally precede others. Ideally, for example, site-based management should be implemented after staff have been trained in how to handle local decision making. An agreement on a performance-based system must precede the creation of assessment instruments.

As the Roundtable works in the 50 states and the District of Columbia, we have made excellent use of what we term a "gap analysis." This is nothing more than an assessment of the reality of education in that state as compared with the model of the Nine Essential Components. The resulting document provides us with a description of the gap between reality and the objective. From this we can create the road map that takes us to our new destination. However, we will never reach that new destination unless we achieve a strong consensus among the political and educational leadership and the voters that we know where we are going and why. Achieving that consensus is at least half of the job that lies ahead of all of us.

The Business Roundtable Education Public Policy Agenda

The Business Roundtable endorses the National Education Goals adopted by the President and the nation's governors. To attain these goals, it believes that a successful education system must include nine essential components that form an integrated whole:

1. A successful education system operates on four assumptions:
   - Every student can learn at significantly higher levels.
   - Every student can be taught successfully.
   - High expectations for every student are reflected in curriculum content, though instructional strategies may vary.
   - Every student and every preschool child needs an advocate, preferably a parent.
2. A successful system is performance- or outcome-based.
3. A successful system uses assessment strategies as strong and rich as the outcomes.
4. A successful system rewards schools for success, helps schools in trouble, and penalizes schools for persistent or dramatic failure.
5. A successful system gives school-based staff a major role in instructional decisions.
6. A successful system emphasizes staff development.
7. A successful system provides high-quality prekindergarten programs, at least for every disadvantaged child.
8. A successful system provides health and other social services sufficient to reduce significant barriers to learning.
9. A successful system uses technology to raise student and teacher productivity and expand access to learning.

Commentary on School Reform

By John F. Jennings

The reform of elementary and secondary schooling was a topic of heated debate in Washington during the last Congress, as Gordon Ambach's paper as well as others in Part I make clear. School reform will continue to be discussed at the national level during the current Congress, especially because the major federal programs of aid to elementary and secondary education must be extended by the end of 1994.

Former Secretary of Education Lamar Alexander presented the Bush Administration's ideas for reform and spoke of his frustrations in dealing with Congress and the national education organizations in seeking enactment of the legislation requested by Mr. Bush. Senator Kennedy (D-Mass.), chairman of the Senate Labor and Human Resources Committee, presented a perspective from Congress, since he was the chief architect of school reform legislation in that body. Mr. Ambach represented the Council of Chief State School Officers, which strongly supported the Kennedy legislation; and Christopher Cross, representing major business groups, spoke of the principles of reform but emphasized that the focus of the Business Roundtable ought to be at the state, and not the federal level.

The key fact in this area of school reform during 1991 and 1992 was that wide differences separated the Republican Administration and the Democratic Congress, and that these differences could not be bridged due to strongly held views on aid to private schools and partisan disagreements linked to the 1992 presidential campaign. Therefore, both the Bush legislation and the competing congressional proposal, the Neighborhood Schools Act, failed to pass.

On the one side, the Republican Administration believed that the Democratic Congress was too beholden to the national public education organizations, especially on the issue of aid to private schools. Secretary Alexander also believed that the Congress was too reluctant to try new approaches to education reform. Consequently, he thought it was better to have no legislation than to accept the bill crafted by the Democratic Congress.

On the other side, the Democratic Congress believed that President Bush was trying to claim credit for improving the schools without spending any significant money on them, and that he would weaken the public schools by encouraging enrollments in private schools through the use of vouchers. The Democrats also were increasingly reluctant, as the presidential election drew near in 1992, to give Mr. Bush the opportunity to sign a piece of legislation he could claim as reforming the schools, and so they rejected many of his ideas, making the final legislation unpalatable to the Republicans in Congress and in the Administration.

The major public education organizations generally held themselves back during this debate, except on the issue of vouchers, which they regard as a "life or death" question. The reason they restrained themselves on the Bush proposal, after some initial enthusiasm, was that they did not see any prospect of increased funding for education to back it up; moreover, they were put off as the Bush Administration became increasingly more aggressive on the issue of private school choice. The national organizations were not eager for the Democratic alternative either, because they again did not see funding being made available to make it a meaningful program.

The Council of Chief State School Officers was unusual among the national education organizations in endorsing and working hard for the Neighborhood Schools Act. That group, under Mr. Ambach's leadership, has become very influential on the issue of school reform.

The business groups are the new actors in these proceedings. In the past they had busied themselves in Washington with worrying about federal taxation and regulatory matters; but recently they have become visible on some social issues as their concern has grown over the quality of the workforce.

But these business groups are unsure of their role at the national level. As the paper from the Business Roundtable shows, many business leaders feel they should concentrate at the state level, since that is where the main constitutional responsibility for education lies. However, another reason they shy away from major involvement at the federal level is that they cannot figure out which side to be on — or, perhaps, how to be on both sides at once.

Many businessmen are inclined to support Republicans and are wary of encouraging too much activism at the federal level because it could lead to higher taxes. But the more they have learned about the social problems of the country, the more they see the need to go beyond simplistic answers like school choice and to support expanded social programs such as Head Start and the Women, Infants, and Children's Program (WIC).

So these four papers depict the policy stew which simmered and boiled during 1991 and 1992 but which was never ready to be served. President Clinton will have his own recipe for reform, but many of the ingredients will be the same as those discussed in the last Congress. A big difference, though, will be that Clinton will have a much greater chance of success than did President Bush.

Partisan disagreements will not exist between the executive and the legislative branches of government because the Democrats will control both. Funding for education should not be the obstacle it was under Bush, since Clinton has declared himself eager to invest in education. The issue of school choice should be less controversial, since both Clinton and the Congress are likely to support public school choice and to oppose private school involvement in such programs.

In addition, the Democrats are avid to show that the gridlock in government in Washington is at an end, and that government can work to help solve our nation's problems. Related to this, of course, is a desire to show that Democrats can govern for the good of the country and therefore should be re-elected.

All of these factors are in Clinton's favor and should help him tremendously in getting his program enacted. He also has going for him the fact that this Congress must renew all the major federal programs of aid to elementary and secondary education. The Elementary and Secondary Education Act and the Individuals with Disabilities Education Act must both be reauthorized in 1994. These programs involve over $10 billion of aid affecting every school district in the country, and the bills to renew them will be the engines pulling new ideas for school reform through Congress. In the legislative process it is always better to attach your proposals to bills that must be enacted to continue ongoing programs than it is to have these proposals considered separately.

This is not to say that Clinton will race through Congress with any proposal he makes. Members of Congress are elected in their own right, and may have strongly held views on education issues. The area of national testing of schoolchildren, for instance, will remain a controversial one. Bush proposed a single national test, but then moved to endorsing a national system of assessment after the National Council on Education Standards and Testing recommended a system and not a test. In 1992 Congress went along with the development of national standards for what children should know and be able to do, but stopped short of approving a national system of assessment.

Some members of Congress believe that tests are a diversion from finding more serious solutions for education problems. Others fear stigmatizing children and do not feel that resources will be provided to help those who fail. On the other hand, many members see the need for greater accountability in education and believe testing will ensure that. This discussion will be a continuation of the debate of 1991 and 1992.

Another difficult issue for Clinton will be to propose changes in current federal programs such as Chapter 1 of the Elementary and Secondary Education Act and the basic program in the Individuals with Disabilities Education Act. These programs are the largest federal aids for elementary and secondary education, and they have been in the schools for two decades.

During 1991 and 1992 the Bush Administration and some members of Congress tried to secure a legislative right to waivers from various requirements under these laws, but many involved with these programs resisted, fearing harm to them. Clinton will have to find some way to make these programs fit in with the conditions of today's schools without lessening the attention they focus on the disadvantaged and disabled.

Another area where Clinton could face serious obstacles is his idea for a youth apprenticeship program. Clinton has proposed a school-to-work transition program that could provide a means for high school youth to connect with employers. Despite the enormous appeal of this proposal, problems exist with the building trade unions, which fear a diminution of traditional apprenticeship and with trying to make schools and companies work together.

These areas, as well as others in which Clinton may make proposals, will be difficult ones to work through Congress; but Clinton has a greater chance to do so than many of his predecessors, because of the political factors mentioned above. In addition, although the debate on school reform in Washington in 1991 and 1992 did not result in successful legislation, it certainly prepared the way for new ideas.

PART II.
POSTSECONDARY
EDUCATION

The Bush Administration's Proposals for Reauthorization of the Higher Education Act

By Barry White

Barry White is chief of the Education Branch, U.S. Office of Management and Budget, Executive Office of the President. He is a career senior executive with 25 years of federal service. Terri Williams, formerly of OMB, and Judy Grew of OMB contributed to this essay. However, the views and opinions expressed herein are Barry White's alone and do not in any way represent official positions of the Bush Administration or the Office of Management and Budget.

In any significant national policy arena with multiple players both in and out of government, no one player "sets the agenda" for a major reauthorization. How each one approaches the issues, however, influences the others. One way of appreciating the issues in a major reauthorization is to understand them from the perspective of the goals of the Administration in office. That is what this paper attempts to do, recognizing that the perceptions of any one participant in a legislative process this big and complex will not accord with all of the perceptions of all others involved.

The Higher Education Act (HEA) reauthorization process of 1991-92 qualified as a significant national policy arena: Its student aid programs alone reached six million students (almost half of all postsecondary students), virtually every postsecondary institution in the country, agencies of every state, and thousands of lenders. Federal cost exceeded $11 billion in 1991 and generated $20 billion in aid.

The fundamental goal of federal student aid programs is to ensure financial access to postsecondary education to otherwise qualified students. Reauthorization issues turn on how well the programs are working and how, or how not, to change them.*

Congress amends the HEA in some way almost every year, but this would be the first major reauthorization in over a decade for which the Administration and Congress started out with more shared goals than differences, as well as a mutual willingness to spend more money (the definition of "more" being open for debate).

The Bush Administration's primary goals were: increased access of the poor to postsecondary education; more grant aid for lowest-income students and larger grants for all income groups; higher loan limits for student borrowers; restoration of financial integrity and public confidence in the programs through stronger laws for policing schools, loan guarantors, and lenders; preventing excessive defaults; instituting rewards for high academic achievement by low-income students; and restructuring precollege assistance to achieve equity and access.

The final legislation fully satisfied little of this agenda, nor the complete agenda of any other single player.

The Context

Who pays? The primary goal of student aid is to lower financial barriers. The central question that should drive student aid policy can therefore be framed as, "How much aid, of what type, should be available to whom, in what circumstances?" Unfortunately, there is no objective method by which one can calculate the answer to this question.

It has long been agreed that the federal government should assist low-income (variously defined) persons and, with less general agreement, that it should ease the financial burden for higher-income families as well. The debates center on the form of assistance (grants, loans, work subsidies) and the amount. Resolving these issues would be easier (though still not easy) if federal aid were the only source of aid, but it is not.

Postsecondary education is financed by family and student resources, state and local government aid, school aid, federal aid, and some pri-

---

*HEA authorizes dozens of programs other than the major student aid programs. There were significant policy debates around many of the other programs and around more issues in student aid than are identified here, but space limitations do not permit coverage.

vate aid.* Some observers believe that the government ought to be the payer of first and last resort, extending the concept of "free public education" that now applies at the elementary and secondary levels to include the cost of education at all types of postsecondary schools, public and private. This is not the theory behind federal law, probably because higher education is not, like a K-12 education, a generally accepted necessity for success for all, either as citizens or in the workplace.

So in order to come to some consensus on the reach of federal policy in this area, the best the federal government can do is to make its decisions through the less intellectually satisfying give and take of subjective political debate over the questions of "fairness" and distributional equity: Who should we help? How much can we afford to do?**

Pays for what? When the HEA was first enacted in 1965, the general image of what student aid would help pay for was "higher education": a two-year "junior college" or a four-year college education. By 1991, roughly $4 billion in Pell Grant and Guaranteed Student Loan subsidies were for vocational training, some provided at two- and four-year colleges, but much in shorter-duration programs at for-profit, "proprietary" schools (which lately prefer to be known as "career colleges").

This is a concern, but not because some people in traditional higher education disparage trade schools or because vocational education is an invalid use of federal subsidies (the federal government spends additional billions on vocational training through a host of other programs). The problem was, and is, that the system designed for traditional higher education has not worked well with these types of programs and institutions. Profits are high and operating costs (not charges) are often low; opportunities to maximize income by misleading students are rife; there are neither cost controls nor required linkages between cost and quality of education (things virtually all postsecondary education sectors fiercely resist); federal oversight was limited in law but more so in practice; offending schools found willing accomplices in some lenders and guarantors to drive up unnecessary borrowing; and the school owners were

---

*See F.J. Fischer, "State Financing of Higher Education," in *Change*, Jan./Feb. 1990, and other sources, for options in policy integration of federal with state aid. No major player proposed such options for this reauthorization. They should be on the table the next time around.

**This may not make public policy theorists comfortable, but it is reality, here and for most major domestic policy arenas. As is not uncommon in such uncomfortable situations, the law has authorized commissions to study the issues. Perhaps they will have new ideas for the next reauthorization.

not political neophytes. The worst aspect of the situation is that most of those hurt are the lowest-income, least-educated persons, those least able to cope with the debt burden (proprietary students had an estimated 45% Stafford Loan default rate for FY 1992) or the bad educational experience they may be left with. And monies misused this way are not available to meet legitimate student aid needs.

By 1991 the Education Department had begun to take more forceful action to deal with offending schools. Congress had enacted a few tougher rules in reconciliation acts and was highlighting these problems in hearings (especially in Senator Sam Nunn's hearings).

The question of what student aid buys is not confined to the question of vocational versus traditional higher education. It reaches the broader issue of the quality of the education that federal money buys in any setting.

One of the hardest things to explain to foreign visitors interested in American higher education policy is that we invest such huge sums without a clear connection to the quality of education purchased (or to student academic effort, an issue I will discuss later). There is a long-standing tradition of nonintervention by the federal government into what goes on inside postsecondary institutions. The HEA has relied on accreditation bodies to ensure quality education. The frequency and intensity of criticisms of the quality of higher education suggest that this approach is not sufficient. The quality question, coupled with the high cost of education to consumers and to government at all levels, seems sure to lead to more intense government inquiry into the cost and quality relationship. Reauthorization debates on accreditation and the state monitoring role opened up the quality issue.

Federal cost. Federal costs rose rapidly in the 1980s. The Administration's commitment to education ensured its willingness to spend more, but also prompted the aforementioned concern for what the money bought. Budget deficit worries cast a shadow over the issue of how much to spend.

HEA Title IV	Billions of Dollars		Percent change
	1980	1991	
Federal costs			
Discretionary appropriation (Pell, SEOG, Perkins Loans, work-study, SSIG) . . .	3.5	6.7	+ 91
Mandatory-outlays (guaranteed student loans	1.6	4.8	+200
Aid available	10.2	20.0	+ 96

The Budget Enforcement Act of 1990 (BEA) put enforceable limits on government spending as follows:

- Discretionary costs, such as Pell Grants, are limited by absolute caps that grow at a rate below inflation each year. Student aid discretionary outlays (Pell, et al.) were $6.3 billion in 1991, more than 3% of all domestic discretionary outlays. All discretionary programs compete for a fixed amount of funds.
- Mandatory costs (mainly entitlements), such as guaranteed student loans (GSL), above current low levels (for example, the cost of legislating higher loan limits, not the cost of more students borrowing under current law limits) have to be paid for with cuts elsewhere in the same or other mandatory programs, or by revenue increases (the BEA's pay-as-you-go, or "PAYGO," rule).

For the major federal education laws, Congress routinely authorizes discretionary spending levels without close regard to what it will actually appropriate for them. This is as true for the Pell Grant program as for elementary and secondary programs. In sharp contrast, executive branch legislative proposals are made to fit a specific spending level the Administration will seek in appropriations. This difference in approach is one of the most important distinctions between executive and legislative branch approaches to authorizing legislation.

Neither the higher education interest groups nor most key congressional players agree with the executive branch approach. Their preference might most favorably be said to be to authorize the highest possible level and hope that, over time, this puts pressure on appropriators to meet it. This fundamental difference doomed hope of agreement in HEA on Pell Grant rules that affect cost.

Budget Structure Issues

Pell entitlement. Although appropriated on the discretionary side of the budget, the Pell Grant program is structured like an entitlement: Individuals receive a grant amount set by the combination of HEA rules and modifications made to them in the annual appropriations acts. The law provided several ways of dealing with any resulting shortfall in a given year's funding.

Some in Congress believe that if Pell were moved to the mandatory side, cost would no longer be an issue; shortfalls would be dealt with routinely, and program growth would be ensured. In one limited way, that is true: Cost growth under current law resulting from unpredicted growth in the number of recipients or changes in their income, employment, and other factors affecting award size could be funded without congressional action.

On the other hand, any legislation to raise benefits (for example, the maximum award) would be subject to PAYGO; another program would have to be reduced to fund the increase. Pressure to reduce the deficit, fueled in large part by mandatory cost growth, has led to the major mandatory program cost-cutting exercises of recent years in nearly annual budget reconciliation acts. Pell Grants as a mandatory program would be vulnerable to such cuts. The program would be competing for resources with student loans, Medicaid, welfare, and other programs with strong constituencies.

Contributing to the entitlement debate as reauthorization extended into 1992 was the growing awareness that Pell cost estimates — by the Administration, the Congressional Budget Office, and interest groups — were increasingly further from reality. Generally, awards are made whether or not the appropriation for a given year is large enough to pay for the sum of all such awards. Among the ways to deal with insufficient appropriations is by using a subsequent year's appropriation to pay for the current year's awards — so-called "borrowing" — which then is replaced by a separate appropriation or by still more borrowing from future appropriations. As long as the borrowing is not too large, it is a more attractive strategy to Congress and the executive branch than the alternatives of reducing award amounts or restricting eligibility. In January 1992, the shortfall was estimated to be $332 million; by spring, it exceeded $1 billion and was rising. Entitlement advocates saw the shortfall as supporting their argument, because if Pell were a mandatory program, these awards would be paid without borrowing or cutting awards.

Given its generic policy of limiting growth in mandatory spending, the Administration never seriously considered proposing Pell Grant entitlement. It threatened to veto any bill that did. Proposals in Congress did not reach the floor of either body.

Direct loans. The idea of replacing the guaranteed student loan programs, which use federal subsidies to generate private capital, with direct federal loans, using federal capital, has been discussed for years for a variety of reasons: to eliminate the administrative complexity of working through banks and intermediary guarantee agencies; to save money by eliminating bank and guarantee agency subsidies; and to make it easier to convert repayment to long-term, income-contingent schemes, using the Internal Revenue Service as the administrator. One major reason such proposals did not become law was that, under most schemes, the federal capital needed — $10 billion to $12 billion per year — had to be appropriated, raising the budget cost of loans far above what Congress would likely provide.

The appropriation issue changed with passage of the Credit Reform Act of 1990. The goal of credit reform is to treat the budget cost of guaranteed and direct lending in a way that permits true cost comparisons. Before credit reform, the annual cost of both types of loans was equal to the cash each needed each year: for GSL, student and lender interest subsidies, default costs, and administrative costs, less origination and insurance fees; for direct lending, administrative costs plus the loan capital disbursed that year, less repayments. Budgeting for the capital this way made direct lending in a given year many billions more costly than guaranteed lending, even though, over the life of the loan and repayments, it could turn out that the net federal cost of direct lending was less than guaranteed lending. Credit reform changed the accounting of all federal lending beginning in FY 1992. (The cost of the outstanding portfolio of pre-1992 loans is, with certain exceptions, still budgeted the pre-credit-reform way).

Under credit reform, federal capital is a "financing" cost that does not appear in the budget authority and outlay totals. Thus the $10 billion to $12 billion was no longer a cost to the program budget (it still adds to the federal debt, but that does not show up in program budgets).

Direct lending now became a front-burner issue of program administration and cost-saving on the mandatory side. Except for the question of how any savings would be used (for example, higher borrowing limits, lower student interest, offsets to other mandatory program costs, deficit reduction), it was not a major issue affecting benefits. It did not, necessarily, affect how much aid would be available to whom and for what; nor would it likely make a material difference in default prevention.

The Administration examined the direct lending issue at some length, but decided early on not to support it. The Bush Administration had taken a strong hand in publicly identifying the many problems in the loan programs, issuing its report, "Improving Guaranteed Student Loan Program Management," in April 1991. Media and congressional investigations highlighted GSL problems much earlier and even more critically. For some observers, direct lending was an opportunity to sweep GSL's problems away. Analysis indicated strong reasons for caution:

- Direct lending could expose the government to greater risks than GSL, by eliminating what risk-sharing GSL had (limited but significant). In light of the S&L experience and the financial failure in 1990 of the largest student loan guarantor, greater financial risk was not desirable.
- Direct lending would add billions to the national debt.
- Administrative savings from direct loans look good on paper; achieving them presents enormous management challenges.
- The outstanding general student loans ($51 billion in 1991) would still need close management for many years. Without the money incentives and other links to new lending that direct lending eliminates, bank and guarantor management of the portfolio could deteriorate rapidly. Some new system would be needed to prevent massive defaults and loss of control.
- Cost-savings estimates were highly speculative (and remain so, as the Government Accounting Office has recently indicated by its sensitivity analyses on its own estimate of savings). Reduced GSL subsidies also were being considered, so direct lending was not the only cost-saving option.
- Among GSL's worst problems were abuses by proprietary schools. Direct lending envisions schools as the loan originators. Proprietary schools would therefore get more control over billions more in federal funds.
- The guaranteed loan program is not a failure. It delivers capital where needed; the great majority of students repay on time, without need for extended repayment terms; and the government's management problems, while acute, are not insurmountable.

Taking into account the program integrity provisions likely to be enacted, it was reasonable to expect reauthorization to produce a much-improved GSL program. This seemed much more preferable to the risks, costs, and unknowns of direct loans.*

Ultimately, Congress agreed; neither the House nor Senate committee brought a full-replacement, direct-loan program to HEA floor debates. Congress did authorize a major demonstration program, now

---

*One frustrated participant in the internal debate went to the press with his views. This led some to make specious claims that the Administration had "supported" direct lending. As a matter of record, the Administration was completely open about the fact that it was analyzing the costs and benefits of a full direct-lending substitute for guaranteed loans; but when the analysis was complete, it lead to the decision not to support such a proposal. That position was never altered.

under way, that should settle many of the key management issues this approach raises, in time for consideration in the next reauthorization.

Program Policies to Carry Out the Goals*

Increasing access; more grant aid for the poor. Administration principles here were straightforward: grant aid is the most costly aid; in the world of limited resources, it must go first to those who most need and benefit from it. Research was clear that past changes in need determination and award rules had shifted the distribution of Pell Grant aid from lower- to higher-income families. Research also showed that grant aid has the largest effect on the enrollment behavior of the poor and that their participation in higher education is particularly sensitive to costs. Award rules sent funding more toward students at higher-cost schools, who were more often those from higher-income families.

All Pell recipients are needy by definition, albeit some are not "poor" by common standards (a very few get awards even with incomes over $50,000, but 80% have incomes under $20,000; more than 50% under $10,000). The Administration's goal was to drive the maximum amount of grant aid to the poorest students. At the same time, the Administration responded to the growing call for aid to families with more income by assuring them that they also could receive larger Pell Grants (see also the discussion below on higher loan limits).

Many of the poorest students attend low-cost schools, so the proposal to raise the maximum award, though a dramatic increase (up 54%, from $2,400 to $3,700), was not enough to get more aid to the poorest. The Administration therefore proposed to replace the three Pell award rules with two, one of which was new: Once "need" was established (cost of attendance less a formula share of family and student income and assets), a higher percentage of the need would be met for the lowest-

---

*Policies were initially set out in the FY 1992 President's Budget (February 1991) and in messages to Congress of April and June of 1991. Some were modified, during House and Senate negotiations, for the FY 1993 budget (February 1992) and subsequently. This paper uses policies as codified for the FY 1993 budget, unless otherwise indicated. Note also that the size of the unfunded Pell liability was unknown when the proposals were made. Its dimensions did not begin to come clear (estimates at this writing are still rising) until late spring of 1992.

income students, a declining percentage for other students. Several scales were proposed. The last was: 80% of need for families with incomes below $10,000, scaling down to 55% for incomes above $20,000.

Scaling awards to need is equitable and easy to explain. Coupled with the proposed spending increase, higher maximum award, and other provisions, Pell funding and average awards in virtually every income category would go up. The following table highlights these effects of the proposals; it appeared in the FY 1993 President's Budget.

Pell Grant Factors	1992 Enacted	1993 Proposed	Change Dollars	Percent
Appropriation (millions)	5,463[1]	6,361[1]	+ 1,178	+ 22
Maximum award (dollars)	2,400	3,700	+ 1,300	+ 54
Average award (dollars)	1,452	1,846	+ 394	+ 27

[1]1992 as of Jan. 1992; 1993 includes short fall funding.

Funds by family income category (millions)

Under $10,000	3,398	3,697	+ 299	+ 9
$10,000 to $20,000	1,355	1,601	+ 246	+ 18
$20,000 to $30,000	616	712	+ 95	+ 15
$30,000 to $40,000	165	221	+ 57	+ 34
$40,000 to $50,000	38	47	+ 9	+ 24
$50,000 and above	10	10	--	--

Average award by income category (millions)

Under $10,000	1,635	2,137	+ 502	+ 31
$10,000 to $20,000	1,466	1,921	+ 455	+ 31
$20,000 to $30,000	1,100	1,305	+ 205	+ 19
$30,000 to $40,000	809	999	+ 190	+ 23
$40,000 to $50,000	649	764	+ 115	+ 18
$50,000 and above	552	752	+ 200	+ 36

The other effects of the proposals, however, were not welcomed by aid advocates. Although it was certainly not their primary purpose, these proposals did reduce the expected number of recipients and the distribution of awards. Key elements:

- Toughen rules for when a student could declare financial independence from his family and thus claim higher awards.
- Require schools to verify data on more aid applications (tests show this reduces error and eliminates ineligibles).

- Eliminate (subject to "mitigating circumstances") high-default schools (that is, extend GSL rules to Pell) to prevent abuse of the more costly grant program. Estimates assume half the students at such schools would transfer to eligible schools while the rest would not.
- Change "expected family contribution" to reduce awards for some higher-income students, for example, require a minimum student contribution from all but the poorest families.
- Institute a modest academic performance requirement.

The net effect of all proposals was to lower estimated Pell Grant recipients from 3.8 million to 3.4 million students. In student aid politics, this was unforgivable, regardless of the merits of individual proposals. The Administration could not convince the Congress or the interest groups of the necessity for accepting any reduction in the number of participants, even if it meant a stronger program and more resources for the remaining 3.4 million.

Moreover, the Administration also proposed to eliminate new federal capital for the campus-based Perkins Loan revolving funds (-$156 million) and to cut spending and increase matching for the other campus-based grant (-$219 million) and work-study (-$161 million) programs. Perkins Loans are much more heavily subsidized than GSLs and less widely available. Perkins and the other programs are less well targeted. Spending more on the uniformly administered Pell program to ensure more grant aid for the poorer students was more important than maintaining the federal share of the other programs.

These proposals were equally unacceptable to Congress and many schools. Schools use these funds to provide aid to students of their choice (albeit still means-tested) and to subsidize on-campus jobs that otherwise would require paying the full cost of staff with their own funds.

Congress did make changes in Pell award rules and need analysis. Some simplify the process, others give a larger share of funds to higher-income persons. The act raised the authorized maximum award to $3,700 for 1993 — presumably to match the level proposed by the Administration — with $200 increases for each year thereafter. But because Congress was not bound by the executive branch rule of authorizing levels expected to be appropriated, it changed Pell without concern for cost. It authorized a Pell program costing an estimated $12 billion in 1993. A few weeks later, Congress appropriated $6 billion.

More loan aid. Subsidizing borrowing has long been a part of federal aid strategy. Views of its place in that strategy vary. Some say subsidized borrowing should be the only aid, since most individuals indisputably reap a substantial economic benefit from higher education and can pay back loans. Others say borrowing creates debt burden whose prospect may deter the poor from higher education. (Evidence here is scant. See "Student Loans: Are They Overburdening a Generation?" The College Board, 1986).

Whatever one's belief, as a practical matter the prominence of loan aid in federal aid strategy is not likely to diminish. School costs are likely to continue to rise faster than grant funds can rise, and grants are about four times more expensive per dollar of aid than loans. Many students really do not need grants, only the ability to spread out payments over time.

How much borrowing to allow is another subjective policy choice. More borrowing means higher subsidy costs for the mandatory side of the budget. The Administration proposed raising limits to make more aid available to all, especially middle-class persons. More borrowing also would replace aid some would lose due to the other policies. The final bill did raise limits. It also provides new, less subsidized (perversely titled "*un*subsidized") loans, regardless of family income.

Financial and program integrity; default reduction. The many Administration proposals in this area followed the principles of broadening financial risk-sharing and toughening penalties for program violations. Key proposals:

- State risk-sharing: require states to provide the equivalent of "full faith and credit" backing to the guarantors of loans in their jurisdiction; penalties on states for highest default rate schools and lenders; financial support to states for enhanced school monitoring.
- Guarantee agency management controls: financial reserve and management standards; more authority to the Secretary of Education to reduce risk of failure; authority to act in the event of failure.
- Lender controls: penalties (reduced special allowance) for high default rates.
- Schools: extension of the GSL high-default school "kick-out" provisions to school eligibility for Pell and other programs; improved "limitation, suspension, and termination" authority; state monitoring; tougher controls on accreditation.

This was an area where all reauthorization players agreed that much needed to be done, but they had significant differences on how to do it. Much-improved guarantor controls were enacted. Congress took the Administration's extremely sketchy notion of state oversight of schools and created a relatively strong state function that could turn out to be one of the most important benefits of the reauthorization. While accreditation controls were strengthened, there is little reason to expect accreditation ever to become a strong component of program integrity strategy. Less was done with the major risk-sharing proposals. In the main, the new HEA provisions do signal congressional expectation of tougher management and give the Department of Education better tools than it had before to carry out the tasks.

Because of highly publicized abuses by some proprietary vocational schools, the issue of how to shape aid for vocational training usually arose during discussions of program integrity. The Administration did not propose limiting access of vocational training schools to student aid. This question opens up the much wider issue of how to resolve the programmatic chaos that characterizes federal subsidies for vocational training. Dealing with that means looking not only at HEA, the largest source of federal vocational training financing, but also the Perkins Vocational Education Act, the Job Training Partnership Act (JTPA), the Welfare/Jobs program, veterans' vocational training, the Employment Service, and many smaller programs. These programs have overlapping eligible populations, different delivery systems, different subsidy rates, no common approach to local or national job markets, and different congressional authorizing subcommittees. Some analysis of these issues was done during development of the HEA proposals, but the inter-agency complexities are substantial and time ran out before a strategy could be developed.

In April 1992, the Administration did propose a first step toward rationalizing this situation, the Job Training 2000 Act. This would have required major programs to have the quality of training they financed certified by states and local entities built on JTPA's Private Industry Council structure, consistent labor market and school quality data, and common referral points. The proposal was made too late to get serious consideration. It was a logical way to make the system accessible and effective, without wholesale redesign of the entire legislative structure.

Pre-college assistance. A number of HEA programs help disadvantaged students in junior high and high school learn about, prepare for, and aspire to postsecondary education. They are competitive (rather than formula) grants and cost more than $200 million. Many of them would give the same grantees awards year after year.

85

The Administration proposed to help states make these services an integral part of their strategies for youth. States would receive a formula share of funds, to be spent in accord with a plan to make services widely available to disadvantaged youth, along with the states' own counseling and support-service resources. Youngsters would no longer get aid only by virtue of the chance presence of an institutional grantee in their area.

The proposal was rejected in favor of authorizing still more competitive grants. The Administration did not mount an effective strategy to market its notion or develop state support. Probably more importantly, it did not propose to grandfather in (or only slowly phase out) current grantees. These are popular programs with laudable goals, few detractors, a strong lobby, and almost no objective data on effectiveness. Absent evidence of failure and without a strong case made for a new policy, the proposal got little attention.

Academic achievement. Traditionally, federal aid addresses only student finances, not academic achievement. The HEA does require recipients to maintain the same "satisfactory academic progress" as a school requires of all its students, but this may not even be a minimum passing grade. At one time, the HEA required a high school diploma or equivalent to qualify for aid, but that was dropped years ago in favor of a determination of "ability to benefit" from postsecondary education. (Reportedly, an effort was made during House committee consideration to restore the degree requirement, but it was overwhelmingly defeated).

The Administration proposed: 1) In general, Pell recipients must maintain at least a C average; and 2) the best students receive $500 supplements to their Pell Grants. These were first steps to show that the government values high achievement. They were part of the Administration's broad goal for all levels of education, of raising education standards, expectations, and achievement.

Neither proposal was greeted enthusiastically by interest groups or most members of Congress. They were said to interfere with school independence and to be susceptible to grade inflation to preserve aid (the latter is a significant issue). The second also was attacked as siphoning away federal aid for financial access. At $170 million out of $7.7 billion proposed for discretionary student aid, this was not an obvious threat, but perhaps was viewed as the camel's nose.

Both proposals were rejected. A Pell Grant add-on was enacted, but not for high achievement. Awards to first-year students go to those who meet course requirements (good in theory, but it is impossible to know, by course name alone, whether course content is true college-prep material), have only a C + average, and either participate in a precollege assistance program (not relevant at all, and discriminatory against those with no formal program in their school) or have high class standing. Subsequent awards go to those who achieve as little as the satisfactory academic progress standard. If the strong movement toward academic standards and performance measures for all levels of education continues in the 1990s, these issues are sure to be revisited in the next reauthorization, if not before.

Conclusion

Because this author was a party to the development of the Administration's proposals, it is likely that this recitation puts them in a more favorable light than other authors in this volume will shine on them. Nevertheless, the record shows that the policies had clearly articulated philosophical underpinnings, followed from a coherent strategic vision of the federal role, and were often (though not often enough) supported by good analysis. They were also fiscally responsible, within the Administration's overall fiscal policy construct.

There are always confrontations and policy arguments during a major reauthorization. In this one, the opening mood of shared goals, though mightily strained during the process and seemingly belied by theatrics by all parties at different times, did result in a bill the President could sign, and did not leave any wounds so deep they will get in the way of future cooperation.

The greatest disappointments seem to me that: 1) Pell rules make so many eligible it is likely it will never be fully funded nor give enough grant aid to the poorest; 2) tensions between benefits for the middle class and the poor are not resolved; 3) unnecessary borrowing has been made too easy; 4) the opportunity to raise academic expectations was missed; and 5) precollege programs remain outside the mainstream of state and local education strategy.

On the other hand: 1) There are now much better guarantee agency, school, and lender management tools; 2) there is a single need-analysis system; 3) loan interest rates are structured more realistically; 4) there are new options for default avoidance; and 5) a large, direct-loan pilot and new commissions will inform the next reauthorization. That is a lot to build on for the next time around.

Reauthorizing the Higher Education Act: Federal Policy Making For Postsecondary Education

By Thomas R. Wolanin

Thomas R. Wolanin is the staff director of the House Subcommittee on Postsecondary Education. From the House side, he managed the reauthorizations of the Higher Education Act in 1980, 1986, and 1992. He has been involved in federal legislation affecting higher education since 1971. He has a B.A. from Oberlin College and a Ph.D. in government from Harvard University. He has taught at Oberlin College and the University of Wisconsin-Madison.

On July 23, 1992, President Bush signed the Higher Education Amendments of 1991. Speaking against a backdrop of smiling students of all ages at Northern Virginia Community College, the President hailed the legislation. "I hope that many middle- and low-income families who dream of a college education for their children will find that this legislation helps to make their dreams reality," the President said. He also saluted the members of Congress who had worked on the legislation for their "bipartisan" and "nonpartisan" efforts. The President's signature at the love feast before the cameras not only made the bill a law but also brought to a temporary conclusion a process that had been going on for almost two years.

The Higher Education Act and Reauthorization

The Higher Education Amendments of 1992 reauthorized the Higher Education Act for six years (FY 1993-98). An authorizing statute such as the Higher Education Act establishes the legal authority for programs to exist. Besides defining the programs, purposes, and structure, it specifies which individuals or institutions are eligible for funds to carry out the act's purposes. It also establishes the upper limit of funding. Funds are provided through the separate annual appropriations process, but no funds can be provided for an activity or program unless it is authorized.

The relationship between an authorization and an appropriation can be compared to a hunting license and a hunt. The license (authorization) is a prerequisite to hunt; it describes the type of game (program purpose) to be hunted, and it sets a limit on the amount of game (appropriations) you can take. However, it does not guarantee a successful hunt; and there are many examples of authorized programs for which no appropriation is made.

The Higher Education Act, last renewed for six years in 1986, was sunsetted (scheduled to expire) on September 30, 1992, thus occasioning its "reauthorization." At its most basic level, the reauthorization is the extension of programs that would otherwise expire. Most importantly, however, since the programs are scheduled to expire, the reauthorization process *requires* that the programs be considered and therefore provides the opportunity to re-examine, change, add to, and subtract from the existing array of programs.

The Higher Education Act of 1965 as amended is nearly 400 pages long; it contains 12 titles and more than 70 programs. The centerpiece of the act is the student assistance programs in Title IV. For the final year of the existing authorization (the 1992-93 school year), these programs are making available approximately $21.5 billion in loans, grants, and work opportunities to students.

The student assistance programs are aimed at helping individuals to overcome financial and nonfinancial barriers to participation in postsecondary education. This goal of equal educational opportunity is premised on the fact that talent and ability in America are not distributed in direct proportion to income and financial resources. Individuals and the nation will be poorer if those individuals with talent, ability, and motivation who lack financial resources are precluded from fully developing their talents and abilities because they cannot afford postsecondary education or because they face such nonfinancial barriers as the lack of information about postsecondary education.

Almost all of this federal student aid is awarded on the basis of financial need. More than seven million postsecondary students, or more than

40% of all students, will receive some form of federal student aid this year. Federal student aid represents about 75% of all student aid awarded in the United States from all sources. In addition, Title IV includes the TRIO programs, which provide encouragement, support, and assistance to low-income and first-generation-in-college students to overcome non-financial barriers to educational opportunity. These programs had an appropriation of nearly $400 million for the 1992-93 school year and served 670,000 persons.

Given the federal share of all student aid, it follows that the federal government is the dominant player in providing student aid to advance the goal of equal educational opportunity. Indeed, support for student financial aid is one of two areas of education policy making where the federal government is dominant as measured by its share of the financing. The other is support for research at colleges and universities.

Also, given the magnitude of the financial commitment and the number of students affected, the federal student aid programs are very important federal domestic programs. Reauthorization of the Higher Education Act, including the student aid programs, is clearly a very important exercise in education policy making specifically and federal domestic policy making generally. Thus, early in 1991 as the reauthorization process was beginning, the *Washington Post* editorialized that reauthorizing the Higher Education Act "may become the most important social legislation of this Congress."

The non-Title IV programs in the Higher Education Act include support for college libraries, historically black colleges and universities, teacher training, international education, construction of academic facilities, cooperative education, graduate fellowships, and the Fund for the Improvement of Postsecondary Education (FIPSE). While these programs make important contributions to enhancing the quality of American higher education, more than 95% of the money appropriated under the Higher Education Act supports the Title IV student assistance programs. The Title IV programs were therefore the primary focus of the reauthorization debate.

The Reauthorization Process

While the groundwork to develop new legislation can extend over many years, all bills (including reauthorization of the Higher Education Act) must navigate all of the stages of the legislative process — House and Senate committee action, House and Senate floor consideration, House-Senate conference committee, House and Senate passage of the conference report, and presidential signature — within the two years of a Congress, in this case the 102nd Congress (1991-92).

In the House, responsibility for the reauthorization fell to the Subcommittee on Postsecondary Education of the Education and Labor Committee. In the 102nd Congress both the Subcommittee on Postsecondary Education and the Education and Labor Committee were chaired by Congressman William D. Ford (D-Mich.). Congressman Ford also had chaired the Subcommittee on Postsecondary Education for the reauthorizations of 1980 and 1986. In the Senate, reauthorization was handled by the Subcommittee on Education, Arts, and Humanities chaired by Senator Claiborne Pell (D-R.I.), who had chaired the subcommittee for the reauthorizations in 1972, 1976, 1980, and 1986. The Senate full committee, the Committee on Labor and Human Resources, was chaired by Senator Edward Kennedy (D-Mass.).

The history of federal policy making for higher education amply demonstrates that only when there is a broad consensus between the legislative and executive branches are there major advances in federal policy. Such a consensus existed for the post-World War II G.I. Bill, the National Defense Education Act of 1958, the Higher Education Act of 1965, the Education Amendments of 1972, and the Middle Income Student Assistance Act in 1978. In the absence of consensus, both branches have the ability to frustrate policies desired by the other and to produce the "gridlock" so often discussed in the 1992 presidential campaign.

The question for the reauthorization of the Higher Education Act was how broad a consensus could be found between the policy preferences of the House and Senate controlled by Democrats and the executive branch controlled by a Republican President, George Bush. Would the reauthorization be a major landmark in federal higher education policy, significantly recasting the programs to meet new and emerging needs? Or would it simply reaffirm the status quo because there was no agreement on how to change it?

Reauthorization Goals

As the House and Senate Democratic chairmen and their staffs made the rounds of association meetings and think tank seminars early in 1991, their remarks made clear that there was broad agreement between the House and Senate Democrats on the reauthorization priorities. Seven issues emerged as the focus of the Democrats' aspirations for the reauthorization.

First, during the decade of the Eighties there had been a dramatic shift in federal student aid from primary reliance on grants to primary reliance on loans. At the beginning of the decade about two-thirds of federal student aid was grants and one-third loans. By the end of the decade the proportions had been reversed to two-third loans and one-third grants. In the Sixties and Seventies grants had been seen as the vehicle for expanding educational opportunities for students from low-income backgrounds, while loans were viewed as a supplement to help middle-income families meet their cash flow needs or to enhance "choice," enabling students to attend higher-priced colleges and universities. Now all students, even the most needy, were required to borrow for postsecondary education. In the eyes of the Democrats, loans were an inferior mechanism for expanding educational opportunities, since many low-income individuals were adverse to borrowing large amounts and would forgo postsecondary education rather than borrow. In addition, loans left low-income students bearing significant debt burdens while their more affluent peers left school debt-free. This seemed inconsistent with the goal of equalizing opportunities among income groups. Redressing the growing "imbalance" between loans and grants was a high-priority objective for the Democrats.

Second, during the Eighties the inflation-adjusted income of middle-income Americans either stagnated or declined, while college costs rose faster than inflation. A Gallup poll released in October 1991 found that more than 80% of the public agreed with this statement, "College costs are rising at a rate that will put college out of the reach of most people." College opportunities for students from middle-income families seemed to be narrowing. In addition, it was a widely held political judgment among Democrats that the student aid programs were not politically viable in the long run if they rested on a narrow base by serving only the lowest-income students. Therefore eligibility for the student aid programs needed to be extended to students from middle-income families.

Third, the student aid programs had been tarnished by reports detailing the exploitation of students by unscrupulous schools, growing default costs, schools offering overpriced and inferior educational programs, and schools and lenders with unacceptably high default rates. These concerns had been highlighted in television documentaries and exposés, investigative reports in major newspapers, reports of the Department of Education's inspector general, and well-publicized hearings held in 1990 by Senator Sam Nunn's Permanent Subcommittee on Investigations. Many persons in Congress saw an urgent need to restore public confidence in the programs as a precondition for expanding aid to students from middle-income families and for redressing the loan/grant imbalance. In particular, the appropriations committees needed to be assured that funds made available for student aid were being well spent.

Fourth, the applications for student aid and the delivery process had become a maze of increasingly daunting complexity, particularly for students and their families. This complexity was in some cases defeating the basic equal opportunity objective of the programs as students from less sophisticated, low-income, and disadvantaged backgrounds gave up in the face of the forms and the process. Thus attention was directed toward simplification of the forms and the delivery system.

Fifth, it became evident that many students in the precollege education pipeline were not motivated to develop their talents because they were unaware of the range of postsecondary educational opportunities available to them and of the availability of financial aid for college. They did not know that they could or should aspire to postsecondary education. There needed to be more attention on outreach programs, early intervention, and early awareness reaching students in the high schools and middle schools.

Sixth, the House committee report on the 1976 reauthorization of the Higher Education Act noted that "The 'typical student' is no longer young, no longer full-time, no longer just out of high school, no longer a stranger to the work world . . . and, to be certain, he is no longer overwhelmingly 'he'." By the early Nineties this statement had become a truism. The student aid programs initially conceived for a student population that was predominantly composed of male, full-time, 18- to 22-year-olds needed to be revised to effectively serve the "nontraditional student" who was the new majority in postsecondary education.

Seventh, education policy discussions in the 1980s were dominated by the need to reform and revitalize elementary and secondary education. Improving the quality of classroom teachers was seen as one key to this effort. Thus there was renewed interest in the programs in Title V of the Higher Education Act to improve preservice and inservice teacher training, facilitate the recruitment of minority teachers, encourage high-ability students to pursue teaching careers, and to reward successful and innovative teachers.

Hearings

Senator Pell's Subcommittee on Education, Arts, and Humanities kicked off the reauthorization process, beginning its hearings on February

21, 1991. By May 13, when its work was finished, the subcommittee had held a total of 19 hearings, eight in Washington, D.C., and 11 outside of Washington. In addition, the Senate full committee held four hearings on the reauthorization.

Before beginning its hearings in February 1991, the House Subcommittee on Postsecondary Education solicited recommendations for the reauthorization from 160 organizations, associations, and governmental bodies. Recommendations were received from 149 respondents representing the spectrum of those interested in the reauthorization, such as American Bankers Association, AFL-CIO, American Trucking Association, Association of Jesuit Colleges and Universities, National Association of Student Financial Aid Administrators, State Higher Education Executive Officers, United Negro College Fund, and United States Student Association. Recommendations received by mid-April were printed in six volumes made available to all interested parties.

The first House hearing was held jointly with the Senate on March 28 to hear from student witnesses. The House subcommittee held a total of 44 hearings, 25 in Washington and 19 in the field, concluding on August 1. The sites for the field hearings ranged from Providence, Rhode Island, to Hilo, Hawaii, and from Great Falls, Montana, to Houston, Texas.

The sites for both the House and Senate field hearings were chosen in the districts or the states of members of the respective subcommittees. Witnesses at each hearing were selected to represent the spectrum of opinion on programs or issues, such as Pell Grants or program integrity or, in the case of field hearings, the range of views in the state or region on the reauthorization.

The Administration got into the game a little late, not submitting a summary of its legislative proposals for the reauthorization to Congress until April 30, 1991. This summary was followed by a draft bill reflecting the Administration's proposals, sent to Congress on June 5. By the time the Administration proposals reached Congress, the Senate hearings had almost concluded. However, the Administration's views were thoroughly aired in the House hearings, at which witnesses representing the Administration testified 13 times.

Consensus in the Hearings

The congressional hearings included more than 600 witnesses, whose testimony comprised more than 4,000 pages in the hearing record. These hearings were a comprehensive survey of opinion and recommendations both inside the Beltway and throughout the country. As the committees looked forward to marking up bills and sending them to the House and the Senate, they found the net result of the hearings was a broad consensus in a number of areas. The House and Senate subcommittees (both Democrats and Republicans), the Administration, and the interested and informed public as represented by the witnesses were in agreement on the following basic thrusts for the reauthorization:

1. The student aid programs needed to be tightened up to minimize fraud and abuse, primarily by strengthening the "gatekeeping" performed by the Department of Education, the accrediting bodies, and the states, to eliminate from eligibility those schools that abused the programs.
2. Significant simplification of the student aid delivery system was desirable.
3. New early outreach programs were required.
4. The federal student aid programs should be modified to better serve the needs of nontraditional students. The President proposed a separate "Lifelong Learning Act" that emphasized this objective.
5. New initiatives in teacher training should be undertaken. Elements of the Administration's America 2000 proposal pointed in this direction.

In sum, five of the seven goals that the Democrats had articulated at the beginning of the process turned out to be broadly shared by almost everyone, including the House and Senate Republicans and the Administration. However, a year of hard work remained, with intense discussions and tough bargaining, before the President signed the bill that turned these broad agreements on principles and goals into specific legislation. It was details rather than basic policy differences that slowed the process.

Outstanding Issues: Loan/Grant Imbalance

There still remained two of the Democrats' original goals on which no consensus existed: what to do about the loan/grant imbalance and whether eligibility for student aid should be extended to students from middle-income families. In addition, a third issue had arisen: Should the existing student loan programs be replaced with a "direct" loan program?

In the hearings there was universal hand-wringing about the loan/grant imbalance. Since the Pell Grant program is by far the largest federal grant program to students, providing about $5.5 billion for the 1992-93 school year, attention focused on the level of Pell Grant funding. It was apparent that the increasing reliance on loans by students resulted in large measure from erosion in the purchasing power of Pell Grants. In 1980 the maximum Pell Grant, which goes to students from the lowest-income families, would pay for about 50% of the average cost of attending college. By the early Nineties, the maximum Pell Grant would buy only about 25% of the average cost of attending college. So the purchasing power of the grants had decreased by about half in a decade. This situation was largely caused by annual appropriations that were insufficient to meet the Pell Grant maximum authorized in the Higher Education Act. During the 20-year history of the Pell Grant program (FY 1973 to FY 1992), sufficient appropriations to fund the authorized maximum had been provided only three times, most recently in FY 1979, 13 years ago. The appropriation bills routinely contained language overriding the authorized Pell Grant maximum in the Higher Education Act and setting a lower maximum. For example, in FY 1992 the Higher Education Act authorized a $3,100 Pell Grant maximum but the appropriations established a $2,400 maximum.

It seemed futile to authorize increased Pell Grant maximums for future years that would in all likelihood be empty promises. The solution was to make the Pell Grant program an entitlement. If the program were an entitlement, funding would be mandatory rather than discretionary. Students eligible for Pell Grants would have a legal right to the full amount for which they were eligible, and the appropriations bills would have to provide enough money to fund the full grants of all eligible students. Among the higher education constituency, particularly students, there was broad support for a Pell Grant entitlement that was expressed in the course of the hearings in both houses. The Administration adamantly opposed a Pell Grant entitlement, and indeed threatened to veto the reauthorization if it contained such an entitlement. The Administration argued that making Pell Grants entitlements would dramatically increase the cost of the program. Depending on the eligibility rules and the level of the maximum award, the program cost would have roughly doubled to about $10 billion to $12 billion. In addition, the Administration argued that the budget deficit was being driven largely by the rapidly increasing cost of entitlement programs. Creating a new entitlement for Pell Grants would increase the portion of the budget that was "uncontrollable" and exacerbate the deficit problem.

Also standing in the way of a Pell Grant entitlement was the 1990 budget agreement. This agreement required that any increase in entitlements be "budget or deficit neutral"; that is, any entitlement increase must be offset either by a reduction in other entitlement programs or by increased revenue. The committees handling the reauthorization neither could nor would engage in the fratricidal warfare of reducing such other entitlements as Medicare, food stamps, school lunches, or veterans' pensions. It also was not within their jurisdiction nor within the realm of political feasibility for them to propose tax increases to generate more revenue.

The Senate Subcommittee on Education, Arts, and Humanities marked up the reauthorization bill on October 23, 1991, and unanimously ordered it reported to the full committee. On October 30 the Senate Labor and Human Resources committee also unanimously ordered the reauthorization reported to the Senate. The Senate subcommittee strongly favored a Pell Grant entitlement, with Senator Pell, the program's author, taking the lead. The Senate committee tried to finesse the strictures of the budget agreement by delaying implementation of entitlement funding for Pell Grants until FY 1997, which was beyond the scope of the agreement. The Administration continued to oppose the Pell entitlement, even if it were delayed to a date beyond the budget agreement. An amendment was offered in full committee by Senator Nancy Kassebaum (R-Kans.), the ranking minority member of the Pell subcommittee, to strike the Pell entitlement provision. The amendment failed, 11-6.

As the Senate began consideration of reauthorization on February 20, 1992, it adopted a "modification" of the bill reported from committee, which was largely technical changes and new provisions embodying ideas that had blossomed only since committee action concluded the previous October. Two innocent-looking lines in this amendment, which took 18 pages of the *Congressional Record*, struck the Pell Grant entitlement from the Senate bill. In the face of solid Republic opposition bolstered by the Administration's veto threat and defections by budget-conscious Democrats, the committee leadership concluded that they did not have the votes to defeat the amendment to strike the Pell Grant entitlement that was expected to be offered. They retained the hope that a Pell Grant entitlement would survive in the House bill, and that it could be accepted in the House-Senate conference. It would be easier to accept the Pell Grant entitlement from the House bill in conference if there had not been a public fight and an affirmative vote against it in the Senate. The Senate passed the bill 93-1.

The House Subcommittee on Postsecondary Education marked up the reauthorization on October 1, 2 ,3, and 8, 1992, and the full committee marked it up on October 22 and 23. The House reauthorization bill provided for making the Pell Grant an entitlement immediately. Attempts to eliminate the Pell Grant entitlement, led by the ranking minority member of the Subcommittee, Congressman Tom Coleman (R-Mo.), were defeated in both the subcommittee and full committee markups. The bill was reported to the House by a vote of 26-14 along party lines, breaking the long tradition of bipartisan action on higher education bills. Republican members of the committee cited the Pell Grant entitlement and the direct-loan program as the primary reasons for their opposition to the bill.

The House began consideration of the bill on March 25, 1992. After the bill was reported from committee in October, a sustained effort was made to generate public support for the Pell Grant entitlement. Unfortunately, although the sail of Pell Grant entitlement was hoisted, the political winds did not blow. As the time neared for the House floor action, the bill had attracted only 97 co-sponsors, including only two Republicans. This was fewer than half of the Democrats and far fewer than the 218 votes that constitute a majority of the House. To take the bill before the House, a waiver of the budget act provision requiring that new entitlements be budget-neutral would have been required. The same forces that were operative in the Senate — solid Republican opposition, the Administration's veto threat, and misgivings by budget-conscious Democrats — were at work in the House as well. In addition, deletion of Pell Grant entitlement from the Senate bill further weakened the chances for its adoption by the House. Given the turbulent political waters and the lack of broad and enthusiastic support for the Pell Grant entitlement, the House Democratic Leadership would not support a waiver of the Budget Act. The committee leadership agreed to strike the Pell Grant entitlement as part of a "committee substitute" that included a large number of refinements and modifications to the committee-reported bill that had risen since the bill was reported from committee in October. The House "substitute" was comparable to the "modification" adopted in the Senate. Thus the Pell Grant entitlement was dead, and with it died any hope of redressing the much-lamented loan/grant imbalance. The House concluded its consideration of the reauthorization on March 26, passing it 365 to 3.

Outstanding Issues: Aid to Students From Middle-Income Families

The second unresolved issue was whether and how much to help students from middle-income families. When Secretary of Education Lamar

99

Alexander testified before the House Subcommittee on May 8, 1991, he made it clear that the Administration did not favor expanding eligibility for federal student aid to such students. "We suggest," he said, "that we take the available money we have and concentrate it on the lowest-income families." His suggestion fell on deaf ears among both Democrats and Republicans. The remarks of Congresswoman Marge Roukema (R-N.J.) were typical. "I hope," she said, "we can deal back in the middle class. And it's not simply because it's our constituency; it's because . . . this group badly needs the help." Across the board in the House and Senate, helping the middle class pay for college became an article of faith, both because of their real needs and because of their attractiveness as a political constituency. So Congress went happily ahead with expansion of middle-class eligibility for the federal student aid program in the reauthorization, objections of the Administration to the contrary notwithstanding. The Administration swallowed its concerns, deciding that vetoing an education bill in an election year because it was too generous to the middle class was a political loser. Instead, making a virtue of necessity, the President took credit for providing more federal help to students from middle-income families in his statement when signing the bill.

Outstanding Issues: Direct Loans

Early in January 1991, sources in the Administration leaked stories to the *New York Times* and the *Washington Post* intimating that the Administration was seriously considering replacing the existing guaranteed student loan program with a direct-loan program. Under the existing program, private capital from banks and other lending institutions is lent to students with the federal government assuring the lender of a return that covered the lender's cost of funds, administrative costs, and a profit margin. These loans are also guaranteed by the federal government should the borrower fail to repay. The basic concept of a direct-loan program, on the other hand, is that the federal government would provide capital directly to the schools, the schools would make the loans to students, and the federal government would be responsible for servicing the loans.

Direct loans were attractive for two basic reasons. First, if administrative costs were constant, the program would be substantially cheaper, because the federal government's cost of funds is less than that of private lenders and the federal government does not need a profit margin to induce it to make student loans. Indeed, analysis done by the Department of Education, the General Accounting Office, and the Congressional Budget Office were in general agreement that completely replacing the existing program with direct loans would be about $1 billion per year less expensive for the same volume of loans.

Second, a direct-loan program promised to be dramatically simpler. In place of 10,000 lenders there would be one lender, the federal government. There would be no need for the 45 guarantee agencies that serve in every state insuring student loans, which are then reinsured by the federal government. There also would be no need for the 35 student loan secondary markets, including the Student Loan Marketing Association (Sallie Mae), which purchase student loans, thereby providing lenders with liquidity to make more student loans. In short, direct loans would "eliminate the need for the cottage industry of middlemen and intermediaries that makes the current system of guaranteed student loans so blasted complex," as one Administration official put it to the *New York Times*.

The idea of having the federal government directly provide the capital for student loans had been around for at least two decades. It had always foundered in large part because of the way the cost of the program was calculated. The entire amount of the capital made available by the federal government was considered a "cost" to the government in the year in which the loans were made, only to be gradually offset years down the road as students repaid their loans. Thus direct loans had always implied tripling or quadrupling the cost of the program in the first year. However, at the Administration's recommendation, "Credit Reform" was adopted as part of the 1990 budget agreement. Under Credit Reform the cost of direct loans would be calculated as the "net present value" of the loans made in any one year. In other words, for budget purposes the "cost" of the loans in any year would be calculated as the amount of capital made available, *minus* the anticipated future repayments of principal and interest, *plus* the future administrative and default costs. With this method of determining cost, direct loans became not only competitive on a cost basis with guaranteed loans but, as noted above, substantially cheaper.

Direct loans attracted supporters in both the House and Senate subcommittees. Simplification of the loan programs was generally applauded. House Democrats were particularly intrigued by the possibility of making savings in the loan program, which would be entitlement savings, to offset some of the costs of a Pell Grant entitlement. The idea of student aid funds being used to pay for bank profits also grated on many Democrats.

101

Congressman Robert Andrews (D-N.J.) introduced a bill in early August 1991 to phase out the guaranteed student loan program and replace it with a direct-loan program. Congressman Tom Petri (R-Wisc.) had been advocating a direct-loan program for more than a decade. Senators Paul Simon (D-Ill.) and David Durenberger (R-Minn.) also had a direct-loan initiative. The lenders, guarantors, and secondary markets, as might be expected, strongly opposed an initiative that would terminate their role in student loans.

The reauthorization bill as reported from the House committee included a phased replacement of the guaranteed loan program with a direct-loan program, basically incorporating Congressman Andrews' bill. While islands of sympathy for direct loans remained in the Administration, the Administration came out in adamant opposition to the direct-loan program, charging that it would increase the federal debt even if this did not increase budget "costs," that it would require the federal government to shoulder all the risk, that schools could not handle the responsibility of originating loans, and that the Department of Education could not administer the program. Indeed, the Administration threatened to veto the reauthorization if it included a direct-loan program (or a Pell Grant entitlement). Almost all of the House and Senate Republican members of the committees handling reauthorization lined up with the Administration in opposition to direct loans.

The House committee leadership was faced with the Administration's veto threat; broad opposition from House Republicans; antagonism from lenders, guarantors, and secondary markets; and uneasiness among some Democratic members reflecting home state concerns, including the anxiety of many colleges about the prospect of a dramatic change in the student loan program that provided $13 billion a year to their students. To smooth the path of the reauthorization on the House floor, it was agreed to back off and include only a direct-loan pilot program in the reauthorization. This direct-loan pilot program was incorporated into the committee "substitute," along with the elimination of Pell Grant entitlement. Despite some sympathy for direct loans, the Senate committee was more impressed by the uncertainties rather than the promise of direct loans and did not include any version of direct loans in its reauthorization bill.

The House-Senate conference committee faced a daunting task. While the House and Senate reauthorization bills were very similar in their broad policy directions, there were approximately 1,500 specific differences between them. Most of these differences were resolved through marathon staff meetings at which about 50 participants representing the 27 House subcommittee members, 14 Senate subcommittee members, committee staff, and legislative counsels discussed each difference and agreed on recommendations to be made to the House and Senate members. While the job was formidable, the staff proceeded in a spirit of bicameral and bipartisan cooperation to fashion a single need analysis for the federal student aid programs, a single free form for applying for federal aid, changes in the student aid delivery system, new loan limits and deferments, a process for state review of high-risk institutions, a redefinition of the role of accreditation, and a myriad other issues. The House and Senate conferees had three meetings in June 1992 to ratify the staff recommendations and to resolve about two dozen issues on which the staff could not achieve a consensus.

Among the conference agreements, the Senate accepted a direct-loan pilot program. However, direct loans continued to stick in the Administration's throat. In a June 16 press release, Secretary Alexander accused the conferees of having "destroyed" the reauthorization by the modest changes in the scale of the direct-loan pilot program that had been agreed to, and he renewed the threat to veto the reauthorization. The issue was not laid to rest until a group of Republicans from the House committee visited with the President and persuaded him that it was not politically prudent to veto the reauthorization because a pilot program that saved money was a little too big. After a bit of last-minute tinkering with the direct-loan pilot, Secretary Alexander pronounced the conference agreement to be "a good bill."

On June 30 the Senate agreed to the conference report by a voice vote. The House considered the conference report on July 8 and adopted it by a vote of 419 to 7.

Outcome of the Reauthorization

The *Washington Post*, the *New York Times*, and the *Congressional Quarterly* all listed reauthorization of the Higher Education Act among the major accomplishments of the 102nd Congress. The Higher Education Act was extended for six years with total authorizations of about $115 billion. Significant changes had been made where there was a legislative-executive consensus on goals or where congressional support was overwhelming and bipartisan, as in the case of expanding aid for students from middle-income families. For example:

1. Students from middle-income families received: a) expanded eligibility for student aid generally through changes in need analysis,

especially the exclusion from consideration of the value of a family's home or farm; b) the ability of all students to borrow regardless of income (but with a reduced federal subsidy for the non-needy); c) the opportunity for most parents to borrow up to the full cost of education; and d) expanded eligibility for Pell Grants (albeit contingent on annual discretionary appropriations).

2. More than 100 provisions were adopted to strengthen program integrity. These included: a) improving the ability of the Department of Education, the states, and the accreditors to terminate the eligibility of schools that abuse the programs; b) prohibiting the use of commissioned salesmen and recruiters; and c) requiring pro rata tuition refunds.

3. The student aid form was dramatically simplified by changes in the independent student definition; elimination of questions (such as those related to extraordinary medical expenses) that applied to only a small percentage of applicants; and exclusion of family home or farm equity from consideration. All students were required to apply for aid by using only the simplified free federal form, and a single need analysis was devised for federal student aid.

4. New early outreach and intervention efforts were launched by strengthening the TRIO programs; by creating a new federal-state matching program to support local partnerships to provide tutoring, mentoring, and increased parental involvement; by providing support for training high school counselors; and by establishing a national computer network of financial aid information.

5. Nontraditional students were guaranteed a fairer share of the federal student aid programs administered on college campuses. Increased support for child-care expenses was provided, along with eligibility for Pell Grants for less-than-half-time students.

6. A variety of new preservice and inservice teacher training programs were authorized, such as the New Teaching Careers program to enable paraprofessionals and support personnel working in schools, who are frequently minorities, to continue their education and become classroom teachers.

7. A direct-loan pilot program was created, perhaps laying the foundation for a major overhaul in the system for delivering student loans.

Loans and grants were not brought into better balance. With the failure of the effort to enact a Pell Grant entitlement, any major increase in grant funding will depend on success in the annual appropriations process. The optimistic view is that the reauthorization lays the groundwork for increased future appropriations by addressing the problem of fraud and abuse, by bringing in an expanded middle-income constituency, by raising the federal profile of the programs through the single federal application, and by making it clear that insufficient appropriations rather than arbitrary and unreasonable need-analysis provisions are what stand between students and the aid they need. The pessimistic view is that loans are here to stay as the dominant source of federal student aid and that the reauthorization only further confirms the fact. Perhaps it is time to concentrate on thinking about how to make student loans more compatible with the goal of equal educational opportunity rather than wait for the happy day when the aberration of student loans will be replaced by grants.

It is, of course, incorrect to view the President's signature of the Higher Education Amendments of 1992 as the final punctuation on the policy-making process. To steal the title of President Kennedy's aide Larry O'Brien's memoir, in policy making there are *No Final Victories*. Budget and appropriations decisions, the regulatory process, the quality of program administration, further amendments, and the education program of the incoming Clinton Administration will all continue to reshape the meaning of his reauthorization.

All in all, in the pantheon of landmarks in federal higher education policy making, the 1992 reauthorization of the Higher Education Act does not rise to the height of the Washington Monument. It is more like a handsome medium-size statue — the mark of a good piece of work if not a masterpiece.

The College Affordability Crisis and Public Policy in the 1990s

By Lawrence D. Gladieux

Lawrence E. Gladieux is executive director of the Washington, D.C., office of the College Board, a national nonprofit association of schools and colleges that provides testing, financial aid, guidance, training, and other services to the education community. He previously served as a staff member of the U.S. Congress and the Association of American Universities. He has written widely on topics related to government and education.

How will students and families be able to afford higher education in the 1990s? Congress sought to address that public concern last summer when it reauthorized and expanded eligibility for many of the federal student aid programs.

The same issue of college affordability surfaced in the 1992 election campaign, as candidate Clinton pressed his plan to provide loans that students could repay through community service or flexible payments geared to their future income. In one of his most frequent and passionate campaign themes, he merged several powerful ideals — removing financial barriers to educational opportunity, tapping youthful energy and commitment to meet public needs, and encouraging students to make their career choices on other than economic grounds. Now the Clinton Administration is working on the nitty-gritty issues of how to implement such an approach, its cost, and implications for existing student aid programs.

It is anybody's guess how postsecondary student aid policies may ultimately be recast in the Clinton years. But it seems certain there will be considerable debate and flux in this policy arena, notwithstanding the fact that Congress extended the Higher Education Act for another five years in 1992 and notwithstanding the fact that congressional education committees will need to focus in 1993-94 on reauthorization of the elementary/secondary programs and issues of school reform.

There remains a wide perception that current student aid policies are not working as well as they should on behalf of students or taxpayers, and this is a point Clinton has stressed in advocating his student loan reform/community service approach. During the campaign he repeatedly cited the defaults, excessive "bank fees," and overall high government cost of the current student loan system.

Let us look first at the historical role of government in supporting the costs of higher education, then review recent trends in tuition, aid, and college affordability. I shall then explore policy challenges of the 1990s, focusing first on the states, where revenue shortages are forcing major adjustments in the financing of public higher education, and then on the federal level, where unresolved problems may have been exacerbated by the 1992 higher education reauthorization. I conclude with thoughts on the emerging policy agenda of the Clinton Administration.

Who Pays for College: A Historical Perspective

Essentially, there are three sources of revenue to pay the instructional (and student living) costs of higher education: the family (students and/or parents); government (federal, state, local); and philanthropy (private donors). It has been roughly estimated that in 1930, families in the aggregate paid almost two-thirds of the college bill, government a little more than one-fifth, and philanthropy the remainder. By 1980 the family share was closer to one-third and government covered about 60% of the total costs.*

Over that 50-year period, taxpayers assumed much greater responsibility for financing higher education:

- State and local governments generated the huge postwar expansion of public higher education, bringing free or low-tuition college opportunities within reach of a much larger segment of the population. By 1970, 75% of enrollments were in state university and community college systems, compared to 25% in 1930.

---

*Michael S. McPherson and Mary S. Skinner, "Paying for College: A Lifetime Proposition," *The Brookings Review*, Fall 1986.

- Meanwhile, the federal government stepped in to pay tuition and living costs for students in both public and private institutions — through the GI Bills (World War II, Korea, Vietnam) and then through the need-tested grant and loan programs that were legislated by Congress in the Sixties and Seventies. Student financial aid, along with sponsored research, became the principal mechanism of federal support of higher education.

Today state governments remain the largest source of *indirect* aid in the form of subsidized low tuition at public institutions. But for the past quarter-century the federal government has contributed by far the most *direct* aid to help students meet their costs of attendance, including tuition and fees, living costs, transportation, books, and supplies. And the great bulk of such aid has been awarded progressively, according to some measure of family and student financial need.

The growth curve in federal support of students ended in the early 1980s with the Reagan budget cuts (and phase-out of Vietnam-era veterans' benefits). In recent years neither federal nor state governments seem prepared to assume a rising share of the college bill, and a relatively greater burden appears to be shifting back to the student and family. The fundamental issue for public policy is how, to whom, and in what form available subsidies will be provided.

Recent Trends Affecting College Affordability

Figure 1 indicates that the federal government in 1991-92 supplied about 75% of direct aid to students, the states 6%, and institutions (using private endowment, donor, or recycled tuition revenue) 19%.

Aid programs benefit students in all sectors of postsecondary education. But according to the National Postsecondary Student Aid Study (NPSAS), the highest rate of participation is in proprietary schools (81%), followed by private nonprofit colleges (63%), public four-year institutions (43%), and public two-year institutions (28%). The average award per aid recipient in 1989-90 was just over $5,000 in private colleges, just over $4,000 in proprietary schools, $3,350 in public four-year institutions, and just under $2,000 in public two-year institutions. (See Figure 2.)

The constant-dollar value of federal student aid declined sharply in the early 1980s, gradually recovered, and leveled off toward the end of the decade (see Figure 3). In fact, the total purchasing power of aid dollars is slightly higher now than it was in 1980. Several factors at

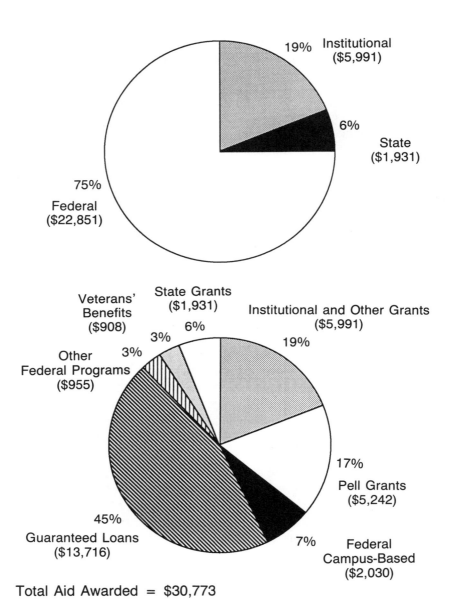

Figure 1
Estimated Student Aid by Source for Academic Year 1991-92
(Current Dollars in Millions)

19% Institutional
($5,991)

6%
State
($1,931)

75%
Federal
($22,851)

Veterans'
Benefits
($908)

State Grants
($1,931)

Institutional and Other Grants
($5,991)

6%

3%

19%

Other
Federal Programs
($955)

3%

17%
Pell Grants
($5,242)

45%
Guaranteed Loans
($13,716)

7%
Federal
Campus-Based
($2,030)

Total Aid Awarded = $30,773

Source: *Trends in Student Aid: 1982 to 1992*, The College Board, 1992.

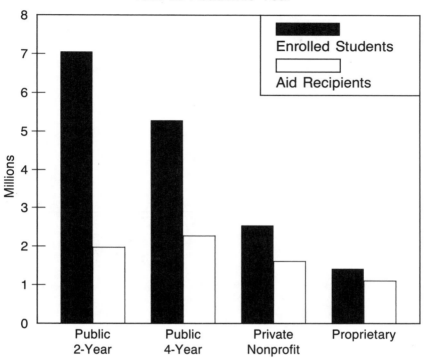

Figure 2
Enrolled Students and Aid Recipients
1989-90 Academic Year

	Public 2-Year	Public 4-Year	Private Nonprofit	Proprietary
Number of Students	7,052,280	5,260,484	2,567,051	1,391,453
Number of Aid Recipients	1,969,278	2,262,618	1,614,358	1,120,897
Percent Aid Recipients	28%	43%	63%	81%
Average Cost of Attendance	$3,324	$4,979	$12,057	N/A
Average Award per Aid Recipient	$1,991	$3,350	$5,163	$4,066

Source: *1990 National Postsecondary Student Aid Study.*

Cost of attendance (tuition, fees, room and board) data from: *Digest of Education Statistics 1990*, U.S. Department of Education, and the *College Cost Book 1989-90*, The College Board.

Figure 3
Amount of Federal Financial Aid
1981-82 through 1991-92 in Constant Dollars

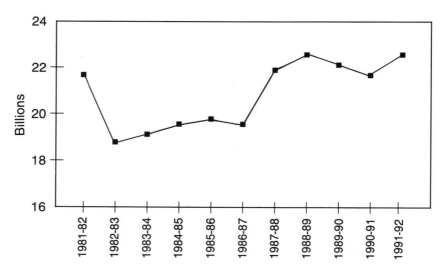

Source: *Trends in Student Aid*, the College Board.

work over the past decade, however, have diluted the real value and significance of federal support in making college affordable:

- The available dollars have been spread over a large student population, including substantially increased numbers of students enrolled in short-term training programs offered by proprietary schools. The proportion of Pell Grant funds going to proprietary school enrollees, for example, jumped from less than 10% in the late 1970s to well over 20% a few years later. Use of federally guaranteed student loans by the proprietary sector also grew dramatically; about one-fourth of loan funds now go to this sector.

- The overall composition of aid has shifted, as indicated in Figure 4. Increasingly, the assistance is in the form of credit — loans rather than grants.

- College tuition increases generally have run well ahead of the Consumer Price Index, while family incomes lagged behind or barely kept pace with living costs.

Figure 4
Composition Federal Financial Aid Dollars
1981-82 through 1991-92 in Constant Dollars

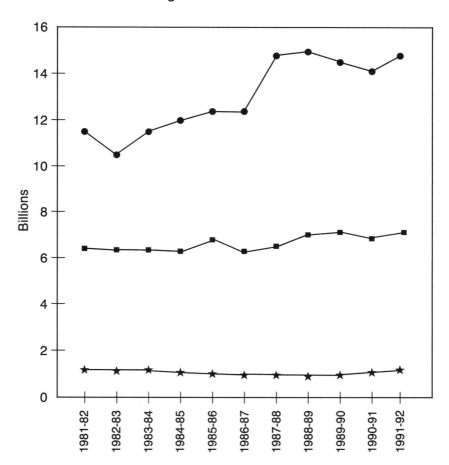

Source: *Trends in Student Aid*, The College Board, Washington Office.

By contrast, in the 1970s the growth of aid outstripped growth in tuition and growth in the eligible student population; grant aid, with the establishment of the Pell Grant program, was more common than borrowing, especially for low- and moderate-income students; and family income levels generally rose faster than living costs. Regrettably, all those trend lines turned adverse to college affordability in the 1980s.

The growing predominance of loan financing during this period has stood the original federal commitment to equal opportunity on its head. The Higher Education Act of 1965 established a commitment to help the disadvantaged through need-based grant programs, while helping middle-class families with government-guaranteed but minimally subsidized private bank loans. Today guaranteed loans are by far the largest source of aid − even for the lowest-income students. Guaranteed loans provide more than $13 billion in aid annually, 2½ times the size of the Pell Grant program that was meant to be the system's foundation. Moreover, as loans became increasingly subsidized and costly to the government, Congress gradually and reluctantly tightened eligibility to exclude much of the middle class for whom the loan program was originally intended.

In the States: Is There a Future for Low Tuition?

For many years the attention of the media has focused on the tuition spiral in the highest-priced independent colleges and universities. But in the early 1990s, concern has focused on the steep rise of tuition and fees charged by public institutions. In the summer of 1992, in fact, a congressional committee conducted an inquiry and held a hearing on college finance and affordability issues, focusing almost exclusively on the *public* sector of higher education.

According to the College Board's annual survey, prices are up 10% (three times the current CPI) on average in public higher education in 1992-93, compared to 6% to 7% (double the CPI) for private nonprofit colleges. Last year's tuition increases averaged 13% in the public sector.

Historically, free or very low-cost public higher education has been a great equalizer and force for assimilation and upward mobility of new populations in American society. The land-grant and state university movement has deep populist roots. And state policy makers have traditionally resorted to raising tuition reluctantly when other revenue sources have run short.

But higher education's share of state revenues has been declining for some time; and the share of public higher education costs financed by tuition has been increasing, from 22% in 1980 to 26% in 1990. In the recent recession, higher education has been hit harder than ever in most state budgets. The early 1990s are bringing deep cuts in appropriations for public institutions, along with double-digit tuition increases for students. States are finding they cannot perpetuate low tuition and generate sufficient funds to sustain quality, so students and families are paying more.

Moreover, there is no assurance that higher education will enjoy a resurgence of state support when the economy recovers. Many observers believe that current austerity for higher education at the state level may be long-term and structural, not simply recession-driven. Higher education will continue to face mounting competition from other pressing claims on discretionary state resources, including health care, prisons, and K-12 education.

These trends suggest a strategic role for need-based student aid, without which college may be priced out of reach for low- and moderate-income students. The question is whether adequate state appropriations will be allocated, or tuition revenue recycled, to protect needy students against the price increases.

For years, analysts of higher education finance have advocated substantially increased public college tuition as a matter of policy, accompanied by greatly expanded student financial assistance based on need. Instead of charging the same percentage of costs to all enrolled students, they urge a more highly targeted use of public subsidies, with wealthier students and their families paying more than those who are less financially able.*

While few state policy makers are eager to embrace a "high tuition/ high aid" philosophy, the strong likelihood is that public-sector tuition will continue to rise as a proportion of instructional costs. To sustain the values of equal access and student diversity, student aid becomes a critical element in state strategies for financing higher education.

Unfortunately, recent changes in federal policy have complicated the task of targeting student aid according to need and of using available resources effectively toward this end.

---

*See, for example, Michael S. McPherson and Morton Owen Shapiro, *Keeping College Affordable: Government and Educational Opportunity*, The Brookings Institution, 1991, for the most thorough recent research in this area and a fully developed proposal for restructuring college finance along these lines.

Reauthorization: Hopes and Promises

The recently completed reauthorization of federal student aid programs started more than two years ago amid much hope and anticipation of greatly expanding the federal commitment in this area. When House and Senate committees started drafting bills in the fall of 1991, expectations of a post-Cold War peace dividend were at a peak and the early versions of both bills reflected the ambitious goals of committee leaders as well as the education community.

But budgetary realities overwhelmed the reauthorization process in the months that followed. In early 1992 Congress could not muster the votes to bring down the "walls" that had been established in the Budget Enforcement Act between defense and non-defense spending, so the much-heralded peace dividend failed to materialize. And if several billion dollars of funds could not be transferred from defense to domestic needs, there was no room under the budget rules to allow the expansion envisioned by House and Senate committee plans for reauthorizing the Higher Education Act, especially proposals to turn the Pell Grant program into an entitlement or mandated spending program with automatic annual increases for inflation.

The grant/loan issue. Leaders in the reauthorization process said they wanted to achieve a better balance between grant and loan support for students, boosting the former and reducing reliance on the latter. But the final legislation is likely to do the opposite over the coming years.

In the end, after the Pell entitlement failed, Congress followed a path of less resistance in boosting the dollar ceilings in most of the existing loan programs. Figure 5 shows the new annual and aggregate borrowing limits; only first-year postsecondary students are excluded from borrowing at higher levels. Loans, unlike Pell Grants, already operate as an entitlement, meaning that all eligible students are assured access to funds up to authorized levels. In estimating the federal costs of this new borrowing authority, House and Senate sponsors were able to assume the continuation of current low market interest-rate conditions, thus minimizing the projected expense of the changes and avoiding violation of the Budget Enforcement Act.

The legislation does raise the *authorized* maximum Pell Grant; but without the entitlement provision, actual funding levels will depend on annual appropriations. Figure 5 shows the widening gap between the authorized and actual Pell maximum over recent years. In fiscal year 1993, reauthorization pegs the maximum at $3,700 while the appropriations committees have only allowed $2,300, a decrease from this year's $2,400.

116

Figure 5
Reauthorization of the Higher Education Act Means More Borrowing Capacity for Students and Families . . .

New federal loan limits, starting in 1993-94:

	Stafford		Supplemental (SLS)		Parent (PLUS)		Perkins	
Undergraduate								
Annual limit:	old	new	old	new	old	new	old	new
1st year	$ 2,625	$ 2,625	$ 4,000	$ 4,000	$ 4,000	(up to	none	$ 3,000
2nd year	2,625	3,500	4,000	4,000	4,000	cost of	none	3,000
3rd year	4,000	5,500	4,000	5,000	4,000	ed., less other aid)	none	3,000
Aggregate debt:	$17,250	$23,000	$20,000	$23,000	$20,000	N.A.	$ 9,000	$15,000
Graduate student								
Annual limit:	7,500	8,500	4,000	10,000	N.A.	N.A.	none	5,000
Aggregate debt:	$54,750	$65,500	$20,000	$73,000	N.A.	N.A.	$18,000	$30,000

. . . But Slim Promise of Increased Grant Aid

How Pell Grant maximums made possible by appropriated funds have fallen far short of authorized amounts since early 1980s:

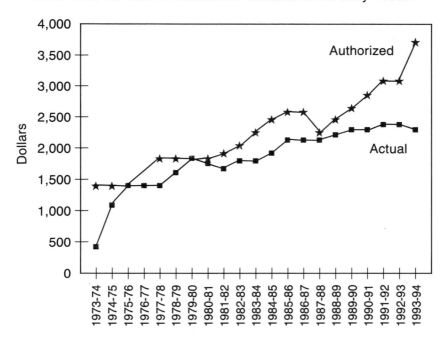

Source: Washington Office, The College Board.

The reauthorization bill also establishes an unsubsidized loan option not restricted by need. This is intended to make loans available to those in the middle-income range who have been squeezed out of eligibility for the regular Stafford Loan; the new loans will be less of a drain on the federal budget in that the government will not pay the interest costs while the borrower is enrolled in school.

All told, the principal impact of the new legislation is clear: Far from correcting the loan/grant imbalance, it will expand borrowing capacity for students and parents at all income levels in the years ahead.

Access to what? Borrowing is an appropriate means of financing for many students, and not all students who borrow are overburdened with debt. For most students in baccalaureate and graduate programs, and in many postsecondary vocational programs, a government-guaranteed student loan is a good bet — both for the taxpayer and the borrower. There is a reasonable prospect that the investment in education and training of the individual will produce future earning power to repay the accumulated indebtedness.

The government's nearly $3 billion annual cost of defaulted student loans, however, suggests that for too many individuals the investment and the risk are not appropriate. As noted earlier, a rising share of the government's student aid commitment over the past 15 years has been used to finance training offered by proprietary schools. And much of that financing has focused on very low-income students who lack basic academic skills and enroll in short-term job-training programs that typically result (at best) in minimum-wage employment. The default rate on student loans in the proprietary sector averages over 40%, four times the average in four-year collegiate institutions.

What types of education and training should be fostered through the mechanism of student aid? In the 1970s Congress substituted the term "postsecondary" for "higher" in the student aid statutes, and eligibility was broadened to include training provided by for-profit schools as well as traditional collegiate programs of public and nonprofit private institutions. Congress embraced a marketplace philosophy; students would "vote with their feet," taking their federal aid to institutions that met their needs.

But the marketplace, students-voting-with-their-feet rationale begged important questions of institutional quality control and accountability as well as consumer protection. No one foresaw the burgeoning of the for-profit trade school industry that was stimulated by incentives built into the federal aid programs. Many proprietary schools are subsidized

118

almost entirely by tax dollars through these programs and set their prices on the basis of the federal aid package available to students.

For several years pressure has been building in Congress to address these problems in the student aid effort. A 1989 House Appropriations Committee report expressed serious misgivings about the aid programs, citing "fiscal integrity and management issues" and the rapid expansion of aid "to nontraditional students for whom the standard student assistance may not be the most suitable." And in 1990-91 Senator Sam Nunn (D-Ga.) led an investigation and issued a committee report calling for overhaul of the aid programs, which he charged were being abused by proprietary schools and other commercial interests.

Restoring "integrity" to the student aid process became a principal theme in the 1992 reauthorization. Congressional sponsors recognized that these issues had to be addressed if the programs under Title IV of the Higher Education Act are to be viable in the intense competition for appropriations. But how effective the new legislation will be in strengthening program integrity is questionable.

The principal new thrust is to place more reliance on state agencies for the gatekeeping function, that is, helping to determine which postsecondary institutions should be eligible to participate in the federal Title IV programs. But the states' responsibility in this regard is not activated until federal funds are provided to support states in carrying out this function, and such an appropriation has yet to materialize. Moreover, states may be reluctant partners in such an endeavor; state officials responsible for licensing postsecondary programs have long complained that they are saddled with regulatory problems the federal government will not confront directly but has itself created by subsidizing the proprietary sector so substantially.*

The crux of the regulatory dilemma is the difficulty of applying the same rules to the sheer number and diversity of schools as well as types of training supported by Title IV. Simultaneously regulating the use of student aid subsidies by more than 8,000 proprietary schools and 2,500 collegiate institutions is awkward at best. Leaders of the reauthorization process, however, were unwilling to consider disaggregating federal student aid policy and differentiating delivery mechanisms by sector or length and nature of training.

---

*See Arthur M. Hauptman's paper in this volume for background on the institutional eligibility issue and a fuller examination of the new program-integrity provisions in the law.

119

The outlook for rethinking and restructuring postsecondary aid in this regard could brighten under the Clinton Administration, given its clear commitment to strengthen education and training policies across the board and its intention to focus on the non-college-bound "forgotten half." Many of the most disadvantaged in this latter group are ill-served by student aid incentives that encourage their enrollment in short-term programs subject to minimal quality control where, at best, they have only modest chances of success and, at worst, are left with no job, a defaulted loan, and a bad credit record. Would not the delivery and accountability for short-term job training be handled better through federal contract authority, coordinated by or with the Department of Labor and counterpart state and local agencies?

Reauthorization did not address this set of issues squarely; perhaps an activist and comprehensive Clinton education and training policy will.

The erosion of need-based aid principles and practice. The heart of Title IV of the Higher Education Act is the method for determining what level of contribution should be expected from the student and family, or "need analysis." As amended in 1986, the law provides for one set of criteria for Pell Grant eligibility and another for other Title IV programs. The 1992 reauthorization consolidates the standards of family and student ability to pay into one system, which has come to be known as the "Federal Methodology" and is scheduled to take effect for awards made to students enrolling in the academic year 1993-94.

The new standards will have significant effects on the actual distribution of dollars among types of students and income groups. Two categories of students, single independent students and dependent students who have earnings of their own, stand to lose Pell Grant eligibility because of the shift from old to new criteria. For purposes of the other Title IV programs, as well as many state and institutional aid awards that may be based on the Federal Methodology, the impact of reauthorization is to stretch potential eligibility up the economic scale and over a much larger population. The new methodology dramatically reduces expected family and student contributions and in the process inflates calculated need by several billion dollars.

This was an election-year bill, and the reauthorization leaders in Congress were intent on broadening the political base of the Title IV programs by expanding eligibility to more of the middle class. But while the new law promises much on paper, there is little prospect of a corresponding increase in available funds from the federal government, states, or institutions. So, more officially recognized "need" will be chasing roughly the same number of available dollars. There is likely to be a surge in applications for aid, and applicants will look more and more alike, making it more difficult to distinguish those most in need.

As always, states and institutions will have to make choices about which students to aid; and the liberalized, federalized need analysis mandated by reauthorization is not likely to serve the neediest well. As suggested earlier in this essay, carefully targeted student aid is becoming more important than ever as tuition outpaces inflation in both the public and private sectors of higher education. But federal policy is currently out of sync with the need to make the most of scarce resources for equalizing educational opportunity.

One day perhaps it will be possible to redirect federal student aid policy toward its original basis in the 1965 legislation: need-based grants for the disadvantaged, loans for the middle class. But that goal will have little meaning if we have in the meanwhile dismantled standards and mechanisms for measuring family ability to pay to the point that the neediest can no longer be identified.

The mid-1990s will be a period of flux in the standards that govern the awarding of student assistance. How many institutions and states will be willing to use the Federal Methodology as a sole standard of need remains to be seen; many colleges indicate that they will look for alternate standards and calculations to guide the awarding of their own funds. A confusion of standards, however, serves no one's interests. Consensus-based solutions and a spirit of partnership are going to be needed once again, as they were in the 1950s, when the practice of need-based aid was formalized among the colleges, and in the 1970s, when a common methodology and application form were devised to serve multiple ends.

Beyond financial aid. Whatever the federal policy and commitment to helping students meet college costs, student aid dollars alone are not sufficient to ensure greater access to higher education by under-represented groups. Too many variables other than finance − quality of prior schooling, family attitudes, motivation, awareness of opportunities − help to determine college participation. Earlier and sustained interventions in the education pipeline are necessary.

And this need is reflected in the new reauthorization bill. The so-called TRIO programs, created as a complement to student aid programs under Title IV in the 1965 legislation, are continued and expanded. But the legislation also calls for initiatives inspired by Eugene Lang's "I Have a Dream" movement in cities around the country and by model programs developed in several states that seek to mentor disadvantaged junior high students, widen their horizons, and see them through to high school graduation and postsecondary opportunities. The new law envisions a federal/state partnership in supporting such endeavors, along with information and advertising to increase awareness of financial aid and special efforts to educate teachers and counselors about college admissions and financial aid procedures.

However, none of these initiatives received an appropriation for fiscal year 1993, and history suggests that new authorizations stand only a slim chance of ever receiving funds if none are appropriated in the first year the program is put on the books. Yet there could scarcely be a more important priority for additional discretionary resources that may become available.

A Look Ahead

The 1992 higher education reauthorization is not written in stone. There will likely be further changes in 1993, including technical amendments to address errors and unforeseen consequences of the new legislation. A "technical" amendments bill could become the vehicle for reopening debate on a number of issues — Pell Grants, student loan reform, standards of family ability to pay, and program integrity provisions. And the agenda surely will be influenced by plans and proposals emerging from the new Administration.

House Education and Labor Committee Chairman Bill Ford has not abandoned his campaign to make Pell Grants an entitlement, and this issue could conceivably work its way into congressional negotiations with the new Administration over national service and other Clinton priorities. Much will depend on President Clinton's early "macro" decisions on the federal budget: whether to press ahead with an economic stimulus package or, alternatively, to stress deficit reduction. In any case, my sense is that a Pell entitlement — another mandated federal spending program — is still not in the cards. And even if room could be found in the budget, a Pell entitlement is not likely to be viable until the issue of "program integrity" and problems in the trade school sector are more effectively addressed than they have been in the recent reauthorization.

But in the final analysis it is pure speculation to comment on what may be advanced by the new Administration and how the 103rd Congress might respond. At this writing, the Clinton policies for education are still in transition from campaign themes to concrete proposals. We do know this much:

- The President is committed to the concept of linking community service opportunities with the student aid system. We do not yet know specifically how this might be proposed. I hope and trust that community service will not be advanced as a blanket condition for receiving need-based federal student aid, but rather as an option for students to exercise before, during, or after their enrollment in higher education. Four years ago the Democratic Leadership Council called for attaching a service requirement to the existing aid programs, a proposal that Congress ultimately rejected on grounds that it would be unfair to expect disadvantaged, needy students to perform service while their more affluent counterparts face no such obligation.

- The President also is apparently committed to reform of the student loan structure and capturing significant budget savings as a result, which might in turn help to support a national service program. Again, we do not know specifics; but it will not be surprising if the Clinton Administration seeks to accelerate and expand the direct-loan demonstration project authorized in the 1992 legislation.

- Further, the President wants to allow student borrowers to repay loans as a percentage of their future income through the Internal Revenue Service. Income-contingent repayment is probably an idea whose time as come, but the devil could be in the details. Not all borrowers should have to repay on this basis, which would unnecessarily complicate the process for many students. It should be an option, and it should be designed to help those who know in advance that they will go into relatively low-paying occupations as well as those who later fall on hard times and need flexibility in repayment. At the same time, income contingency should not become a vehicle for encouraging unnecessary and excessive debt burdens by needy students.

Finally, it is a good bet that systemic reform of education will be a principal theme of the Clinton program, and "systemic" will probably encompass higher as well as elementary/secondary education. Systemic reform may mean a number of things, including accelerated development of national standards and assessments for measuring progress toward the National Education Goals, a process which so far has not impinged substantially on higher education. But in the Clinton years, a great deal more may be expected of the higher education establishment.

All of which is to say: Expect change. Exciting and challenging times are ahead.

A Changing Federal Role in Providing Student Financial Aid?

By Arthur M. Hauptman

Arthur M. Hauptman has been an independent consultant since 1981, specializing in issues relating to higher education finance and federal budget policies. Recently, he has written on reforming student aid programs, the growth in college tuitions and costs, and the financial condition of American higher education. He previously served on the staff of the U.S. House Budget Committee and the U.S. Senate Labor and Human Resources Committee. He received a B.A. from Swarthmore College and an M.B.A. from Stanford University

The discussion here of the 1992 reauthorization is derived in part from a paper Mr. Hauptman prepared for the Consortium for Policy Research in Education.

In 1992 two activities focused particular attention on the federal role in providing financial aid to individuals participating in postsecondary education or training. One was the reauthorization of the Higher Education Act, the principal legislation that governs the federal government's student aid programs. The other was the presidential campaign, in which one of candidate Bill Clinton's principal proposals was to scrap the existing student loan programs and replace them with loans that borrowers would repay either through designated forms of national or community service or as a small percentage of their income once they completed their educational program.

It was ironic that these two activities occurred in the same year, since the Clinton proposals, if adopted, would radically change much of what the Congress and the Bush Administration agreed to as part of the reauthorization. As I write, a primary question of interest is whether the 103rd Congress, when it convenes in 1993, will be willing to reopen the higher education legislation to accommodate one of the principal campaign promises of the 42nd President of the United States.

This essay explores the question in three ways. First, it describes a number of the issues that were addressed during the reauthorization process that could be subject to review and revision early in the Clinton Administration. Second, it attempts to explain why congressional pride in what was accomplished in reauthorization seems so at odds with the popularity that greeted candidate Clinton in his proposal to scrap the existing student loan system. Finally, the essay speculates on how differences between provisions of the reauthorization and proposals made during the campaign might be resolved as President Clinton deals with the 103rd Congress.

A Look Back at the 1992 Higher Education Act Reauthorization

A number of issues that were prominent during the debate on the reauthorization could well be re-opened when President Clinton comes into office. These issues include:

- Should Pell Grants be made into a federal entitlement program?
- What steps should be taken to stem and reverse the imbalance between grants and loans?
- What should be done to relieve the growing pressure placed on many middle-class families in paying for college?
- Should a new system of direct loans replace the current set of bank-based loan programs?
- How can the federal government ensure that the programs in which students enroll are of adequate quality to merit federal aid?
- What should be the federal role for improving the quality of the students who graduate from college?

Pell Grants as an Entitlement. Of the issues debated during the 1992 reauthorization of the Higher Education Act, perhaps the most prominent was whether Pell Grants should be made into a federal entitlement program. When Pell Grants were created as the basic grant program in 1972, it was envisioned as a foundation of financial support so that low-income students would know with assurance that a certain basic level of assistance would be available to them if they chose to attend college. But this initial purpose has not been achieved over time. Low-income and minority students continue to participate in college at much lower rates than wealthier and white students.

Many attribute this continuing disparity in college participation rates to the fact that the Pell Grant maximum award has not kept pace with inflation over time. One reason for this lag is that the program is part

126

of the discretionary portion of the federal budget. For discretionary programs, annual appropriations levels determine how much will be available to recipients, thus subjecting the programs to annual uncertainty over funding levels. To combat this uncertainty and to help ensure adequate funding levels in the future, leading Democratic representatives and senators sought to make Pell Grants into a federal entitlement program, where the level of funding would no longer be subject to annual appropriations decisions.

The Bush Administration opposed such a change, arguing that too much of the federal budget is already entitlements, and entitlements are one reason the federal deficit has grown so large. Most Republican members of Congress supported the Bush Administration on this issue, as did the Budget Committee leaders from both parties in both houses. As a result of this opposition, the Pell Grant entitlement provisions were withdrawn from both the House and Senate bills before final passage.

But the Pell Grant maximum also has not kept up with inflation because more middle-income and trade school students have been added to Pell Grant eligibility over time, thereby diluting the effectiveness of the program for lower-income students going to college. Roughly one-fourth of all Pell Grant dollars, for example, now go to students in trade schools. Making Pell Grants an entitlement would have made this current distribution of dollars more permanent and should give pause to those who advocate entitlement status.

It was unfortunate that while Congress was debating the concept of a Pell Grants entitlement, persistent mis-estimates of program costs by both the Administration and the Congressional Budget Office (CBO) led to a shortfall in spending well in excess of $1 billion, spread over two years of activity. A major cause of this shortfall was the economic recession, which led more students to enroll in college, particularly in community colleges. It appears that the funding models and projection assumptions used by the Department of Education and the CBO did not adequately provide for this effect of recession.

The impact of this shortfall in funding is made much worse by the prohibition against the federal government borrowing to make up for mis-estimates of spending in a program that has historically operated as a quasi-entitlement, in that eligible students have never been denied aid. (The history of the Pell Grants is that when funding has been insufficient to meet the awards of all students who applied for aid, then the size of at least some awards was reduced rather than deny aid to any eligible student.) The existence of this funding shortfall, in combination with the expansion in program eligibility, will no doubt add to the difficulty of increasing the maximum Pell Grant award in the future.

Righting the Loan/Grant Imbalance. Much of the support for Pell Grants as an entitlement was premised on the notion that this change would help to correct the loan/grant imbalance in the federal student aid programs. In the early 1970s, loans constituted a relatively small share of all federal aid; but the mix of loans and grants changed decidedly over the next two decades, in part because the Guaranteed Student Loan program is a federal entitlement while the federal grant programs are not. Loans have become the largest form of federal aid, constituting two-thirds of all federal aid and roughly half of the $30 billion in aid from all sources in the early 1990s.

Many in Congress and in the higher education community decry this imbalance between grants and loans, fearing that the growing reliance on loans is acting to inhibit participation in postsecondary education and training. This concern has led many to argue for greater funding of grants, thus reducing the need of students to borrow.

But with the rejection of the Pell Grant entitlement provision, the 1992 reauthorization will probably result in a further deterioration in the ratio of loans to grants. Loan limits in all of the federal loan programs were increased in the reauthorization in an effort to keep up with increased tuitions and other costs of attendance. This was particularly true in the PLUS program, where the only limit now is the total costs of attendance. In addition, Congress created a new unsubsidized component of the Stafford Loan program in which students without financial need can borrow at the same terms and conditions as needy students, except that they owe the interest while in school. These changes have raised concerns that greater loan availability will increase the linkage between student aid and tuition inflation. While loan limits were increased, the growth in future funding for grant programs is likely to be slow or negative in inflation-adjusted terms, since these remain as discretionary programs subject to the limits of annual appropriations.

The reality of this growing dependence on loans led a number of representatives and senators to push for systematic income-contingent repayments as a means for helping student borrowers deal with anticipated growth in debt burdens. Congressman Tom Petri (R-Wisc.), a long-time advocate of income-contingent repayment in the House, was joined in the 1992 reauthorization by a bipartisan group of legislators, including Democratic Senators Bill Bradley (N.J.) and Paul Simon (Ill.), Republican Dave Durenberger (Minn.), and Democratic Representatives

George Miller (Calif.) and Sam Gejdenson (Conn.). But the debate over income contingency occurred late in the reauthorization process, and committee leaders who seemed unenthusiastic about the concept were able to defer consideration of the issue.

The reauthorization instead takes a modest step to redress the effects of the loan/grant imbalance by providing greater flexibility in repayment options for a limited number of borrowers who are in danger of defaulting. These flexible repayment options include graduated and extended repayment terms as well as an option for some borrowers to repay through the Internal Revenue Service on an income-contingent basis. Some borrowers who already have defaulted also will begin repaying on an income-contingent basis.

Such provisions hold the promise of mitigating the adverse effects of increased borrowing. But these repayment options are limited in the legislation to a very small proportion of the borrowers who could benefit. Most of the nearly one million individuals who annually default on their student loans, and the even larger number of individuals who defaulted in previous years, will still be without assistance in trying to make their repayment obligations more manageable. In addition, many borrowers who do not default but who nonetheless are having difficulty in making their payments would benefit from being eligible for flexible repayment options.

Easing the Middle-Class Crunch. The debate over making Pell Grants an entitlement program occurred at the same time that Democrats and Republicans in both the House and the Senate wanted to aid more students from middle-class families. This congressional desire to extend federal financial aid to more middle-class students is a long-standing one. It is rooted in the belief that the viability of the student aid programs is tied to convincing the politically active and vocal middle class that these programs are not just for the poor. This political assessment is reaffirmed when members of Congress return to their states and districts and are barraged by struggling middle-class constituents asking what is being done for them.

To accomplish this purpose, the 1992 legislation increases the amount of income that is set aside for a family's basic living costs in the calculation of what it is expected to contribute to college expense. This change will reduce the family contribution of many middle-income students. In addition, the equity value of the parent's home in the future will be ignored in the determination of a student's financial need. Many members of Congress expressed pride in these changes because they will enable many currently ineligible middle-income students to receive federal grants and subsidized loans.

What very few members of Congress were willing to say, however, is that without sufficient additional funds, the effect of expanding eligibility for aid for the middle class is a dilution of the benefits for more disadvantaged students who truly need the assistance. In the past, this financial reality is what prevented substantial extension of aid eligibility further up the income scale. Apparently, Congress decided in 1992 that it was more important to appease the middle class than to help the neediest students.

Making Loans Directly. Another principal focus of the reauthorization debate was whether loans should be financed directly by the federal government, with educational institutions serving as administrative agents, rather than continue the traditional reliance on banks and other private lenders in the Guaranteed Student Loans (GSL) programs. Proponents of direct lending argued that federal expenditures could be cut by $1 billion or more per year without reducing student access to loans by using the federal borrowing authority and its lower interest rates instead of paying market rates of interest to private sector middlemen. Analyses by the CBO and the General Accounting Office (GAO) confirmed this view that large-scale federal savings were possible under direct loans. These savings could in turn be used to increase loan limits, increase grant awards, permit redirection to other federal activities, or reduce the federal budget deficit.

Credit reform changes in federal budget accounting rules adopted in 1990 altered the parameters of this debate, in that henceforth the federal costs of loans will be calculated on the basis of the present value of federal subsidies provided over the life of the loan. Thus, with credit reform, direct-loan programs in which the federal government provides the initial capital and is repaid over time will be able to compete on a more equal basis with guaranteed loan programs in which the private sector is the source of capital and is paid over time for the use of its money. A number of legislators in both the House and the Senate expressed support for the direct-lending concept, and a sizable direct-lending program was incorporated into the House bill.

Opponents of direct lending, including representatives of the various banking associations, the Student Loan Marketing Association (Sallie Mae), and the state guaranty agencies, argued that the current loan system works well, having provided billions of dollars of loans to deserving students over the years, and that the difficulties and start-up costs entailed in establishing a direct-lending system would actually increase the federal costs of loans and reduce access to loans relative to the current programs.

The Bush Administration, despite its role in other areas as a proponent of spending/deficit reduction in the face of congressional inclination to spend more money, was a leading opponent of the direct-lending concept. The Bush Administration arguments against direct lending, principally formulated by its Office of Management and Budget, included opposing having the government borrow money even if it were cheaper to do so than to pay private lenders for the use of their funds, as well as a concern that the Department of Education would be unable to administer such a program. The Bush administration also was heavily influenced, apparently, by the banking community and others who have a vested interest in seeing the GSL programs continue more or less in their current form.

The conference committee of the House and Senate initially agreed to a fairly substantial direct-lending demonstration program that would possibly have allowed up to 500 colleges to participate, with annual lending volume probably in the $1 billion to $2 billion range. But the Bush Administration threatened to veto the legislation because of the inclusion of a direct-loan component. Congressional leaders were unwilling to test this veto threat, and the final legislation includes a much scaled-back direct-lending demonstration project that will be limited to $500 million in annual loan volume and will be restricted to a smaller number of institutions.

Improving Program Integrity. Another focus of attention during the reauthorization process was the question of program integrity: What is the federal government's responsibility for ensuring that the institutions eligible for federal student aid provide a quality program? Much of the emphasis in the 1992 reauthorization debate on the need for greater program integrity was a function of the continuing high default rates in the student loan programs. Since students attending proprietary trade schools account for a disproportionate share of all defaults, the issue of program integrity cannot be separated from the question of how to regulate participation of these schools in the federal student aid programs. In addition, there is concern that many of these schools set their tuitions in line with the availability of student aid.

These problems with the current student aid structure lead some to suggest establishing separate programs for trade school students or, at a minimum, limiting how much the federal government reimburses these

131

schools to the reasonable costs of providing different kinds of training. Senator Sam Nunn (D-Ga.) in his role as chair of the Investigations Subcommittee of the Senate Government Affairs Committee, conducted an extensive investigation of the loan programs with special focus on the proprietary schools. He issued a stinging report on abuses in the programs, including a comprehensive set of recommendations for reform.

But calls for separate programs or extensive restructuring of how to help proprietary school students pay for their training fared poorly in the relevant authorizing committee debates, where leading committee members defended the current system and the critical role of proprietary schools in providing access to postsecondary education and training. The question, Access to what? was largely swept under the rug. The Nunn subcommittee recommendations were mostly ignored, as were many other suggestions for substantial restructuring of the current aid programs.

Instead, the issue of program integrity was addressed primarily through a re-examination of how schools become and remain eligible to participate in the federal student aid programs. Traditionally, institutional eligibility for the federal student aid programs has been based on the so-called triad of instructional accreditation, state review, and federal approval to help ensure adequate quality control in institutional program offerings.

The history of this triad approach can be traced to the 1960s, when the current federal student aid programs were created. At that time, the question was raised about how students could be assured that the programs in which they enrolled were legitimate. Many national and regional accreditation bodies had been in existence for several decades at that time and seemed capable of providing reasonable reviews of educational program quality.

Lacking a better alternative, the authors of the 1965 Higher Education Act required that institutions be accredited in order for students to be eligible for aid. Over time, state higher education agencies also became more involved in the oversight of institutions participating in federal aid programs. The federal leg of the triad stool consists of the U.S. Department of Education certifying accrediting agencies to judge institutional eligibility for federal aid, as well as a requirement that the ED directly approve institutions to participate in the federal aid programs.

However, this triad arrangement has become increasingly ineffective in ensuring program integrity and eligibility for federal student aid.

The role of the federal government in approving institutions has been largely pro forma. That was also the case for federal certification of accrediting agencies, although Secretary Lamar Alexander ended that tradition when he challenged the right of the Middle States accreditation agency to use diversity as a criterion for accreditation. (After more than a year of negotiations, Alexander did recertify Middle Schools, although the decision was subject to further review.)

In many cases the state review role has been weakened because a number of agencies are responsible for reviewing different types of institutions, so that the overall impact of state review is often uncoordinated and diluted. In addition, many states apparently view proprietary schools as small businesses and therefore minimize their regulation of them.

Probably the weakest link of the triad, however, remains the accrediting agencies themselves. These agencies rightly remain focused on their principal purpose of reviewing the academic merits of institutions, a function that often bears little relevance to whether the institutions are financially viable enough to qualify for federal aid to their students. In addition, the fact that the institutions themselves provide the bulk of the revenues of the accrediting agencies creates a less than arm's-length environment and surely compromises the ability of some agencies to make negative judgments against their members.

In the discussions leading up to the 1992 reauthorization, Congress sought to improve this system by giving more authority to the state agencies. But a wide range of postsecondary institutions and accrediting agencies opposed this move for a variety of reasons. Many colleges and universities bristled at the notion that a state agency would be in the position of advising them about the quality of their academic programs. Other schools worried that state agencies would be more difficult to deal with than the accrediting agencies in which they were dues-paying members. The accrediting agencies worried that they would lose the responsibility of reviewing institutional eligibility for federal student aid, which has become one of their major roles. Key legislators responded to these concerns, and the 1992 legislation was much less restrictive and intrusive than at least some of the initial proposals.

As a result, the provisions that prohibit students at institutions with high student loan-default rates from participating in the federal student aid programs remain the primary vehicle for providing program integrity. This dependence on default-rate cutoffs is problematic for several reasons. First, the measure of default rates is flawed in a number of ways, thereby giving institutions many opportunities to appeal. Second, the burden of proof remains on the government to prove abuse, so schools have wide latitude in appealing government decisions. Third, the cut-off rates were set at levels that allow a number of schools where there are legitimate problems to escape scrutiny and termination. Finally, using a single cutoff figure encourages institutions to take the steps necessary to get below the cutoff, at which point no further activity is necessary. A better approach would be to require institutions (and lenders, for that matter) to pay fees on each defaulted loan above some threshold level, thus providing incentives to prevent defaults over a much broader range of borrowing activity.

Improving Student Quality. The possible role of the federal government in promoting better quality in higher education is not limited to the question of program integrity. Another aspect of the quality issue is whether the federal government should adopt policies that would promote better quality and greater achievement by students enrolled in postsecondary education and training, both by improving the academic preparation of students entering college and improving their performance while in college.

The question of improving the academic preparation of students before they enter college is obviously primarily a function of the elementary and secondary education system. But is there some federal policy that would encourage better preparation of students in high school? One suggestion along these lines made by columnist Robert Samuelson and others is to require that students meet some minimum standard in order to qualify for federal aid. There are a number of reasons to believe that this approach would be an effective way to achieve better performance from an American high school system that is generally given low marks. But Congress implicitly rejected this approach, apparently because of fears that it would restrict access to postsecondary education for students who failed the tests.

The Congress and the Bush Administration chose instead to encourage better performance of high school students by creating a supplemental Pell Grant award, called Presidential Access Scholarships. These would be restricted to students otherwise eligible to receive Pell Grants who met such academic criteria as graduating from high school with a certain grade point average. But these scholarships require a separate appropriation, which is unlikely to be forthcoming in the near future, thus effectively blunting this policy thrust.

In order to continue receiving this award while in college, recipients would have to maintain satisfactory academic progress, the same as has traditionally been required of all federal student aid recipients. There has been much criticism over time, however, that this standard of satisfactory progress has not been effective, in that it is too loose a definition to provide adequate quality controls. But Congress has typically been unwilling to strengthen the satisfactory-progress standard for the same reason that it has not imposed minimal academic standards for the receipt of federal aid: It does not want to disenfranchise individuals from being able to try to make the grade in college despite inadequate preparation.

Another means of getting at the quality issue is to measure the quality of institutions according to their success in graduating the students that enroll. An initial step in this direction was taken with passage of Student Right to Know legislation, which requires that all institutions publish graduation rates in their catalogues and that institutions that give athletic scholarships provide that information to the federal government. An obvious further step in this direction would be to use these graduation rates as a determinant of the eligibility of institutions to continue their participation in the federal student aid programs, a move that likely would be strongly resisted by most of the higher education associations.

Impediments to Change in Federal Student Aid Programs

When discussions of the 1992 reauthorization first began several years before it was passed, there was a sense that this might be the first revision of the Higher Education Act since 1972 that would entail major changes in the federal student aid programs. The *Washington Post* at one point considered this "the major piece of domestic legislation in the 102nd Congress." Key members of Congress and their aides talked openly about the need for bold, innovative approaches to address widespread concerns with the existing set of programs, including lagging participation rates of low-income and minority students, unreasonably high default rates and costs, and an excessively complex system that too often served as a barrier to entry.

But congressional unwillingness to grapple with many of the tough issues associated with possible major changes and a distinct lack of leadership on the part of the Bush Administration resulted in legislation that can more appropriately be described as one of marginal change. And because a number of the major thorny questions were not answered by the 1992 legislation, many important issues in federal student aid policy remain unresolved.

For example, not making Pell Grants into an entitlement, congressional insistence on expanding eligibility for aid to middle-class students, higher loan limits, and a continuing excessive reliance on loans to finance training in which borrowers have only a modest chance of success means that lower-income students will still have insufficient grant aid to go to college. Therefore, the "loan/grant imbalance," which so many in Congress deplore, will probably grow rather than decrease with the passage of the 1992 reauthorization legislation; and student loan defaults are likely to increase rather than fall as a result.

One unfortunate consequence of the substantial attention paid to direct lending during the reauthorization process is that relatively little attention was paid to needed reforms in the Guaranteed Student Loan program. As a result of this inattention, many of the basic shortcomings of the program are still very much in place, including its excessive complexity and relatively high federal subsidy per dollar loaned. (At current interest-rate levels, the long-term federal cost of student loans is roughly 25 cents for every dollar loaned. If interest rates increase, the federal cost will be much higher.) The changes that were made in the reauthorization — a small decrease in the federally paid rate of return for lenders, a slight increase in the interest rate charged to borrowers, and the creation of an unsubsidized program within the Stafford Loan program — will not substantially reduce the underlying federal cost or the complexity of the existing student loan structure.

Similarly, while there was much discussion during the reauthorization debate of the concept of income-contingent repayment, the final legislation contains little in this regard. The debt-management options for borrowers having difficulty making their repayments, and a component of the direct-lending demonstration that requires income-contingent repayment, are the only vestiges in the legislation of the debate over income contingency.

In addition, the 1992 reauthorization does very little to address the many calls for strengthening the linkage between student aid and the performance of national or community service. A set of small authorizations for community service were inserted at various places in the legislation, but it is questionable how much funding will accompany these provisions. Moreover, by consolidating and reducing the activities that qualify for deferments in the student loan programs, the legislation may discourage some forms of service.

The reauthorization also did very little to address the very real needs of nontraditional students — those who are older, part-time, and not dependent on their parents for financial support. In fact, for nontraditional students who are single and not financially dependent on their parents, the 1992 legislation severely reduces eligibility for aid, both by raising the age at which independence is allowed from 22 to 24 and by substantially increasing the amount that single independent students will be expected to contribute to their education.

For long-time observers of federal higher education policy, the fact that the 1992 legislation did not yield major innovations should come as no surprise. In many respects, the legislative history of the federal student aid programs over the past several decades is a case study in why it is so difficult to introduce substantial reforms in a broad range of federal policies, such as health care, housing, welfare, and other areas.

The congressional decision-making process, in sorting out the federal role in student aid, has been dominated by a few senior members and their staffs who, because they have been responsible for writing the existing legislation, tend to have a great attachment to the status quo. This traditional dominance by senior members and staff has become even more evident in recent years as turnover in junior members and their staffs has created a greater gap in expertise within the relevant committees. The influence of staff was particularly noticeable in the 1992 reauthorization, when virtually all of the differences between the House and Senate bills were worked out through meetings of staff members; the formal conference committee work of representatives and senators was completed in one day!

As a result of the growing dominance of senior members and staffs, the relevant interest groups — the higher education associations, the banks, guaranty agencies, and others involved specifically with the student loan program — have had time to cultivate relationships with those who remain in power. This trend also tends to reinforce the status quo. In addition, many staff members, when they have left Capitol Hill, have become employees of the interest groups or their lobbyists, thus strengthening the hands of these groups in advocating their positions.

It has been clear for a long time that for change to occur in federal higher education legislation, it is necessary for the incumbent administration to take a lead role. When major changes were last made in the Higher Education Act of 1972, the Nixon Administration was a key player, despite the fact that there was a Democratic majority in both the House and the Senate. In contrast, during the past four reauthorizations (1976, 1980, 1986, and 1992), the administration in power did not play a lead role in formulating policy. In 1986, for example, the

137

Reagan Administration under the stewardship of William Bennett as Secretary of Education provided its plan for reauthorization after the full House of Representatives had already voted on the legislation.

Two exceptions to this two-decade rule of ineffectual administration leadership occurred in 1978, when the Carter Administration was willing to negotiate with Congress on the specifics of the Middle Income Student Assistance Act, and in 1981, when the incoming Reagan Administration forced Congress to accept some cost cutting in the federal student aid programs as part of its omnibus budget and tax legislation.

Nor are the problems with administrations limited to political appointees. The culture of the bureaucracy within the Department of Education also contributes greatly to the problem. Many government officials view institutions and lenders as their clients, and they want to help rehabilitate the bad apples rather than eliminate them from the program. The revolving door between government and vested interest groups is not limited to Capitol Hill. A number of high-ranking executive branch officials have moved to organizations they previously regulated. There are several instances where the move was to a chain of proprietary schools that had received favorable rulings while these officials were in power.

Another example of how the bureaucracy can contribute to the problem is that after several years of developing a plan for reorganizing the Office of Student Financial Aid, a group that most observers would agree has some very serious organizational problems, a decision was made not to make any hires from outside the agency. The result was a substantial shifting around of existing personnel, including promotions for some officials who, many observers would agree, have been part of the problem.

In a similar vein, in the 1992 reauthorization Congress decided to subject a number of student aid issues to a process called negotiated rule making, in which the regulations that implement legislation are developed through formal meetings and negotiations between administration officials and representatives of various interest groups. One problem with this approach was that some Bush Administration officials apparently decided that they would strive for consensus at the public hearings that preceded the formal decision making despite the fact that many of the issues slated for negotiated rule making are either highly contentious or can cost the federal government large sums of money. As a result, seeking consensus either was foolish or costly. The selection of the negotiating teams also raised questions, as many of the interest groups who were the targets of the regulations would have prominent seats at the table, while other groups were excluded.

The higher education associations and other interest groups with a stake in the student aid programs have traditionally been defenders of the status quo, spending much of their time worrying about how federal funds are distributed among the various sectors of higher education. When major changes were introduced in the federal legislation in 1972, the associations were staunchly against them, arguing instead for federal support to institutions. Once it became clear, however, that student-based aid rather than institution-based aid was the wave of the future, the associations climbed on board and became the greatest defenders of the Pell Grant and other aid programs, for all of their blemishes.

During the process leading up to the 1992 reauthorization, however, the associations broke away from their traditional allegiance to the status quo by proposing a major shift in the Pell Grant award formula and in backing a move toward direct loans. The change in Pell Grants advocated by the associations would have made the award formula much more tuition-sensitive by designating that a portion of the award would be based on a proportion of the tuition charged. The associations were willing to propose such a change, despite some substantial shifting in sector shares of funds, because of their strongly perceived need to reform how Pell Grant funds were distributed.

Congressional leaders expressed amazement that the associations were able to put aside their normal attachment to the status quo and come forward with a reform plan of this magnitude. But after initially embracing the change in the legislation as reported out of committee, the final legislation watered down the tuition-sensitivity provisions in the Pell Grant program to the point that they will largely be irrelevant for the six years for which the legislation is reauthorized.

The process by which the direct-loan demonstration program became part of the legislation is also instructive. Because the relevant committees are oriented toward education-related issues and not experts on financial matters, the groups with the most direct interest in the loan programs, such as the bankers' trade associations and Sallie Mae, have traditionally been relied on to formulate legislative language for the loan programs. Thus, when interest grew in the direct-loan approach, these groups were instrumental in developing the particulars of the direct-loan demonstration. As a result, the final legislation is unlikely to produce an adequate test of the direct-loan concept because of the restrictions inserted by the affected interest groups.

Resolving Differences Between President Clinton and Congress

Given that Congress raised student loan limits as part of the 1992 reauthorization at the same time the presidential campaign was occurring, some have asked, Why would President Clinton continue to pursue his reform agenda for student financial aid if much of it in the form of higher loan limits has already been accomplished through the just-passed legislation?

One answer is that Congress did the easy part of raising loan limits without taking care of the more difficult tasks: cutting federal costs per dollar loaned, providing adequate repayment alternatives that will allow borrowers to repay these larger amounts of loans in the future without defaulting, and instituting procedures that would prevent these higher loan limits from leading to higher tuition and other costs of attendance.

Another answer is that the Clinton campaign proposals were premised on the notion that the current student aid programs, particularly loans, are not working well and should be replaced. Candidate Clinton made it clear that he wants to redesign the student aid system to encourage more community and national service, including using federal funds that currently are designated for need-based student aid. The absence of these reforms should make it easier for President Clinton to pursue the proposals he made during the campaign.

These positions are in sharp contrast to the dominant congressional view during reauthorization that the existing student aid programs work pretty well and would work much better if additional funding were provided. In addition, Congress historically has seemed disinclined to use the student aid programs to encourage service if that would detract from what Congress views as the primary purpose of the student aid programs: promoting access and choice in postsecondary education. How are these seemingly large differences between Clinton and the Congress likely to be resolved when the 103rd Congress convenes and Clinton takes office?

If Clinton's willingness as governor to negotiate with the Arkansas legislature is any indication, one likely scenario is that soon after taking office, President Clinton will sit down with William Ford, chairman of the Education and Labor Committee, and Claiborne Pell, chairman of the Senate Education Subcommittee, and ask what congressional leaders would need in order to push forward on the agenda of national service and student loan reform that they effectively rejected the preceding year.

One plausible horse trade would be for President Clinton to agree to a Pell Grant entitlement in exchange for an extensive national service program, a much-expanded direct-loan approach, and a large-scale income-contingent repayment system. The notion of entitlement, of course, runs against Clinton's oft-stated philosophy that the beneficiaries of government programs should not view those benefits as a right, and that receipt of government benefits entails certain responsibilities on the part of the beneficiary. The creation of another entitlement also will make the job of reducing the federal budget deficit that much more difficult. Nonetheless, Clinton's obvious desire to encourage service might well lead him to agree to such a deal.

To reduce the impact on the deficit, however, a Clinton Administration agreement to a Pell Grant entitlement would probably be conditioned on a much slower growth in the maximum award than what is called for in the 1992 reauthorization. There will also be those in the Clinton Administration with a particular interest in bringing down the deficit, such as Office of Management and Budget Director Leon Panetta and the House Budget Committee chairman in the 102nd Congress, who will continue to oppose creation of a Pell Grant entitlement. One reasonable compromise would be to permit borrowing authority for Pell Grants to prevent future shortfalls in funding, while stopping short of creating a true entitlement program that would cut out the executive branch and appropriations committees from any real decision-making power.

Direct loans hold the promise of large-scale federal cost savings, which could be used to augment funding of Pell Grants, finance a national service program, or help reduce the deficit. Congress hotly debated the direct-loan issue during the reauthorization, but opted for a demonstration program in the face of opposition from the Bush Administration. With anticipated support from the Clinton Administration, greater or total dependence on direct loans seems likely.

The large federal costs entailed in adoption of a full-scale program of national service reduce the probability of this happening. Instead, a phasing in of national service seems far more likely.

This scenario still leaves a number of questions unresolved. For example, the Clinton campaign focused on encouraging service once student borrowers had completed their education and were ready to begin repaying their loans. But the initial Democratic Leadership Council (DLC) proposal that formed the basis of the campaign proposal was premised on the notion that in order to receive federal aid students would have to serve before they got to college. Some of Clinton's advisors seem inclined to push once again for the service requirement and cashing out of the federal student aid programs as called for in the DLC proposal, while others are working more specifically from the campaign proposal. Congress and the colleges are likely to balk at the notion of a service requirement or a cashing out of the existing student aid programs. In my opinion, a better approach would be one in which service was encouraged but not required before, during, and after college, rather than focus on any particular time period.

There also is likely to be disagreement between the Clinton Administration and the Congress on the particulars of how student loans will be repaid in the future. The Clinton campaign proposal called for all loan borrowers to repay as a portion of their income through the Internal Revenue Service. But the Internal Revenue Service has been reluctant to get into the business of student loan collection, and Congress has traditionally been of the same view. One possible compromise that I would favor would be to provide borrowers who are having difficulty repaying their student loans with a set of repayment options, including graduated and extended terms as well as income-based repayment schedules. The bulk of borrowers who are not having trouble making their repayments could continue to repay on a fixed amortized basis, a development that would greatly reduce the administrative burden on the IRS or any other agency responsible with providing alternative repayment schedules. For the income-contingency option to help the most borrowers, it is important that it be extended to those who have already borrowed, not be limited only to new borrowers.

These and many other issues are unresolved as the Clinton Administration assumes control. One thing seems certain, however, the federal role in helping students participate in postsecondary education and training will be a much more hotly debated topic in the 103rd Congress than it would have been had George Bush been re-elected.

Commentary on Postsecondary Education

By John F. Jennings

After presenting these four papers, it may be redundant to state that the issues involving postsecondary education at the federal level are mostly limited to questions of the distribution of financial aid to students and families to assist in securing education and training after high school. The vast bulk of federal funds (95% of aid provided under the Higher Education Act) is used to support these student aid programs; and the remainder is targeted at select areas, such as grants to historically black institutions.

In 1972 Congress made the basic decision to concentrate federal aid for postsecondary education on providing assistance to students rather than on giving aid directly to institutions of higher education to fund their operating expenses. If direct aid to institutions had been adopted as the policy, instead of aid to students, it is more likely that the federal role in postsecondary education would have become more directive than it has. As a general rule, whoever provides direct operating revenues tends over time to want the implementation of certain policies by recipients.

The decision made in 1972 to fund student aid and not institutional aid has shaped the national debate since then. When the President and Congress review these programs for renewal, the questions considered are not those dealing forthrightly with the quality of the education being offered as measured by student achievement or required coursework; rather, they revolve around what types of students should be favored in distributing financial aid. Of course, the national organizations representing higher education discourage any discussion of quality on the ground that institutions ought to be free from government influence in order to pursue academic excellence.

Although the debate in Washington is therefore mostly limited to issues of the distribution of student aid, the decisions made are very important to millions of students and their families. As noted in the previous papers, approximately 75% of the funds providing loans and grants for postsecondary education comes directly or indirectly from the federal government.

The federal student aid programs tend to be very complicated in their provisions, since they must balance the distribution of this aid among students from different income levels, among students from different stages in life (for example, financially dependent on parents or independent), and among students at institutions charging very different amounts for tuition and fees. Furthermore, a single policy cannot be adopted without affecting the other parts of the system for distribution of aid. For example, if the value of a family's home is excluded from consideration of the assets available to pay for a child's education, and the total amount available for student aid remains the same, then there is a shift of aid from students whose parents rent an apartment to students whose parents own their home.

Since these issues are so complicated, we asked four experts well-known in the field of student aid to contribute papers to this publication. Barry White, who works for the White House in the Office of Management and Budget, is the executive branch's foremost expert on student aid. Thomas Wolanin, who works for the U.S. House of Representatives, is unrivaled in the Congress for his expertise in this area. Lawrence Gladieux is another well-regarded expert who works for The College Board, which administers the SATs and processes applications for student aid. The last contributor is Arthur Hauptman, a consultant widely sought for his knowledge of student aid, whose work has included advising the American Council on Education, the national umbrella group in Washington for higher education organizations.

The three principal issues they discussed in their papers were: how to expand aid to students from middle-class families, whether to ensure funding for grant aid by creating an entitlement for Pell Grants, and whether to create a loan program directly funded and administered by the federal government. These were the major contentious questions the Congress and the Bush Administration grappled with while renewing the Higher Education Act in 1991 and 1992.

A fourth major issue involved how to reduce the default rate in the student loan programs. That issue received considerable attention, but it proved easier for Congress and the Bush Administration to agree on solutions respecting that topic than it did in the first three areas mentioned.

In fact, the final bill enacted by Congress and signed by President Bush incorporated more than 100 provisions aimed at tightening the administration of federal loan programs in order to reduce defaults and curtail other abuses of the program by schools and students. As already noted by the writers in the section, that same legislation resolved the first three issues by 1) expanding the grant and loan programs to include more middle-income students and 2) requiring an experiment involving hundreds of colleges to test the idea of a federal directly funded and administered loan program. But the proposal to ensure grant aid by creating an entitlement for the Pell Grant program was not included.

The four papers in this section present the factors that went into these decisions and describe the anticipated results of these policies. To fill out the picture, it might be helpful to describe how the various actors in Washington dealt with these issues.

On the question of expanding loan and grant programs to include the middle class, the Bush Administration showed great reluctance to propose or endorse any ideas in this area. The principal reason was that the Administration was afraid of greatly expanding the costs of these programs. In fact, the initial proposals from the Bush Administration were to focus the Pell Grant program even more than it is now on the very poor, thus eliminating many near-poor. The idea was to concentrate limited aid on the neediest, since there was not an inclination to expand the total amount of funds available for student aid.

Congress moved on a bipartisan basis to expand loan and grant programs to include middle-income students. The Democrats could have been accused of shifting limited aid from the poor to the middle class, but they countered by asserting that the funds saved in the loan programs by the 100 toughening provisions would be used to offset any expansion of those programs to the middle class. The Democrats on the education committees also proposed an entitlement for Pell Grants, thereby assuring advocates for the poor that poor students would be guaranteed grant aid by law, even though the eligibility of the Pell Grant program would be expanded to include middle-income students.

The national postsecondary education organizations were on record as supporting an expansion of aid to the middle class; but they were less sanguine than the Democrats on the education committees that an entitlement would be created for Pell grants, thereby safekeeping aid to the poor. Consequently, during congressional deliberations these groups would raise questions about the effects of the various provisions assisting the middle class, while endorsing that goal.

On the Pell Grant entitlement issue, the education organizations were almost universally supportive; but they suffered from a common problem among national organizations representing higher education: They had trouble marshaling broad support among professors, students, parents, and administrators. Therefore, no flood of mail from constituents appeared on the desks of congressional representatives and senators.

This is an endemic problem in postsecondary education. Many national organizations are focused on college and university presidents and do not enjoy a broad base of support among those affected by decisions made in Washington. There are exceptions, such as the National Association of School Aid Administrators; but most of these groups are much weaker than their counterparts in elementary and secondary education, which generally do have broad support.

The Bush Administration was opposed to the idea of an entitlement for Pell Grants; but it did not have to do much work against the proposal, because Congress was itself divided, owing to the lack of popular support for the idea. The Senate and House education committees both sent to their bodies bills containing entitlements for that program; but, as already noted by the writers, those provisions were never voted on by the full Senate or House because the budget committees in both houses objected and thereby imperiled passage of both bills. The sponsors of those bills, Congressman Bill Ford and Senator Clairborne Pell, had to remove those sections creating Pell Grant entitlements before the bills could be brought up for a vote. The budget committees objected because creating an entitlement might make it more difficult to control costs.

Republicans in both the House and Senate were overwhelmingly opposed to the idea of an entitlement, as was the Bush Administration. But it was the fact that the Democrats on the budget committees were opposed that doomed the bill from even being brought up for a vote, much less from being approved and sent to the President for his approval or veto.

On the question of creating a direct-lending program, there was a different mix of actors. The Bush Administration was opposed to the idea because it feared the costs could mushroom. The Republicans in the House and Senate were mostly, but not universally, against the concept. Congressman Thomas Petri (R-Wisc.) and Senator David Durenberger (R-Minn.) were noteworthy examples of Republican supporters.

Democrats in Congress were mostly in favor of the idea, although cautious enough to propose as their last offer establishing a large-scale experiment rather than changing the whole program immediately from one going through the states and using private capital raised by banks to one using federally raised funds and making colleges the distributors of the loans. Congressman Robert Andrews (D-N.J.) and Senator Paul Simon (D-Ill.) were the principal sponsors of the demonstration amendments.

The national organizations were divided. Some supported the concept; but many were somewhat equivocal, fearing the effects on colleges of having to administer millions of dollars of aid. The state guarantee agencies that now operate the loan programs were opposed, as were the organizations representing the banks that now raise the funds on the private market and distribute them to students and families.

As can be readily discerned, enacting legislation is difficult because of all these crosscurrents. Sometimes elected officials will line up with one another on one issue, then oppose one another on the next issue. The organizations have to reflect their constituencies while trying not to antagonize those who generally support them in Congress. The Administration has to know what it wants and zealously pursue it through the thicket of congressional interests and organizational alignments. A major reason the Bush Administration was not more successful than it was on the higher education bill was precisely because it was not so persistent. It seemed there was more interest from the U.S. Department of Education in marshaling support in the country for the school reform effort, "America 2000," than there was in shaping the reauthorization of the Higher Education Act.

Ordinarily, when Congress reauthorizes a major education law, it likes to leave the area alone for five or six years so that the legislated policies can be fully implemented. President Clinton, though, campaigned on the idea of linking the receipt of student aid to providing community service.

Because Clinton has the benefit of factors mentioned in the commentary on school reform, the House and Senate have announced that they will depart from the usual policy of resisting changes for five or six years and instead will reopen these programs for possible change in 1993.

As of this writing, details of Clinton's proposals have not been written, so it is impossible to predict outcomes with any accuracy. An interesting question, though, will be whether other issues thought to be closed will be reopened. For instance, without Mr. Bush resisting a large-scale direct-lending experiment, will the demonstration legislated in 1992, which involves only several hundred institutions, be broadened? Will the advocates of a Pell Grant entitlement again raise that issue, hoping for a more favorable response from a President who has said he wants to invest more in education and training? And so on.

If I can return to remarks made in the introduction to this volume, congressional consideration of Clinton's ideas in 1993 underscores how Washington, D.C., is a continuous debating society, with many of the same issues appearing again and again. Clinton's idea of community service was considered in reauthorizing the Higher Education Act in 1991 and 1992, but support for it was not strong. There will be strong support in 1993; but during the consideration of that issue, other questions that had been very recently decided will be raised and debated again.

PART III.
EDUCATION RESEARCH

Critical Issues in the Office of Educational Research and Improvement

By Diane Ravitch

Diane Ravitch is author of The Troubled Crusade: American Education 1945-1980 *and editor of two acclaimed anthologies,* American Reader *and* The Democracy Reader. *She served as Assistant Secretary for Educational Research and Improvement at the U.S. Department of Education from 1991-1993. She currently is a visiting scholar at the Brookings Institute.*

Every study of the federal role in education has concluded that the U.S. Department of Education has two fundamental responsibilities: 1) to support the education of students who are disadvantaged and/or needy (through such programs as Chapter 1, Pell Grants for college students, and special education); and 2) to provide leadership in research and statistics about education.

The weakness of the linkage between these two responsibilities is startling. The Department of Education appropriately devotes most of its funds to programs for those who have the greatest educational needs. But relatively little is spent for research to evaluate the effects of these and other educational programs or to assess alternative ways to improve education. While the department's budget has grown steadily and is now funded annually at more than $30 billion, its investment in research and development has not kept pace. Indeed, research and development receive less than 1% of the department's budget; a recent study by the National Academy of Sciences concluded that only about $58 million is actually spent on education research by the department's Office of Educational Research and Improvement, and that spending on education R&D has declined by a startling 88% in the two decades since the agency was created.

An outside observer would likely conclude, regarding federal support for education research, that the consistently meager levels of support for sustained inquiry have produced little. That production is slim should not be surprising; nothing ventured, nothing gained. Neglect of education research and development has been bipartisan. Indeed, as we spend more and more on schooling, we have spent proportionately less on understanding how children learn, what happens in the classroom, and how to improve education.

The Office of Educational Research and Improvement (OERI) in the U.S. Department of Education has a wide variety of roles. It includes the National Center for Education Statistics (NCES), which gathers data about the condition of education here and abroad and administers the National Assessment for Educational Progress (NAEP). OERI oversees the work of 10 regional laboratories, a score of national research centers, the ERIC system, the STAR Schools (distance learning) program, the National Diffusion Network, the Blue Ribbon Schools Recognition Program, the Javits Program for Gifted and Talented Students, the Eisenhower National Mathematics and Science Program, the Fund for Improvement and Reform of Schools and Teaching (FIRST), Educational Partnerships, and the Office of Library Programs.

While this may seem to be a potpourri of diverse activities, all are linked to the theme of educational improvement. Even the collection of data and statistics, which was the original mission of the Department of Education in 1867, has as its purpose the improvement of education. We don't gather data for the sake of gathering data but to understand the condition and progress of education and recognize what needs to be done to improve it for American children.

During the 18 months I served as Assistant Secretary for the Office of Educational Research and Improvement, the two overriding organizational issues that the agency confronted were 1) to increase appropriations for R&D in support of the National Education Goals, with particular emphasis on research to identify effective ways to educate disadvantaged children; and 2) to renew the legislative charter of the agency (reauthorization). Secretary Lamar Alexander, who began his tenure early in 1991, placed high priority on a strong program of education research and on the development of high standards and improved assessments. He embraced the National Education Goals developed by the President and the nation's governors in 1989, and he collaborated with Congress to establish the bipartisan National Council for Educational Standards and Testing (NCEST) in 1991.

The national education goals helped to focus the R&D agenda of OERI, as did the report of the NCEST panel. This panel (which included leading members of Congress) called for voluntary national standards and a new system of assessments (not a single national test), and OERI sought to implement those recommendations. First, acting at Secretary Alexander's request, we made grants to independent organizations (representing teachers, scholars, and the public) to develop voluntary national standards in the sciences, history, the arts, civics, geography, English, and foreign languages. The recipients of these grants agreed to develop a national consensus-building process within their discipline that would identify what American students should know and be able to do. Thus, with a relatively small allocation of discretionary dollars, we launched what may well be a historic development in American education. Unlike most other modern societies, this nation has never established explicit standards as goals for student achievement; those nations that do have such standards view them as an invaluable means of ensuring both equity and excellence.

To support research and development activities on behalf of the national goals and the NCEST proposals, the department requested a 57% increase in OERI's 1993 budget. (While this appears large, it actually would have increased the investment in R&D from 0.9% to 1% of the department's budget). The increase was to have been used for the following purposes: to provide assistance to states that wanted to develop new curriculum frameworks and new student assessments; to fund new research to understand how disadvantaged youngsters succeed under difficult circumstances; to initiate international studies to improve our knowledge of standards, assessments, and instruction in other nations; and to commission research on new forms of student assessment, especially performance assessment. The increase would have doubled the appropriation for field-initiated studies (from $1 million to $2 million). It would also have started the development of an interactive on-line electronic network devoted to education that would link every school and library in the nation (SMARTLINE). The proposed budget also would have supported NCEST-related expansion of statistical activities, including more frequent and more diverse state testing by the NAEP, the development of better performance measures for NCES student assessments, and studies to improve our ability to link and equate different testing programs.

It was an ambitious agenda, intended to reflect and support the bi-partisan agreement between the governors and the President that has produced the six National Education Goals. It also reflected the underlying commitment in the national goals to set high standards for all students and to support changes in instruction and assessment that will encourage higher expectations and higher achievement in every classroom.

This agenda for research and development did not receive a friendly reception. Some members of Congress, annoyed that Congress was not a partner in shaping the National Education Goals, were hostile to any effort to support them and treated them as partisan, even though leading Democratic governors (most notably Bill Clinton of Arkansas) helped to write them. Many members of Congress simply don't like education research, and they make no bones about it; they say, "We know what works, and we shouldn't waste any more money doing education research." There is a stereotypical view of education research that undercuts its legitimacy: that it is a waste of time and money; that it is theoretical and unrelated to what happens in the classroom; that every dollar spent for research is a dollar taken away from the classroom; that it produces nothing worth knowing. Actually, the paucity of federal funding for education research has, if anything, served to strengthen the nay-sayers, because the field has lacked the resources necessary to attract top-flight researchers or to sustain long-term investigations. The circle is indeed vicious, and the price paid is our continued ignorance about the improvement of education.

The other interesting and difficult issue during this period was the question of reauthorization. Periodically, every federal agency gets what amounts to a new charter, when a congressional committee rewrites its authorizing legislation. The legislative statute governing OERI's research activities was due to expire in September 1992. New legislation had to be written and passed — or the existing legislation had to be renewed — during the 1992 session of Congress.

The current authorizing statute for OERI's research activities spells out the agency's mission clearly and succinctly in seven printed pages. The statute strongly emphasizes the twin goals of "quality and equity." Research is not an end in itself; it is expected to support the nation's policy of providing "to every individual an equal opportunity to receive an education of high quality regardless of his race, color, religion, sex, age, handicap, national origin, or social class."

Certain needs are described as priorities for OERI, such as: "improving student achievement . . . improving the ability of schools to meet their responsibilities to provide equal educational opportunities for all students . . . collecting, analyzing, and disseminating statistics and other data related to education in the United States and other nations . . . encouraging the study of the sciences, the arts, and the humanities, including foreign languages and cultures . . . improving the data base of information on special populations and their educational status. . . ."

The specific functions of the office are clearly delineated: "1) conduct educational research; 2) collect, analyze, and disseminate the findings of educational research; 3) train individuals in educational research; 4) assist and foster such research, collection, dissemination, and training through grants, cooperative agreements, and technical assistance; 5) promote the coordination of educational research and research support within the federal government and otherwise assist and foster such research; and 6) collect, analyze, and disseminate statistics and other data related to education in the United States and other nations."

The legislation also authorizes regional educational laboratories, national research and development centers, and the ERIC clearinghouses. In addition, it establishes a "National Advisory Council on Educational Research and Improvement" composed of 15 persons who are broadly representative of the public, policy makers, practitioners, and researchers.

The authorizing statute seemed reasonable and thorough; and the Administration intended to ask for more flexibility and discretion so that the agency could support a vigorous and balanced set of research activities, including the capacity to sponsor research on state and local education reforms and emerging policy concerns, as well as to respond to congressional inquiries for information. In the absence of this kind of flexibility and staff resources in OERI, Congress creates independent commissions − often at a large cost − to explore issues and answer questions that should be within the scope of OERI. However, the Administration's proposal was rejected out of hand, because the House subcommittee that oversees OERI (the Select Subcommittee of the House Education and Labor Committee) had prepared its own proposal to reorganize the agency.

When it became known that the broad mandate that currently governed the agency would not be renewed, the Department of Education suggested to the committees in the House and Senate that OERI's research priorities should be organized thematically in support of the National Education Goals. These goals represent a broad consensus that is likely to remain stable for at least the next decade. Indeed, the goals provide a useful focus for research around the enduring themes of American education, which (like OERI's mandate) express the dual importance of equity and excellence. The goals identify six challenges for the nation, challenges that are ambitious but not impossible, and measurable outcomes around which the nation can focus its energies.

The department proposed a research agenda for OERI that was fitted broadly to the goals, pursuing the following lines of inquiry:

1. research on early childhood education, families, and communities (Goal 1);
2. research on the education of children who are at risk of failing in school (Goal 2);
3. research on student achievement, and especially on the connections among curriculum, instruction, and assessment (Goals 3 and 4);
4. research on postsecondary education and adult education (Goal 5);
5. research on school organization, finance, policy, and management (Goal 6).

The Senate Labor and Human Resources Committee worked with the Department of Education to shape a bipartisan bill for reauthorizing OERI. This bill would have created five research directorates, organized around the themes of the national goals; and it would have explicitly permitted OERI to support the development of voluntary national standards, state curriculum frameworks, and new state or regional assessments.

However, the Subcommittee on Select Education of the House Education and Labor Committee framed its legislation reauthorizing OERI without discussion with the Department of Education. The chair of the subcommittee, Congressman Major Owens (D-N.Y.), outlined his plan for the agency in a speech to the American Educational Research Association in April 1991. On this occasion, Congressman Owens harshly criticized the agency, calling it "an unprofessional, ideological, and partisan toy." In his view, OERI as a research agency had neither integrity nor professionalism.

When I took office in late July 1991, I wondered whether I was entering a hotbed of ideological and political intrigue. However, I soon learned that the charges of politicization were untrue. In fact, the agency has little control over the research agenda. Congress directs or earmarks most of the agency's research dollars to specific recipients and programs, and the small proportion of the budget that is discretionary is generally subject to peer-reviewed competitions. There is not a single study, project, conference, or report that could be accurately characterized as partisan or political or ideological. Although the charges of politicization had become commonplace through repetition, the reality was that the agency has no partisan agenda, no ideological control, no raging controversies. OERI is an agency in which more than 90% of the staff is civil service, where the research agenda is set by Congress through earmarks and directed appropriations, where most of the long-term employees are highly professional public servants, where there is extreme reluctance to touch anything that might be construed by anyone as controversial, and where there is a strong desire to do a good job of satisfying the expectations of Congress and the Administration for a solid program of research and development. It is also an agency where many people are deeply demoralized as a result of constant battering by critics and where the persistent underfunding and earmarking of research has produced resignation and, in some cases, cynicism.

Among leading features of the House bill (introduced first as H.R.3458, then in a second version titled H.R.4104) were these:

1. There was to be a large policy-making board, nominated by specific organizations. In the first version of the bill, the board was to have 24 members, appointed by the President and confirmed by the Senate; in the second version, it was to be 20, appointed by the Secretary of Education. The board was to have broad powers, unusual for a subcabinet agency, effectively reducing the Secretary of Education's control of OERI. Among the board's functions were to devise a long-term agenda for the agency, review all grants and contracts, and establish policies for the conduct and evaluation of research. It would hire its own staff, convene its own workshops and conferences, make grants, and collect data. Although the board would meet only four times a year, its powers were extensive, including involvement in both policy and management.

2. The first House bill, H.R.3458, proposed the creation of two research institutes, a National Institute for Education of At-Risk Students and a National Institute for Innovation in Governance and Management. The first institute was to have a presidentially appointed board of 33 members, and the second was to have a presidentially appointed board of 12 members. The second bill, H.R.4014, proposed the creation of three additional research institutes (early childhood education, student achievement, and postsecondary education). The five institutes in H.R.4014 brought the bill into alignment with the Senate bill, which proposed to create five directorates reflecting the National Education Goals.

The Department of Education supported the concept of large, well-focused research directorates (the term used in the Senate bill) or institutes (the term used in the House bills). In particular, it welcomed the idea of an institute/directorate on the education of at-risk students, which was already a major focus of federal research efforts (four existing national research centers concentrate on finding ways to improve the education of disadvantaged youngsters: the Center for Research on Effective Schooling for Disadvantaged Students at Johns Hopkins; the Center on Families, Communities, Schools and Children's Learning at Boston University; the National Research Center on Cultural Diversity and Second Language Learning; and the National Center on Education in the Inner Cities).

However, the House bill contained some features that were problematic for the department. The board — specifically its composition and its powers — was objectionable to the Secretary of Education. Customarily, a board for a subcabinet agency is chosen either by the Secretary or the President. In this instance, the appointing official would have to choose from nominees selected by designated organizations and interest groups. If the Secretary or President did not like their nominees, the organizations would offer new names. This was an unusual proposal. No other subcabinet agency has a board selected in this manner. Neither the National Institutes of Health nor the National Science Foundation, nor any other major federal research agency, has a board chosen by interest groups and nongovernmental organizations. The Secretary concluded that it was a usurpation of his authority to restrict his (or the President's) appointing power as H.R.4104 proposed to do. This was not a partisan issue but a question of separation of powers. If the Congress wishes to retain oversight of appointments, the customary means is to require Senate confirmation of the President's appointments.

Another concern about the board was that it would itself become an instrument of politicization by giving control of the agency over to representatives of organizations that in some instances have a direct interest in funding decisions by the agency. The proposed board was rife with potential conflicts of interest. The department believed that it would be inappropriate to have the research agenda for a federal agency set by a board that includes representatives of interest groups that lobby for research funding from the agency. Certainly there was no precedent in any other federal agency for such an arrangement.

The extensive powers of the board were also a cause for concern. The department's position was that OERI should have a distinguished *advisory* board of researchers and practitioners. But the House reauthorization bills proposed not an advisory board but a board that exercised executive authority. The board proposed in the House bill would have exercised nearly the same powers as the agency itself — collecting data, holding conferences, awarding grants and contracts. The potential for conflict between the board and the agency loomed large.

The report from the National Academy of Sciences about the future of OERI recommended a board structure that struck a useful compromise between the House proposal and the Administration proposal. It recommended a diverse 24-member board, appointed by the President for six-year staggered terms (as well as a fixed, six-year term for the Assistant Secretary). Though called a policy-making board, the NAS board did not have the broad and intensive involvement in the day-to-day management of the agency that was projected in the House bill. The primary functions of the board proposed by NAS were to set the agency's priorities and to issue a biennial report on federally funded R&D. Unfortunately, the NAS proposal was not incorporated into the House bill.

Another critical sticking point occurred when H.R.3458 was replaced by H.R.4014. The new House bill included specific prohibitions that would have barred OERI from supporting research and development activities in the area of student assessment, other than the current program of research; would have barred the agency from supporting the development of content or performance standards for students; and would have barred OERI from supporting states that wished to develop curriculum frameworks. These prohibitions were unacceptable, because they would have prohibited the activities that OERI was already supporting to implement the NCEST recommendations and the National Education Goals. It seemed strange to prohibit OERI from pursuing activities that were currently authorized by law and that had been recommended by the NCEST panel, which included prominent members of Congress. There would be no way to reach Goal 3 or Goal 4 without explicit standards to aim for, and no way to assess progress without new assessments tied to these high standards. And it was precisely these implementing activities that H.R.4014 sought to prohibit.

The problem with the House reauthorization legislation went far beyond the board and the prohibitions. H.R.4014 sought to impose organizational changes on the agency without regard to the agency's capacities. Imposed reforms seldom work, in schools or in any other complex institution. The effort to micromanage the agency through legislation and to impose radical change without consulting those who do

159

its work was inherently unwise. OERI cannot be transformed by re-naming things, or by declaring the existence of institutes for which there is neither funding nor staff depth. Unless there is a sustained commitment to strengthen and renew the internal research capacity of the agency, it will be unable to meet the often-admirable expectations embodied in the House legislation.

In the spring of 1992, the Department of Education repeatedly urged a compromise between the House and Senate bills, hoping that the best features of both would survive a conference. The Senate bill (S.1275) included an advisory board that would be comprised of distinguished researchers and practitioners, and it did not include the prohibitions in H.R.4014. Nor did the Senate bill attempt to micromanage the agency nor to identify every conceivable research question that should be addressed.

OERI's reauthorization was repeatedly put on hold by other, more pressing matters. In the spring and well into the summer of 1992, OERI's reauthorization was set aside while the Congress reauthorized the Higher Education Act, a complex bill involving the disposition of billions of dollars and affecting millions of college students. Then when Congress returned after the summer break, everyone's attention was turned to a major education reform bill. A small agency, OERI got lost in the shuffle, forgotten in the rush to adjourn. The House passed H.R.4014; the Senate never took up its own bill, S.1275. The two bills were never brought to conference. The agency's authorization was extended for a year, and the 103rd Congress will now consider the future of the agency.

When the process of reauthorization begins again, the new Secretary of Education should give careful attention to OERI's reauthorization. The reauthorization of this agency will allow the new Administration to integrate research and development, standards and assessments, statistics and data-gathering, education technology, and the various other functions of OERI in support of educational improvement. They should have full opportunity to see that their views are reflected in the legislation that reauthorizes the agency.

My own judgment as a historian of education is that OERI's problems stem from the controversial nature of the questions that are imbedded in education. Over the years, OERI has served as a lightning-rod for controversy; similar issues and controversies have recurred during the two decades of this agency (whether called the National Institute of Education or the Office of Educational Research and Improvement), as well as in its predecessor agency within the federal Office of Education.

Education policy and education research are such that everyone has an opinion, based on either their own experiences or those of their children. And the work of OERI, dealing as it does with policy, practice, research, equity, and student environment, invariably enters into questions on which people hold very strong and often divergent opinions. Anyone familiar with the history of education in this country knows that communities have been torn apart by education controversies; nothing raises passions more than education disputes.

In addition, the agency has been the victim of two decades of underfunding and suffered the generalized obloquy that attaches to education research as a field. The malady is serious indeed, but it need not be fatal. What is needed is the funding that would permit the agency to support R&D of sufficient scale to address the twin challenges of equity and excellence. It is possible to build the agency into a first-rate program, dedicated to the highest-quality education research in the service of educational improvement for all Americans. However, certain things must happen to ensure OERI's vitality and stability:

First, the agency's mission should be codified in simple direct language: It is responsible for advancing the national aims of equity and excellence in American education; and toward those ends it collects data and statistics, conducts national assessments, sponsors research and development, supports the use of education technology, advances information technology, and furthers the art and science of education.

Second, it should be the responsibility of a distinguished advisory board of scholars, practitioners, and public members to establish research priorities (as envisioned in the report of the National Academy of Sciences) and to assure Congress and the American people that all education research, development, and improvement activities are conducted on a strictly meritorious, nonpartisan basis.

Third, the agency must have sufficient funding to support a balanced portfolio of research and development activities, some produced within the agency and some contracted with outside agencies and individuals; within that balanced portfolio there must be adequate funding for mission-oriented basic research, applied research, planned variations (for example, analyzing the effectiveness of different instructional strategies in significant numbers of classrooms), and field-initiated studies, possibly as much as $40 million to $50 million annually (rather than the current level of $1 million).

Fourth, the more than 20 national research and development centers, each funded at about $1 million to $2 million per year, are too many and too small; they should be replaced by a smaller number of larger centers, where critical issues could attract the sustained attention of the best people in the field. These larger centers should have funding sufficient to allow both research and development activities, working when appropriate in collaboration with the regional laboratories.

Fifth, the internal staff capability of the agency must be strengthened. OERI needs to gather an internal staff of expert researchers within the Office of Research, who would be responsible for synthesis and analysis of education research from across the government and universities. Each year, the Office of Research should be enabled to appoint two to three senior scholars on one-year appointments; the current paucity of researchers is a serious handicap to the organization.

Sixth, the Office of Research should have funds necessary to engage in regular evaluation of the research and development activities of the national centers and laboratories, with *quality* as the sole criterion for judgment. Without this sort of systematic evaluation of all grants and contracts, the staff of the Office of Research is reduced to monitoring without standards of quality, and the recipients of federal research dollars are led to believe that standards of quality do not exist.

Seventh, the Department of Education needs an on-line interactive electronic service through which to disseminate and learn about best research findings, best practices, and best programs, as well as to disseminate information about federal grant competitions and other requests for proposals. Such a service should contain a wide variety of resources and networking possibilities for researchers, practitioners, policy makers, community leaders, and parents.

Eighth, OERI should have the funding to support a well-planned program of publications and to develop videotapes and audiotapes based on best research and practice for dissemination to parents, teachers, policy makers, administrators, community groups, and others concerned about improving education.

Ninth, congressional appropriators should recognize the value of research and development in education as they have in health, transportation, labor, agriculture, and other areas vital to the well-being of the nation. The nation invests hundreds of billions of dollars each year in education; that investment would be safeguarded and multiplied by a thoughtful program of scientific inquiry to understand how best to improve education and student achievement.

The new reality is that the same party now controls both the White House and the Congress. Perhaps now Congress will not feel that it must keep a tight leash on research and development. Perhaps now Congress will provide both the appropriations and the administrative discretion that are needed to support a well-planned program of R&D. Perhaps now Congress will allow the Department of Education to support high standards and improved assessments. Only with strong congressional support can OERI help to implement the nonpartisan agenda of excellence and equity that our nation needs.

The Educational Research, Development, and Dissemination Excellence Act: Imperative for OERI Reform

By Congressman Major R. Owens

Congressman Major R. Owens represents the 11th Congressional District of New York. He has chaired the House Education and Labor Committee Subcommittee on Select Education since 1986.

When President Bush and the nation's governors promulgated six goals for the improvement of education in America by the year 2000, they posed a formidable challenge to the nation. We can bridge the wide gap between what exists now and what should be by the year 2000, but it will require more than high hopes and good intentions. Nothing less than an overwhelming campaign is needed to improve education throughout America. As with every ambitious goal pursued by the nation, from the exploration of space to the prevention and treatment of disease, our efforts to realize the National Education Goals must be built on a solid foundation of research and development to shape and guide our quest. Intuition, guesswork, and individual trial and error will not get us there. Sound, research-based knowledge is needed to point the way.

Yet our federal system of education research and development is not prepared today to fulfill these pressing new demands for leadership and enlightenment. Most educators throughout the nation know well how more than a decade of budgetary retrenchment and backward thinking in Washington has affected the delivery of services to children in the classroom. Less familiar to them has been the devastating impact on education research and development. Starved of resources and denied effective and consistent direction, the federal education research and development system has been permitted to dissolve into irrelevancy.

By any standard of measurement or comparison, this system is dangerously underfunded. Between 1973 and 1988, finances for the Department of Education's Office of Educational Research and Improvement (OERI) was cut a dramatic 88%. Federal spending for the Department of Education as a whole, in contrast, increased modestly during this same period. Federal expenditures for education research and development amount to one-third of those for research and development in agriculture and transportation and only 4% of federal expenditures for research and development in health. Research and development spending amounts to less than 1% of federal education expenditures, but represents 13.6% of federal health expenditures, 3.2% of federal transportation expenditures, and 6.9% of federal agricultural expenditures. At a moment when a solid and broad foundation of knowledge is needed, the federal investment in education research and development is scarcely enough to buy a handful of bricks.

Despite the education research and development system's obvious need for more federal dollars, greater resources are unlikely to be forthcoming unless action is first taken to address more fundamental weaknesses in the way OERI funds and carries out research and development activities. Policy makers in Washington and educators throughout the nation now have little confidence that funds provided to OERI will be invested wisely or productively. Unlike other federal research agencies, OERI's decision making is controlled by a handful of political appointees with little input or participation by the research community and other stakeholders. This decision-making structure has deprived OERI of a coherent long-term agenda to drive its investment in education research and development. Research priorities have fluctuated rapidly, shifting with changes in key personnel and presidential administrations, and have been dominated by short-term and sometimes partisan considerations. The needs and concerns of teachers and school administrators have often been overlooked. Critical areas of research, including the education of at-risk children, have been neglected for extended periods of time. And once these priorities have been set and the investments made, little sustained attention has been given to translating the knowledge gained into real improvements in practice.

While these dysfunctions and deficiencies are long-standing, they are not impervious to correction. But that will require nothing less than a complete overhaul of the system. Tinkering on the margins and making minor, incremental changes has not worked in the past and it will not work today. Only wholesale reform will suffice.

Since 1987 the House Subcommittee on Select Education has been working to forge a consensus on what should be the necessary elements of this urgently needed overhaul of OERI. In that time we have held 15 hearings and heard from 92 witnesses about the kinds of changes that are needed. The operations of other more respected and successful research agencies, such as the National Institutes of Health (NIH) and the National Science Foundation (NSF), were closely examined. With financial support from OERI, the National Academy of Sciences convened a study group to evaluate the structure and functioning of OERI; their subsequent report, *Research and Education Reform: Roles for the Office of Educational Research and Improvement*, provides us with numerous insights and useful recommendations. Countless meetings also were held with the staff of the Republican members of the Education and Labor Committee in an effort to ensure that the legislation that emerged reflected their ideas and contributions and was a truly bipartisan effort.

The legislative product of this extensive process was the Educational Research, Development, and Dissemination Excellence Act (H.R.4014), which was introduced in November 1991. The legislation's central provisions include the restructuring of OERI into five research institutes, the establishment of a governance framework modeled on those of the National Science Foundation and the National Institutes of Health, and the creation of new dissemination and development initiatives to ensure that the knowledge gained from research would be fully put to work to improve the quality of education.

OERI is currently organized according to the manner in which research is conducted, and not by the topics being studied. Different administrative units, for example, manage the field-initiated research program and the research and development centers program. This structure has contributed to the overall incoherence, fragmentation, and instability that have plagued the agency. New topics, ideas, and points of emphasis drift in and out with changes in top personnel. There is no enduring, permanent focus to drive the agency's work. For this reason, H.R.4014 adopts the recommendation made by the National Academy of Sciences and many other observers that OERI be organized programmatically instead of functionally, focusing its activities on five enduring priority areas: the education of at-risk students; education governance, finance, and management; early childhood development and education; student achievement; and postsecondary education, libraries, and life-long learning.

The bill creates five research institutes with first-year funding authorizations of $20 million each to carry out comprehensive research and development activities in these priority subject areas. Each institute, for example, could support university-based research and development centers, field-initiated research, and special studies addressing issues pertinent to its subject area. In this way, the agency's efforts would be more permanently focused on solving critical, persistent problems in education and would be less likely to experience the often abrupt shifts of emphasis that have marred its work in the past. Important areas of inquiry would no longer be neglected for years at a time merely because they were not of great interest to the particular Education Secretary or Assistant Secretary in power at the time.

H.R.4014 also realigns the governance framework of OERI according to the models that have proven so successful at other federal research agencies. Federal research in education stands alone among all other kinds of federally funded scientific research in the extent to which it concentrates decision-making authority in the hands of a few political appointees and provides for such scant participation in those decisions by members of the research community and other stakeholders. The administration of other kinds of scientific research both within and outside government relies heavily on collegial decision-making processes that provide for maximum participation of individuals with expertise or an interest in the issues under consideration. This tradition of collegial decision making, diffuse authority, and peer review is embodied in the organizational structures of the two largest federal research agencies: the National Science Foundation (NSF) and the National Institutes of Health (NIH).

The National Science Foundation is governed by the 24-member, presidentially appointed National Science Board (NSB), which consists of leading scientists and other experts in the disciplines supported by the NSF. The NSB has exclusive authority to prescribe policy for the NSF. These policies may be originated by the board itself or initiated by the NSF director and other NSF personnel and submitted to the board for its approval. The board also plays a significant role in approving individual grant and fellowship awards. Board approval currently is required for any grant that represents or entails a change in NSF policy and all other proposed grants exceeding $1,500,000. All grant proposals, including those submitted to the board for approval, are first evaluated by peer reviewers with appropriate knowledge of the science involved. The only area in which the board has exercised little authority or influence has been the organizational structure of the NSF, which has largely been determined by the director and the Congress with only minimal participation by the NSB.

Although somewhat differently configured than NSF, the governance structure of the National Institutes of Health also emphasizes the importance of collegial decision making. Each institute has an 18-member advisory council appointed by the Secretary of Health and Human Services (HHS) in consultation with the institute's director. Two-thirds of the members of each council are scientists with expertise in disciplines relevant to the purposes of the institute; and the remainder are policy makers, economists, and other members of the public who have an interest in the purpose of the institute. Each of these councils makes recommendations to the Secretary of HHS and the director of the institute about institute policies and the kinds of research it supports; while these policy recommendations are not binding on the secretary or the director, traditionally they have carried great weight. Each council also must review and approve every proposed grant that exceeds $50,000. As with NSF, all grant proposals first are evaluated by peer reviewers with appropriate expertise.

The structure of the Office of Educational Research and Improvement is in dramatic contrast to that of NSF and NIH. Decision-making authority is vested exclusively with the Assistant Secretary and the Secretary; and the only formal mechanism for participation by the research community and other stakeholders in these decisions is a general biennial notice in the Federal Register, which solicits public comment about OERI's research priorities. While there is a presidentially appointed advisory council for OERI, its membership is not considered representative of the research community or particularly well qualified; and it is universally regarded as irrelevant both within and outside OERI. Between 1972 and 1986, this council did have policy-making authority; but it never attained the same degree of influence as either the NSB or even the NIH advisory councils, because its powers were vague and its membership was not fully representative of the research community and other stakeholders in education research and development. In 1986 this board finally was stripped of its policy-making authority because the quality of its membership had become so poor — consisting generally of persons who received their appointment as a political favor and who were neither knowledgeable nor even interested in education research — that it was widely seen as an embarrassment.

OERI's authoritarian, centralized decision-making structure is outmoded and dysfunctional and must be changed. The consensus on this point could not be more clear. For more than 30 years — since at least 1958 — every major study of the federal education research effort has consistently recommended that it be restructured along the lines of the National Science Foundation and the National Institutes of Health to provide for more collegial decision making about research priorities and the allocation of resources. These studies, by such authorities as the National Academy of Sciences and the RAND Corporation, have concluded that this kind of restructuring is essential to provide for a more stable and coherent research agenda, to insulate research from partisan influences, and to ensure that education research meets the same standards of excellence as all other types of research supported by the federal government.

H.R.4014 heeds this consensus call for more collegial decision making and public participation at OERI by creating a 20-member Educational Research Policy and Priorities Board consisting of both education researchers and representatives of teachers, parents, school administrators, and other stakeholders in the nation's education system to guide OERI's activities. This board would have some policy-making authority, but overall its authority would be substantially less than that of the National Science Board at NSF.

The Educational Research Policy and Priorities Board has two essential functions in H.R.4014. First, it is responsible for developing a comprehensive research priorities plan to end the incoherent, "flavor of the month" approach to research that has limited OERI's effectiveness for so long. This would be a long-term agenda for OERI's research and development efforts, reflecting a consensus of both educators and researchers, which would set out priorities and objectives for OERI, including areas that merit further inquiry and the most effective means of addressing them. This agenda would not be simply an aggregation of the personal preferences and ideas of the members of the board. Rather, H.R.4014 requires the board to develop the plan through a broadly participatory process that includes regional forums and other mechanisms for enabling the diverse constituencies of education research and development to express and exchange their points of view.

The purpose of the research priorities plan is to provide a broad, long-term agenda to drive decision making by the Congress and the Administration. The board would not have the authority to compel the Assistant Secretary — or the Congress — to implement each and every detail of the research priorities plan. But the board would be able to ensure that the broad parameters and priorities set out in the plan are followed, through its review of large-grant and contract solicitations. Before the Assistant Secretary could proceed with a solicitation for grants or contracts that exceed $500,000 in any single fiscal year or a total of $1,000,000 over several fiscal years, the board first would have to review the proposal and determine that it was consistent with the long-term research priorities plan.

The second critical function of the board is to establish a broad set of binding quality standards to govern the conduct of research carried out by OERI. These standards would address procedural issues only, including such matters as the process by which applications for assistance are to be reviewed and how and when funded activities are to be evaluated. Nearly every procedure and administrative policy related to the conduct and evaluation of research funded by OERI is now determined on an ad hoc basis, with minimal participation or input provided by the research community itself. Here again, OERI is unique among federal research agencies. NSF, NIH, and other agencies that fund scientific research have issued detailed regulations and internal policy manuals addressing these procedural issues. This haphazard, improvisational approach to research is dangerous because it creates opportunities for political mischief and manipulation and, even if these opportunities are never actually exploited, contributes to the overall impression that OERI's activities are highly politicized.

H.R.4014 seeks to address this problem by giving the board responsibility to develop comprehensive, permanent standards to govern the conduct and evaluation of all of the activities carried out by OERI. As with the research priorities plan, H.R.4014 directs the board to develop these standards through a broadly participatory process and actively solicit and consider the views of the research community and other stakeholders in the system.

The Educational Research Policy and Priorities Board can succeed only if its membership is both well qualified and broadly representative of both the producers and consumers of education research and development. Unfortunately, the history of policy making and advisory councils at OERI and its predecessor, the National Institute of Education, is not very encouraging in this regard. At no time has there been a council that met this essential dual test of appropriate expertise and representativeness. Little or no care has been taken by the President or the Secretary of Education — irrespective of political party — to ensure that such councils included representatives of the research community and the diverse constituencies that have a stake in education research and development. Incredibly, for example, not one teacher and very few education researchers have been appointed to such councils. Clearly, then, if the membership of the Educational Research Policy and Priorities Board is to be both qualified and representative, a new approach to its appointment must be tried.

H.R.4014 calls for the 20 members of the board to be appointed by the Secretary within 10 separate categories (that is, education researchers, teachers, parents) from among nominations made by professional associations and other national organizations representing such individuals. For example, the parent representative on the board would be selected from among nominations made by the National PTA, the National Coalition of Title I/Chapter 1 Parents, and the National Committee for Citizens in Education. It is only though this framework for the appointment of the board, which has precedent in other laws and approximates the manner in which the National Science Board is selected, that we can ensure that all of the diverse stakeholders for education research will be fully involved and represented.

Though the creation of research institutes and the establishment of a governing board to provide coherent, long-term direction to their work promises to improve the quality, breadth, and relevance of the knowledge generated by the federal investment in education research and development, this is only half the battle. Greater attention also must be paid to ensuring that this knowledge is fully put to work in the classroom and in the community to improve the practice of education. One critical reason for the persistently weak link between education research and practice is that there has been no single entity within OERI that is centrally responsible for directing the dissemination of the knowledge generated by the office and for improving its utilization by educators, parents, and others. Each individual research and development center, for example, is responsible for disseminating and marketing its research and resources within the education community. This diffusion of responsibility has resulted in wasteful redundancies in some areas and little or no activity in others.

H.R.4014 seeks to end this inefficient, scattershot approach by consolidating authority over dissemination in one single location by establishing an Office of Reform Assistance and Dissemination within OERI to be responsible for carrying out a broad range of dissemination and technical-assistance activities to support reform and school improvement efforts undertaken by local education agencies, teachers, school administrators, policy makers, parents, and others.

As the National Academy of Sciences pointed out in its *Research* report, the weak link between research and practice is both a supply-side problem, stemming in part from the quality, format, and orientation of the research supplied by researchers, and a demand-side problem, stemming from the failure of educators to seek out and use research-based knowledge more systematically in practice. For this reason, H.R.4014 authorizes multiple, complementary approaches to dissemination and technical assistance, recognizing that no single "magic bullet" will be sufficient to do the job.

The new Office of Dissemination would administer the existing 16 ERIC Clearinghouses, which index, abstract, and synthesize research results and other education-related information; the network of regional education laboratories, which work with educators and policy makers to apply research to improve existing education programs and to develop new ones; programs to deliver research syntheses and other information to parents and educators through Internet-based electronic networking and other new technologies; and a new program to train teachers in the use and conduct of education research. H.R.4014 also establishes the America 2000 Communities Special Assistance Program to provide intensified technical assistance to schools and communities located within the 50 poorest congressional districts in the nation. Inspired by the Agricultural Extension Agent program that proved so successful in improving the productivity of American farmers, the America 2000 Communities Special Assistance Program would support a district education agent who, in conjunction with a local institution of higher education, would work with teachers, school administrators, parents, and others in the community to apply research to solve particular educational problems and to support overall reform and improvement of education in the community.

The House Education and Labor Committee reported H.R.4014 by voice vote in May 1992. Although the legislation enjoyed broad support among education researchers and within the larger education community, the bill's progress was temporarily sidetracked by a ferocious campaign of opposition mounted by the Bush Administration and Assistant Secretary for OERI Diane Ravitch.

The intensity of Dr. Ravitch's opposition to H.R.4014 was somewhat surprising, because prior to her appointment as Assistant Secretary she had been co-director of a 1991 National Academy of Education study that was supportive of creating a policy-making board at OERI and made other recommendations that were consistent with the provisions of H.R.4014. Once installed at the helm of OERI, however, Dr. Ravitch apparently saw things differently. She continued to endorse the consensus diagnosis of the multiple maladies afflicting OERI, but now offered up an altogether different prescription: investing the office of the Assistant Secretary with maximum flexibility and discretionary authority. Given such power, she insisted, she could set right all that was wrong at OERI.

The problem here, of course, was that this approach had already been tried. Every other Assistant Secretary before Dr. Ravitch had made a similar vow about using the office's ample discretionary authority to clean up all of the problems at OERI, with less than stellar results. Nor did the experiences of other federal research agencies, with their emphases on collegial decision making, offer much support for the idea that what OERI needed now was one powerful czar to fix it. And even if Dr. Ravitch managed to succeed where all others had failed, this promised to be a short-term solution at best, since the average tenure of an Assistant Secretary was less than two years.

The Bush Administration rejected the new approaches and sweeping reforms of H.R.4014 out of hand. Every provision of the bill that might in some way limit the discretion of the Assistant Secretary was bitterly opposed. After initially supporting the idea of creating research institutes, the Administration ultimately opposed it because it would reduce OERI's "flexibility." Similarly, the Administration insisted that while the Office of Reform Assistance and Dissemination might be a worthwhile idea, it should not be established through legislation but through unilateral action by the Assistant Secretary. Necessary illustrative language that described but did not mandate possible research topics for each of the research institutes was inaccurately attacked as "micromanagement" of OERI.

Another point of conflict centered on the Administration's efforts to use appropriations for OERI's research account to make grants to states to improve their curriculum frameworks. This was probably a useful activity, but it has almost nothing to do with research. Moreover, instead of dipping into the already meager funds available to support research, it would have been more appropriate to fund the activity through the Fund for Innovation in Education or through other education-reform legislation then pending in Congress. For this reason, H.R.4014 included language that prohibited the use of OERI's research funds for this purpose. This outraged Dr. Ravitch and the Administration.

But the brunt of the Administration's ire was directed at the concept of creating a board with policy-making authority at OERI. The successful examples of the National Science Foundation and the National Institutes of Health notwithstanding, the Administration argued that anything more than a purely advisory board would be unworkable and destructive. Hard pressed to make their case on its merits, the Administration took to wildly misrepresenting the decidedly limited powers of the board, claiming inaccurately that it would be vested with authority to make nearly every day-to-day decision at the agency.

The Administration's objections were not totally unexpected. Since education research is one of the few areas of the Department of Education's budget over which the Secretary can exercise almost complete discretion, it is not surprising that any Administration would be reluctant to make the kinds of changes called for by H.R.4014. Dr. Ravitch's lack of any prior administrative experience was probably another contributing factor; had she had some experience in the public or private sectors in working with the kind of board set out in H.R.4014, she might have found the concept less threatening. But understandable or not, the Administration's opposition to a policy-making board was most certainly wrong-headed, given the resounding failure of the OERI's centralized, command-and-control governance model. The chief concern of the Congress and the Administration must be to provide for the kind of high-quality education research the nation needs to improve our schools — not providing for the personal or political gratification of a Secretary or Assistant Secretary.

The Administration opposed the appointment process for board members for much the same reason that it opposed the creation of the board itself: It did not want to share power. Attacking the organizations given responsibility for nominating board members as "special interests," the Administration complained that board members would be unable to "make decisions in a neutral, impartial way." This argument was more than a little disingenuous. President Bush and his predecessors have not traditionally appointed "neutral and impartial" individuals to decision-making positions within the Department of Education; rather, each President has appointed persons who represent a definite point of view and ideology — his own. But when it comes to education research, it is imperative that decision making reflect a diversity of views — and not just one — if the end product is to be useful and credible.

More ridiculously, the Administration argued that board members would be beholden to the organizations that nominated them and would be chiefly occupied with trying to "logroll" among themselves to steer OERI funds to these organizations. This would simply not have been possible — not only because board members were governed by the same conflict-of-interest protections as other federal officials but, more importantly, because the board's authority was limited to setting priorities — it could not award funds to carry out those priorities.

The Bush Administration's determined campaign against H.R.4014 succeeded in delaying floor consideration of the bill for several critical weeks. Though the committee remained confident that it had sufficient votes to turn back any Administration-supported amendments on the House floor, further delay so late in the session would imperil the enactment of the legislation. In an effort to advance the process, a package of amendments designed to address the Administration's chief objections was offered. Deleted from H.R.4014 were the restrictions on the use of research funds for grants to improve curriculum frameworks, the board's authority to develop standards, and the requirement that board members be selected from among nominations by organizations. With these amendments, H.R.4014 was passed by voice vote by the full House of Representatives on September 22, 1992.

Unfortunately, these concessions were deemed insufficient by the Administration, which continued to object to even the last vestiges of policy-making authority for the board remaining in the bill. Largely as a result of the Administration's continued opposition, the Senate was unable to take up consideration of H.R.4014 before the 103rd Congress adjourned.

The Bush Administration had succeeded in derailing enactment of H.R.4014 in the 102nd Congress, but it was a definitively Pyrrhic victory. The decision to mount a blisteringly negative campaign against H.R.4014 rather than work with Congress in a joint effort of building consensus alienated many in the education community and demoralized OERI employees. OERI's research budget was cut significantly by the appropriations committees, leaving it barely enough funds to maintain its current activities, let alone initiate new ones. Dr. Ravitch still had maximum discretion, but it was not discretion over much.

It was a temporary victory because reason will eventually prevail. During the initial congressional consideration of legislation to establish the National Science Foundation nearly 50 years ago, the Truman Administration, too, strenuously objected to the creation of a board with policy-making authority at NSF and insisted that the National Science Board be made an advisory council only. In 1947, in fact, President Truman vetoed the first NSF bill passed by the Congress over just this issue. Some three years later, however, reason prevailed and President Truman accepted the concept of a policy-making board and signed the National Science Foundation Authorization Act into law.

Just as it took three years before the Congress convinced the Truman Administration of the wisdom of the governance structure it devised for the NSF, it is now necessary to stand fast and continue to press for the meaningful structural reform of the Office of Educational Research and Improvement. The Educational Research, Development, and Dissemination Excellence Act will be reintroduced in the 103rd Congress and the Subcommittee on Select Education will act on it quickly. Working alongside the new, more enlightened Clinton Administration, it should be possible for Congress to reform and revitalize OERI, enabling it to produce, systematically and abundantly, the knowledge the nation now so urgently needs to support education improvement and reform. We must have this knowledge if we are ever to attain our six ambitious National Education Goals.

OERI Cure Must Wait for New Congress

By Gerald E. Sroufe

Gerald E. Sroufe has served as director of the Governmental and Professional Liaison Program of the American Educational Research Association for four years. His other Washington policy experiences include serving as executive director of the National Committee for Support of the Public Schools and work in the Office of Education while participating in the Washington Interns in Education Program (now the Institute for Educational Leadership). Sroufe earned his doctorate at the University of Chicago. This paper appeared originally in the Educational Researcher *for December 1992. Copyright 1992 by AERA. Reprinted by permission of the publisher.*

Some may take exception to the implied assertion that the Office of Educational Research and Improvement (OERI), the major research agency of the U.S. Department of Education, is ill and requires congressional attention. Certainly, OERI staff and programs do much good; and some in the research community are doing not only good but well by virtue of participation in federal programs in education research and statistics. However, viewed in the context of the nation's need for dependable knowledge and informed perspectives, OERI's anemia is apparent.

Legislation intended to address the major obstacles facing OERI was drafted by both the House and Senate and passed in the House. It died in the Senate, ensuring that the present difficulties will continue for at least one, and possibly two years more. How this came to happen and what is likely to happen next form the primary subject of this article. Those familiar with the symptoms of the problem and various cures prescribed by the National Academy of Education and the National Research Council, the American Educational Research Association (AERA), and the House and Senate, may wish to fast-forward to the sections on "malpractice" and "prognosis."

Symptoms

One symptom of OERI's frailty is the paltry flow of funds to support field-initiated research, the mainstay of scientific investigation in the United States. In FY 1993, OERI will have less than $1 million to award on a competitive basis to individual researchers. Since few awards can be made and since they provide support for only one year and will be only about $75,000 each, little is expected to result from the program despite the best intentions and efforts of all involved.

This constricted flow of resources to support the work of individual investigators does not represent a temporary blockage but a chronic condition. Since 1986 the appropriated funds have seldom reached beyond $1 million, despite energetic efforts of OERI administrators. In 1989 OERI was able to fund only 10 field-initiated proposals, depleting the $500,000 appropriated. The National Science Foundation, in comparison, funded 1,300 individual research studies from an appropriation of $1.5 billion in that year.

A frequent lament of AERA members is that the research centers and regional laboratories supported by OERI "soak up all the money." This is true only in a relative sense: The amount of research money available within OERI has diminished over time, and a relatively large portion of what currently is available is allocated to centers and labs. It is a false diagnosis to the extent that it assumes centers and labs are adequately funded, which is patently not the case in either absolute or relative terms (Sroufe 1991). More disheartening is the fact that even if the total research funds appropriated for centers and labs ($64 million in FY 1993) were shifted to field-initiated research, the program would still be inadequately funded. The NRC study recommends an annual appropriation of $150 million for field-initiated research (Atkinson and Jackson 1992).

An additional symptom of fiscal weakness is that federal funds for education R&D declined 82% between 1972 and 1988 (Atkinson and Jackson 1992). Can this decline be attributed to budget constraints or the contracting economy? Unfortunately, no. While federal funding for educational R&D declined 33% in real dollars between 1980 and 1987, federal funding for all other R&D increased 24% (General Accounting Office 1988). Clearly, more is required to fix the problems of education research than renewed effort; the reauthorization bills designed by the House and Senate attempted to provide conceptual and organizational bootstraps on which the agency might tug.

Diagnosis

The problems of OERI were brought to the 102nd Congress, just concluded, because the five-year reauthorization customary for federal education programs had expired. In order to gain information, the House Subcommittee on Select Education, under the leadership of Chairman Major Owens (D-N.Y.), held more than 15 hearings and received testimony from nearly 100 witnesses, beginning in the 101st Congress. The subcommittee served as a clinic for diagnosis of the problems of OERI and for proposing and assessing recommendations for strengthening the agency. Testimony was provided from representatives of the Education Department, including four Assistant Secretaries of Education heading OERI during the period. Testimony was also provided by representatives of the business community, teachers, researchers, and professional associations. The AERA provided formal testimony before the subcommittee on four occasions during the period of information gathering prior to legislative drafting.

Consultations

In addition to the information developed at the hearings, Congress had available for consultation formal studies from two independent scholarly committees. The first was prepared by the National Academy for Education (NAE) under the direction of professors Mike Kirst and Diane Ravitch. The second was prepared by the National Research Council of the National Academy of Science (NRC). The studies have been reviewed in the *Educational Researcher (ER)* ("National Academy of Sciences," 1991; "Research and the Renewal of Education," 1991). They were complementary in that the NAE study fixed the unique responsibility of the federal government for supporting education research, decrying the absence of corporate or state support, and the NRC study provided a blueprint for actions necessary to resuscitate OERI.

Prescriptions

Following the advice of a member of the Senate education staff, AERA offered its prescription for OERI early and often. Arthur Wise and I addressed the question in "A Response to America's Reform Agenda:

181

The National Institutes for Educational Improvement" (1990). The AERA Council endorsed the "institutes" or mission approach to reauthorization and reorganization of OERI, and efforts were made to call the advantages of this approach to the attention of appropriate members of Congress and professional education associations.

Bills were drafted and redrafted in the House and Senate. The House bill proved to be the most closely aligned with AERA's understanding of legislation required to address the major problems of OERI. While the House bill (H.R.4014) was subjected to several substantial revisions and a host of extraneous amendments, it consistently sought to define and organize OERI in terms of five mission-driven institutes within which significant R&D programs could be created, sustained, and supported. Each of the institutes would have supported research centers, and each would have set aside 15% of its funds to support field-initiated research. The bill provided authorization for the appropriation of nearly $100 million for the institutes; if fully appropriated, the bill would have ensured at least $15 million for field-initiated research and at least $30 million for national research centers.

The House bill would have provided full-strength medicine to treat what many have regarded the central problem of OERI: too close affiliation with the Administration in power. The bill provided for a somewhat independent Policy and Procedures Board responsible for establishing a long-range agenda for OERI; it was intended to parallel the structure of the National Science Foundation in the hope of eventually gaining a reputation for scientific investigations unclouded by partisanship. In the substitute bill ultimately approved by the House, the functions of the board were curtailed and the title changed to Board of Governors.

S1275 was almost entirely the work of Senate staff. Only one hearing was scheduled on OERI in the Senate, and that was devoted mostly to consideration of testing issues. The Senate bill preferred the term "directorate" to institutes but was in keeping with the AERA idea that it was necessary to design research programs around a limited number of compelling problems and to devote greatly increased resources toward understanding and resolving them. Set-asides were provided to promote larger, and fewer, research centers and to provide for increased field-initiated research.

Each congressional body developed at least one unique approach to dissemination. In the House, the National Education Dissemination System included provisions for creation of a new entity: field-based technical assistance for the nation's most impoverished urban and rural districts. The plan called for learning grant institutions to augment and support activities of district education agents, who would work to develop and implement a comprehensive, communitywide plan for school improvement. Community school-improvement plans would have made extensive use of R&D, training, and demonstration of effective programs. The legislation would have authorized $40 million for this program.

In the Senate, Senator Nancy Kassebaum (R-Kan.) and her staff provided for the creation of a network of Teacher Research Dissemination Experts (TRDE). TRDE was to be a multipurpose program for training teachers to participate in research, be better consumers of research, and become knowledgeable about federal research resources. Participants were to be trained during the summer and then return to their districts to share their knowledge and expertise, acting as continuing resources for other teachers. TRDE was to be assigned to the regional laboratories and authorized an appropriation of $20 million (Senate report); similar provisions introduced by Representative Pat Williams (D-Mont.) in the House bill authorized $30 million. In both bills the rationale for the new program was to stimulate the use of research in the classroom to enhance learning.

Both Senate and House bills provided for the establishment of research programs of sufficient breadth to create a platform for sustained future growth. However, the governance structure proposed by the Senate more nearly resembled over-the-counter medication. The Distinguished Board of Governors, the Senate counterpart to the House Board of Governors, was given nine functions with regard to the assistant secretary; six involved "recommendations," and three involved offering "advice."

Resistance

As might be anticipated, primary resistance to the medication proposed by the House was from the Administration, especially OERI, and particularly Diane Ravitch in her position as Assistant Secretary of Education. Dr. Ravitch had more influence in the Senate drafting process than in the House and focused the considerable influence of the Administration behind efforts to avoid the remedies proposed by the House in favor of the more conservative prescription offered by the Senate.

The issue was a familiar one: how to provide sufficient independence to a policy board to remove it from charges of partisanship while not making it impossible for the Administration to govern the agency. The gridlock resulting from Democratic control of Congress and Republican control of the Administration had been exacerbated in education because of unusually contentious ideological controversies. White House education reform proposals, such as represented in America 2000, were anathema to most congressional Democrats. Worse for OERI, many in Congress have come to regard the agency in terms of its role in implementing or supporting a controversial policy agenda, rather than as an "independent" research agency such as NIH. Early versions of the House bill included governance provisions that many felt took too much authority from the Administration and gave too much authority to the Policy and Procedures Board. The Administration and Republican representatives were strongly united on this issue, although Congress was comfortable with the compromises finally reached. Dr. Ravitch, while acknowledging the difficulties resulting from not having an authorization, held out to the end for the Senate version of an OERI reauthorization, which would not have diminished the current authority of the Secretary of Education to make appointments to the board or the Assistant Secretary to develop the research agenda and procedures regarding awards.

The decision to stand by the Senate plan proved unfortunate, at least in the short run. As had been foretold, the appropriations panels provided funds (FY 1993) for OERI only sufficient to continue programs already in place. Funding for the statistics account was increased; funding for centers and laboratories was increased slightly; field-initiated research was level-funded, but the Assistant Secretary's discretionary account was decimated. In what became his final budget, Christopher T. Cross was given $10 million in discretionary funds for developing new programs and initiatives, sponsoring symposia, and creating new publications. OERI will have $1.5 million in FY 1993 for the same purposes, further diminishing the possibility of the agency to heal itself.

Malpractice

The legislative process is frequently compared to the process of making sausage; it is best to avert one's eyes. However, *malpractice* seems to be the best term for characterizing the legislative process as revealed in the reauthorization of OERI, partly because it fits without our belabored medical metaphor, partly because the bill did not die so much from natural causes as by intent.

It is seldom possible to tell the complete story of passage, or failure, of legislation. There are simply too many actors, too many partisan views, too many actions occurring in too many places for anyone to assemble all the important pieces in the right relationships. Moreover, those who know the most often have most reason to hold the information closely. However, recounting those aspects of the legislative history of this bill about which there is much agreement may shed light on what might happen in the next Congress.

Legislative Politics in a Presidential Election Year. Democratic strategy, under the leadership of Senator Edward Kennedy (D-Mass.), included seeking to embarrass President Bush by forcing him to sign or veto a school reform bill (S2) that did not include support for private school choice. It was assumed that he would veto the bill, intended to reach his desk just a month before the election. To ensure that this would happen, Senator Kennedy issued the word that the Senate would take up no education legislation until S2 "was passed or vetoed." Obviously, this tactic slowed down the legislative process and meant that action on OERI was not possible in the Senate until the final days of the session.

Actually, President Bush turned the tables on the Democrats. The Administration made opposition to S2 a matter of party loyalty and was able to defeat a cloture vote necessary to take the bill to the floor, where it would have passed. President Bush was not called on to veto an education bill, and Congress was unable to take credit for passing one. Because of the controversy over fetal tissue research, a similar fate befell the National Institutes of Health.

In addition, because of the elections, Congress was anxious to adjourn. While some sessions of Congress run as late as November, this year it was clear that the stipulated adjournment on October 3 would be observed as closely as possible, no matter what legislation did not get passed. Adjournment fever created great competition for floor time to debate bills and discouraged consideration of controversial or less than essential measures.

Timing in the Legislative Process. In retrospect, it is appealing to believe that if OERI had been coupled to the Higher Education Act, as it had been in the past, it would have had smooth sailing and would now be authorized. Similarly, even without OERI being treated independently, if it had been possible to pass it in the House and Senate early enough, it might have been possible to arrange a successful conference before the end of the Congress.

Difficult Situations Create Difficult Relationships. While it might have been desirable to reach early agreement on the provisions of a bill to reauthorize OERI, major important issues separated the parties and precluded early resolution. For example, the Senate sought to defer action until all necessary compromises were reached within the education committee. This procedure ultimately resulted in unanimous passage of S1275 from the full Committee on Labor and Human Resources, but required months of private negotiations. In the House it was clear that Representative Owens and Dr. Ravitch were not likely to agree on much of consequence. For months, Ravitch and Education Secretary Lamar Alexander prevailed on the Republicans to refuse to accept the bill "under suspension" (meaning it was uncontroversial and had bipartisan support). Near the end of the session, Owens agreed to enough compromises with Republican members that they permitted the bill to go under suspension of the rules. The bill was passed by voice vote, Dr. Ravitch's continued objections notwithstanding. In voting approval of the bill, both Representative William Goodling (R-Pa.), the ranking member of the House Education and Labor Committee, and Representative Cass Ballenger (R-N.C.), the ranking member of the House Subcommittee on Select Education, spoke in favor of the bill (U.S. Congress 1992).

A House Is Not the Senate. The House bill that was ultimately passed had a good chance, but only one chance, of becoming law. The Senate would have to "leave it at the desk" for amendment and vote to return it to the House with stipulations avoiding the need for an extensive conference. In order to make this feasible, the House had accepted a number of provisions from the Senate bill and added them to its bill, essentially compromising in advance. This appeared to many to be a viable plan, and most of the staff on the Senate committee proceeded as though the bill were alive and action would be taken soon. AERA, and most professional education associations, urged the Senate to amend the bill and return it to the House without going to committee.

This was not to be, however. Labor and Human Resources Committee staff did not request that the bill remain at the desk, which would have required unanimous consent; and after one day it was sent to committee. Senators Kennedy and Claiborne Pell (D-R.I.), chair of the Subcommittee on Education, Arts, and Humanities, hoped to introduce a new "substitute bill" modifying S1275. Few people — not even all members of the Senate Labor and Human Resources Committee — had an opportunity to review the substitute bill, and so it is not possible to report fully on its contents. However, Dr. Ravitch had indicated that

186

she expected the Senate to produce a better bill than the House; and it is reported that the substitute reflected her thinking regarding the troublesome governance issues.

Consequently, the House bill designed to cure OERI was itself stone dead sooner than most realized. Ironically, many House Republicans and Senate Democrats thought the bill was alive and at the desk two days after it was sent to committee and killed. The modified House bill seemed to have gained broad support among those on the relevant committees in the House and Senate, but the support was too weak and too late to achieve success in this Congress.

Prognosis

Congress and the Administration were unable to pass a bill addressing the serious problems of OERI this year; consequently, an improved federal program of education research is probably two years away.

Whatever the outcome of the presidential election,* there is likely to be a new administration in the Department of Education, which means much time will pass before personnel are in place who feel comfortable addressing the needs of OERI. Of course, either party could mount a "first 100 days" campaign of education reform actions that include the reorganization of OERI; but nothing was proposed in the election campaign to suggest that such action is likely.

It is anticipated that the House will continue in Democratic control and that Owens will continue to chair the Subcommittee on Select Education, which will continue to have jurisdiction over OERI. This being the case, it is anticipated that the House will pass legislation similar to H.R.4014 early in the session, unless requested not to do so by a new Democratic Secretary of Education. However, the Senate has fewer members and fewer committees and will prefer to combine OERI — a very small program — with the reauthorization of the Elementary and Secondary Education Act (ESEA) — a very large program. This would mean that OERI will have to survive in very much its present form until the 1995 appropriations cycle, because ESEA will probably not be authorized until the second session of the 103rd Congress.

The "two more years" prognosis raises two questions for education researchers. The first is, How bad will things be? The second is, What might be done?

---

*Editor's Note. Although published in the December 1992 *Educational Researcher*, this article was written before the November 1992 election.

For those comfortable with the status quo regarding federal support for education research, the next two years may be as predictable and comfortable as the Arizona sunshine. Programs specified in the existing authorization (for example, research centers, regional laboratories, field-initiated research, ERIC) will continue to be funded at present levels; no new research programs will be funded; there will be tiny increments, if any, in total research dollars. The National Center for Education Statistics is authorized under different legislation and may be expected to continue its recent pattern of growth.

For those who believe the sweeping reforms called for in the recommendations of the National Science Academy are the proper direction for OERI, failure to achieve a new authorization represents a serious setback. The agency is unlikely to be a better place to work with or work for over the next two years.

What can be done? Researchers with ties to the incoming education administration can press the case for an expedited reauthorization of OERI, independent, if necessary, of the ESEA reauthorization. Additionally, all will have to work to establish the idea of an independent research agency within the Department of Education as an important component of education reform at all levels. The reports on federal research prepared by NAE and NRC provide an excellent basis for making the case that must be made, but neither is likely to be on the top of the "things to be read" by new members of Congress or the Administration without vigorous efforts of researchers.

The failure to achieve reauthorization of OERI during the Congress just concluded provides a benchmark of how much remains to be done to educate federal policy makers to the importance of this work and this agency.

References

Atkinson, R.C., and Jackson, G.B., eds. *Research and Education Reform: Roles for the Office of Educational Research and Improvement*. Report of the National Research Council. Washington, D.C.: National Academy Press, 1992.

General Accounting Office. *R&D Funding: The Department of Education in Perspective*. Washington, D.C.: U.S. Government Printing Office, 1988.

"National Academy of Sciences Announces New Study of Federal Education Research Policy." *Educational Researcher* 20, no. 1 (1991): 27.

"*Research and the Renewal of Education*: Executive Summary and Recommendations." *Educational Researcher* 20, no. 6 (1991): 19-21.

Sroufe, G.E. "Education Enterprise Zones: The New National Research Centers." *Educational Researcher* 20, no. 4 (1991): 24-29.

U.S. Congress. "Proceedings and Debates." *Congressional Record*. 138 (130 part II) (1992): 9007-9029.

Wise, A.E., and Sroufe, G.E. "A Response to America's Reform Agenda: The National Institutes for Educational Improvement." *Educational Researcher* 19, no. 4 (1990): 22, 25.

The Department of Education's Support of Education Research

By Richard C. Atkinson and Andrew C. Porter*

Richard C. Atkinson is chancellor of the University of California at San Diego and professor of cognitive science and psychology. He formerly served as director of the National Science Foundation and president of the American Association for the Advancement of Science. His research on problems of memory and cognition has been used to develop computer-controlled systems for instruction in the primary grades. Atkinson is a member of the National Academy of Sciences, the Institute of Medicine, the National Academy of Education, and the American Philosophical Society. He obtained a Ph.B. degree from the University of Chicago and a Ph.D. degree from Indiana University.

Andrew C. Porter is a professor of educational psychology and director of the Wisconsin Center for Education Research at the University of Wisconsin-Madison. He has also served on the faculty at Michigan State University, where he was associate dean for research and graduate study and co-director of the Institute for Research on Teaching. He was a visiting scholar and an associate director of basic skills research at the National Institute of Education. Porter has published on psychometrics, student and teacher assessment, teaching research, and education policy. He has served on the editorial boards of eight professional journals including, currently, the American Journal of Education *and* Educational Evaluation and Policy Analysis. *Porter has a B.S. in education from Indiana State University and a master's and Ph.D. in educational psychology from the University of Wisconsin-Madison.*

*Our thanks to Alexandra Wigdor, director, Division of Education, Training, and Employment, Commission on Behavioral and Social Sciences and Education, National Research Council, and Carolyn Sax for assistance in preparing this paper.

The Office of Educational Research and Improvement (OERI) in the Department of Education is responsible for a broad range of research, development, and dissemination activities. Over the years, OERI and its predecessor agencies have been subject to widespread criticism. Researchers often have claimed that support for education research has been insufficient, misguided, and poorly managed; teachers and principals often have been unaware of the office or claimed it has not done much to improve their schools; and members of Congress often have expressed dissatisfaction and frustration — as much with their votes as with their words.

With these historic problems in mind, with heightened national attention on educational issues, and with its scheduled congressional reauthorization approaching, OERI asked the National Academy of Sciences in the fall of 1990 to consider how it could better carry out its mandate to improve education in the U.S. The academy, through its National Research Council (NRC), convened 15 distinguished experts to conduct the study. The following remarks are drawn from the resulting report, *Research and Education Reform: Roles for the Office of Educational Research and Improvement* (1992).*

Background

The nation expects a great deal from its education system. Not only do we expect the schools to impart the rudiments of learning, to equip citizens for economic survival, and to produce the kind of informed populace needed to sustain the nation's democratic institutions, we expect them to mitigate economic and social inequalities, find ways to circumvent difficult barriers of language, disability, and disadvantage, and to provide an increasing array of social services. Even to approach these expectations, schools need to be extraordinarily resilient and resourceful.

In the past decade, dozens of reports have identified serious problems with schooling in America. Every state has mandated initiatives for reform, and countless local programs and alliances have tried to bring about change and improvement. Intense pressures have built up nationally for renewed attention to education, as indicated by the call for national edu-

---

*The National Academy of Sciences' Committee on the Federal Role in Education Research was chaired by Richard C. Atkinson. The study director for the project was Gregg B. Jackson. See National Research Council, *Research and Education Reform: Roles for the Office of Educational Research and Improvement*. Committee on the Federal Role in Education Research, Commission on Behavioral and Social Sciences and Education (Washington, D.C.: National Academy Press, 1992).

cation goals (National Education Goals Panel 1991), the congressionally mandated rapid growth of the Education and Human Resources Directorate at the National Science Foundation, and former President Bush's America 2000 proposal for improving education (Alexander 1991).

There is no question about the significance of the challenges now facing U.S. education. Part of the imperative for today's reforms comes from increasing academic and intellectual demands of the workplace. Part of it comes from the mediocre educational attainments of a significant proportion of youth in the United States, particularly those in low-income families and those of minority status. Demographic trends also have quickened the reform impulse. The U.S. population is an aging population, so there will be proportionately fewer workers to support retirees in the foreseeable future. In addition, the population groups that are expanding most rapidly, African-Americans and particularly Hispanic-Americans, are also at highest risk for school failure and the accompanying likelihood of a marginal economic existence.

Many people have concluded that ad hoc improvements will not suffice to meet these challenges; rather, a fundamental rethinking of education is necessary. The core idea is that schooling should promote conceptual understanding, problem solving, and the ability to apply knowledge and skills in new contexts and to real-world problems (Porter, Archbald, and Tyree 1991). A variety of solutions has been proposed, both structural and substantive. Among the most talked-about are a national system of standards and assessments; school-site management; school choice; abolition of ability grouping; outcomes-based curricula; team teaching; ongoing staff development; deep coverage instead of broad coverage as a curriculum principle; community-based learning; small, stable, family-like instructional units of students and teachers; the use of portfolios of student work to replace standardized tests; and parental control of schools.

Whether these many suggestions can be knit into a workable and effective program for improving the nation's schools remains to be seen. As a society, the United States has been good at launching reforms; it has been less good at continuing them to completion (Cuban 1990; Elmore and McLaughlin 1988). And despite the growing national consensus that the nation faces a major problem in education from kindergarten through high school, fixing the problem — or even defining it adequately — remains a daunting challenge.

Education in the United States exists on a vast scale, with annual budgets of $240 billion for just the K-12 component and more than $375 billion for the total education enterprise — encompassing higher education, industrial education, and supporting organizations. Both the scale and the decentralized character of education make the imposition of central solutions impossible. If schools in the U.S. are going to get better, it will require the combined efforts and commitment of all concerned — parents, teachers, administrators, and government officials. The challenge for federal and state policy makers is to create conditions that will make education reform more likely — to help schools and communities equip themselves with the tools of reform.

The Role of Research

At the present time, the formulation of education policy is running far ahead of education research — and this is cause for concern. Whether the initiative is school choice or national standards and assessments, new ideas are being advanced and implemented with little knowledge of how they will fare.

Few Americans would deny that research has been a potent force for improved medical care or the emergence of modern agriculture in the 20th century. So axiomatic is this to the business of agriculture, for example, that one of the nation's foremost seed companies invested 40 years of effort in developing the seedless watermelon. When it comes to education, however, it is difficult to find an equivalent example. Education research is more likely to be dismissed as trivial or irrelevant than it is to be considered a fundamental ingredient in understanding how children learn and in improving how they are taught.

Telling evidence of the low status of education research is the very small portion of federal education funding that goes to research — just $350 million of $64.1 billion in FY 1991. In comparison, the federal government spends three times as much for space research and development and 30 times as much for research related to health. Policy makers are not alone in their general low regard for research as an integral part of a robust system of education. Teachers commonly indicate that they do not use research and do not see its connection to what they do on a daily basis in the classroom (Louis, Dentler, and Kell 1984).

There are many reasons for the undistinguished reputation of research in education, only some of which are well-founded. Part of the cause can be found in the practical orientation of teacher education. Schools of education generally do not prepare the nation's future teachers to value disciplined inquiry or even, at a more mundane level, to keep track of relevant research. Once on the job, the conditions of work do not encourage school teachers to study the research literature. No matter how enlightening research may be, it cannot contribute to improvements in education if it is not understood, used intelligently, and refined in the context of local experience.

This situation is aggravated by the national tendency to want quick solutions to problems — even if the problems have been generations in the making. Much of the public discussion of education research has a distinctly utilitarian cast; it assumes that researchers conduct studies, their findings are translated into products or programs for use in the schools, and education is improved. This view is at once too narrow and too grandiose. It implies that the only valuable research is research that can be directly translated into classroom practice, a view that gives short shrift to much research. And it encourages unrealistic expectations about what research can — or should be able to — accomplish.

The effects of research on education practice are seldom straightforward and quick. As in other fields, there are few definitive studies, but rather a gradual accretion of knowledge drawn from overlapping studies in many fields of study, conducted over a long period of time, punctuated by an occasional breakthrough. In physics and chemistry, as well as social and behavioral science, decades of basic research provide the seedbed for new approaches and methods. Improvement in education will occur only if all participants — parents, students, teachers, the public, and policy makers — are willing to make strong intellectual commitments to work together using new insights, approaches, and techniques to improve education.

Although the undistinguished reputation of education research may be partly attributable to some of the work, the NRC committee did not share the widespread negative judgments about the contributions of research to the reform of education. Its review of research-based programs to improve teaching, strengthen curricula, restructure institutions of learning, and assess and monitor progress in U.S. schools led to the conclusion that research has been demonstrably useful and can improve education.

Basic research and theory building in cognitive science, for example, have produced important insights into how children acquire knowledge and make sense of new experience. Many of the current generation of cognitive scientists are now taking these insights into applied settings — that is, classrooms — to develop teaching strategies that encourage children to develop progressively more effective thinking strategies.

In a very different vein, the data collected by the OERI National Center for Education Statistics provide crucial information to federal, state, and local policy makers and to social scientists, education associations, and others about the character, status, and problems of the education system. The National Assessment of Educational Progress, for example, is an important source of information about students' knowledge and how their knowledge has changed over time. Trend data indicate that reading and mathematics skills have increased only slightly over the past two decades (National Center for Education Statistics 1991), information that has helped fuel the desire for thoroughgoing reform. One of the lesser known trends apparent in these data is that the reading and mathematics scores of African-American and Hispanic students have been rising faster than the national average, which many analysts interpret to mean that the basic skills movement, for all its limitations, has had some positive effects.

If, as the NRC committee argues, a sustained investment in research is an essential ingredient in the overall effort to improve education, what can OERI, which is after all a very small player in a very big enterprise, do to strengthen the effectiveness of education research? First, successful education research tends to require a sustained investment of time and money. (Should we be surprised at this if the seedless watermelon took 40 years to develop?) Second, we can benefit from innovation only if we can distinguish worthwhile programs from fads. An important shortcoming of almost all federally funded (and other) education research is the lack of money and time allotted to evaluation. Third, even its brief review of research quickly convinced the committee that no one mechanism and no one discipline should be given priority in federal funding. Although OERI funds virtually no field-initiated research, most of the innovative programs reviewed were built on a research base supplied by the works of individual social and behavioral scientists. A vigorous program of support for field-initiated research is as important as the current support of laboratories and centers. Moreover, advances in education have been built on research in the cognitive sciences, psychology, sociology, anthropology, organizational behavior, and clinical work. Education research will be substantially strengthened to the extent that it embraces a broad array of disciplines and fields of study.

All of these recommendations — support of long-term research efforts, serious evaluation, much greater support of individual scholars and scholars from many disciplines — suggest a bigger dollar outlay, and indeed the NRC committee strongly recommends a large increase in OERI's research budget. But that sort of financial commitment on the part of Congress is likely only if OERI can be strengthened. The next section of this essay briefly describes OERI's checkered institutional past before discussing some structural changes that the NRC committee recommended to lend it greater independence and strength.

Appraisal of OERI

Governance. The National Institute of Education (NIE) was created in 1971 as a separate agency within the Department of Health, Education, and Welfare (HEW) to consolidate education research and development activities, give responsibility for management of these activities to professional scholars, and provide higher status for the work. Its director reported to the Assistant Secretary for Education, who was also in charge of the Office of Education and, starting in 1974, the newly established National Center for Education Statistics (NCES).

A National Council on Educational Research was created by legislation to set overall policies for NIE. The 15 members were appointed by the President and, in the 1976 reauthorization of NIE, Congress specified that the council was to be broadly representative of the general public, of the education professions, and of the various fields of education.

With the creation of the Department of Education in 1979, the Office of Educational Research and Improvement (OERI) was established. It was conceived as an umbrella organization to house a semi-autonomous NIE, NCES, Library Programs, and some discretionary and dissemination activities. The National Council of Educational Research was retained.

During the 1980s OERI was reorganized and NIE eliminated. The policy-making council was replaced with a National Advisory Council on Educational Research and Improvement. The responsibilities of the new council were somewhat more limited, since it was not given authority to prescribe the duties of the head of OERI, and it was to provide advice to the Secretary of Education and to the Assistant Secretary of OERI, rather than to determine policy.

It is not clear which governance structure — the policy-making council of NIE or the advisory council of OERI — has been more effective. There is widespread agreement that the advisory council has not been influential within OERI or outside of it. The policy-making council, under both Republican and Democratic Administrations in the 1970s, generally was considered competent and hardworking; but it was unable to help NIE gain the support of educators, the public, or Congress. In the early 1980s it was considered less distinguished, more politicized, and even less effective in securing support.

Another key issue in the governance of OERI has been the roles played by the top administrators. Each new director or assistant secretary of OERI (and NIE) has sought to make his or her mark by pursuing a distinctive agenda, but most have not remained long enough to enact more than a small portion of it. Seven of the ten former top administrators of OERI and NIE have held their positions for less than two years.

However, even with their short tenures, most of the directors and assistant secretaries have reorganized the agency. It is not clear whether the reorganizations have been due to a persisting belief that there are structural solutions to the problems of federal support of education research or to the lack of opportunities for discretion in other areas of managing the agency.

Politicization. The National Institute of Education was born in the midst of political maneuvering. It was proposed by President Richard Nixon, a Republican, at a time when he was simultaneously proposing cuts in federal funding for many social and education programs to a Democratically controlled Congress (Sproull, Weiner, and Wolf 1978). Political conservatives, wanting to limit federal involvement in the nation's life, were generally against the institute. So were many liberals, who were unwilling to trade federal support of local school programs for education research. Senator Warren Magnuson, a powerful member of the Senate Appropriations Committee and chair of the subcommittee responsible for HEW, was angered by Nixon's proposals to cut $3 billion from that department and sought to extract revenge through NIE.

Ever since, there has been a widespread perception that NIE and OERI have been inappropriately and dysfunctionally politicized. The examples of politicization, however, vary markedly, depending on who is citing them. Members of Congress and their staffs frequently charge that the Administration's ideological and political agendas have skewed the appointment of top administrators, the selection of topics to be studied, the determination of how the topics are to be studied, the awarding of contracts, and the editing of reports and timing of their release. For instance, it is claimed that there was little research on the educational effects of dual-earner families during the Carter Administration (for fear that the results might impair women's employment opportunities,

198

which were supported by the Administration) and little research on women's equity issues during the Reagan Administration (because excellence, rather than equity, was that Administration's focus). In turn, members of the Administration frequently charge that Congress has politicized the research by favoring constituency desires rather than substantive merit, by large set-asides for the laboratories and centers, by mandating specific centers and studies, by limiting the focus of some congressionally mandated studies (such as the lack of examination of student achievement in the 1980s Chapter 1 study), by pushing other pet projects with threats against OERI's appropriations, and by making "big cases" over trivial complaints from constituents.

Some researchers complain that those who hold views unpopular with the members of proposal review panels are precluded from funding and that various interest groups have distorted OERI's agenda. Organizations of professional educators frequently complain that OERI (and NIE) has been the pawn of the researchers and ignored the needs of practitioners. Education writers complain of political coloring of research reports, especially those on issues of major concern to the Administration.

Thus, for almost three decades, charges of politicization have swirled around NIE and OERI. Many people view the agency as politicized, and that perception inevitably affects the credibility of its work. The diversity of the allegations, however, does suggest that these charges are partly a function of the dissension that often accompanies education. Over and over again, what one group views as leadership, other groups view as politicization.

Sustained Efforts. The Office of Technology Assessment's (1988) recent report on R&D for technological applications for education provides a good discussion of the importance of sustained efforts in R&D work:

> The Department of Education has had an off-and-on love affair with technology. Where research support has been consistent, as in support of children's television programming in the late 1960s through the 1970s, or long term as in support for technology in special education, important milestones were reached. These are exceptions. Most research projects did not have opportunities to proceed from laboratory research through to development of products and processes, much less to testing in the classroom, with real students and teachers.
>
> In the 1970s, the department supported quite a few projects lasting five or more years. . . . During the 1980s few projects received comparable long-term support.

. . . [The 1987-88 plans] fall short of focused, long-term commitments called for by the National Governors' Association, the National Task Force on Educational Technology, and the National School Boards Association. . . . Significant improvements in education can be made if sustained support is made available for development of new tools for teaching and learning. The private sector, while a contributor to this effort, does not have the primary responsibility or appropriate vision for making this a priority. States and localities do not have the capacity.

Instability often results in mediocrity. Most of the research-based innovations that are currently available to educators provide only modest improvements, partly because of the complexity of human learning and behavior, but also partly because these innovations are seldom subject to successive iterations of research, development, and evaluation aimed at strengthening effects, ensuring effectiveness in a wide range of settings, enhancing market appeal, and minimizing costs. Funding for such work is rarely available, and universities often do not consider the second and subsequent iterations to be scholarly work.

As the nation moves from innovation to comprehensive reform, the need for sustained efforts becomes even more important. As Elmore and McLaughlin (1988) have observed:

> Reform of the basic conditions of teaching and learning in schools requires "steady work". . . . Lags in implementation and performance are a central fact of reform. . . . [T]he time it takes for reforms to mature into changes in resource allocation, organization, and practice is substantially longer than the electoral cycles [four years] that determine changes in policy.

Balanced Portfolio. OERI supports many kinds of education R&D activities. Each makes different contributions, and a mix of them is necessary to fulfill its mandate.

Two critical types of R&D activity have been severely underfunded at OERI. First, the agency invests very little in field-initiated research — research whose topics and methods are suggested by scholars around the country rather than in response to requests by an agency for specific work. Field-initiated research harvests the insight, creativity, and initiative of researchers widely dispersed across the country; it has been a major contributor to knowledge and technology in all fields of science. NIH invests 56% of its R&D budget in field-initiated research and NSF devotes 94%, but OERI, in 1992, invested only 2% of its R&D budget for this purpose. It seems to have been congressional action that has constrained field-initiated research at OERI by imposing set-asides on virtually all of the agency's primary appropriations and specifying very low levels of support for this work.

The second underfunded critical type of R&D activity is basic research. Basic research in education is aimed at expanding understanding of the fundamental aspects of human development, learning, teaching, schools, and their environmental contexts; such research generates new views of what exists and new visions of the achievable. While federal government overall, excluding the Department of Defense, invests about 40% of its R&D budget in basic research, in 1989 only 5.5% of OERI's R&D budget was allocated for this purpose.

In 1977 a National Research Council report, *Fundamental Research and the Process of Education* (1977), recommended that the federal government "increase . . . the proportion of the federal investment in education research and development designated for fundamental research" and that NIE "take immediate steps to implement a policy of strong support for fundamental research relevant to education." Support for basic research at NIE increased substantially for a few years after the report's publication (Timpane 1982). During the early years of the 1980s, the entire Department of Education invested about 11% of its R&D budget on basic research; since 1986 it has spent only about 2% (National Science Foundation 1991).

Basic research has been slighted at OERI primarily because Congress, teachers, administrators, and the Administration have repeatedly urged that the agency quickly solve the pressing problems in schools. Since basic research seldom yields practical applications in less than a decade, the agency has responded to demands for solutions by focusing on applied research, development, and dissemination activities. Although this is an understandable response, it ignores the fact that several of today's most promising innovations in education have been heavily influenced by findings from basic research in cognitive science — work that was conducted not only by education researchers but by investigators in several of the behavioral and social sciences.

Funding. NIE was established to enhance the federal role in education R&D, yet within a year its budget began spiraling downward. That trend continued when NIE's functions were assumed by OERI, reaching a low point in 1989. This downhill slide inevitably extracted a heavy toll on the agency. Careful agenda setting became futile; "quick fixes" replaced thoughtful investments; and few sustained research and development activities could be maintained. Resources were spread so thinly that mediocrity was virtually ensured. Individual researchers, with less political clout than institutions, were squeezed out. Agency staff focused on required administrative functions and survival strategies rather than fulfilling the agency's substantive mission. Top-flight personnel often shunned working in the agency.

Researchers, watching resources for field-initiated work dwindle, blamed the loss on the set-asides of funds for the laboratories and centers, which have taken increasingly large percentages of the budgets. Some observers suggest a quite different view: that the centers and laboratories, especially the latter with clients spread across the country, have provided most of the constituent support for NIE and OERI, and that without their efforts the agencies would have disappeared.

However, the centers and laboratories also have suffered from the declining budgets: In 1973 NIE provided $80 million for their operations (in 1990 constant dollars); by 1979 that had declined to $52 million; and in 1991 the amount was $47 million. For individual laboratories and centers, the effect has been more dramatic because there are now twice as many of them as there were in 1973.

The budget cutting also has been reflected in congressionally requested studies. For instance, in the mid-1970s Congress directed NIE to conduct a nationwide study of the administration and effectiveness of compensatory education. The equivalent of $34 million (in 1990 dollars) was appropriated for the 3.5-year study. In 1990 Congress directed OERI to conduct a nationwide study of school reform efforts — a much broader topic — but just $9 million was made available for the 3.5-year study.

These budget cuts have had a marked effect on the work and products of OERI. A U.S. General Accounting Office report that reviewed the work of NIE, NCES, and the department's Office of Policy, Budget, and Evaluation concluded:

> During the past decade, the production of federally sponsored research, statistical, and evaluative information on education has declined notably . . . so much so that the availability of up-to-date information to disseminate to teachers and other practitioners may be threatened (U.S. General Accounting Office 1987).

Plan for a More Effective OERI

At the outset, it is important to recognize that much that needs to be done about U.S. education is beyond the responsibilities and authority of OERI. OERI's mission is to expand understanding and assist in the improvement of education. It has no authority over teacher education institutions, state education agencies, school boards, district administrators, principals, teachers, or parents. The agency also is tightly constrained in the extent to which it can promote or induce change. The role of OERI (and its predecessor, the National Institute of Education) has always been limited to generating new knowledge, developing new techniques and approaches, disseminating information about both, and assisting interested parties to apply the education research and development.

In addition, the mission of OERI is inherently difficult. The disagreements and conflicts over education are endless. Probing the mysteries of human learning is not easy. Linking research with practice remains a challenge. And improving schools is always difficult.

But OERI also is faced with many problems that are not inherent in its mission or responsibilities. If these problems are eliminated or reduced, the agency could be more effective. Frequent changes in leadership have caused organizational instability, false starts, abandoned efforts, and unfulfilled agendas. Having the head of any research agency serve at the will of a high political appointee creates the appearance, if not the reality, of politicization. So does requiring a research agency to submit its reports for clearance by a politically controlled public affairs office. Congressional actions also have weakened OERI. In addition to substantial budget cuts through most of the 1980s, set-asides in the appropriations have almost eliminated field-initiated research; and mandated studies have occasionally been politically skewed.

Fragmentation within OERI, and between it and other federal agencies, has resulted in agenda setting with little benefit from what the others have learned and accomplished. The paucity of sustained research often has limited the advance of understanding. The paucity of sustained development efforts has resulted in many innovations that are less effective and more expensive than necessary. Inadequate mechanisms for quality control and accumulation of results have forced practitioners and policy makers to wade through large literatures with little guidance as to what is valid, important, and widely applicable. Weak links with teachers, administrators, and policy makers often have limited researchers' knowledge about the realities of schools and making public policy and denied practitioners the benefits of R&D. Inadequate funding has contributed to most of these problems and undermined OERI's capacity to deal effectively with them.

When Congress passes legislation to reauthorize OERI in 1993, we (the 15-member National Academy of Sciences Committee) recommend a number of changes in leadership structure and in the mechanism for setting research priorities:

1. OERI should have a director appointed by the President, in consultation with the agency's board and with the advice and consent of the Senate, for a six-year renewable term. The rapid turnover at OERI has been dysfunctional to an agency that needs sustained leadership in planning for, investing in, and supporting the long-term efforts that are required for major scientific and technological advances.

There are several precedents for four- or six-year terms of office in federal research agencies. These arrangements have been instituted to ensure sustained professional management and to minimize the opportunities for politicization. Although they cannot ensure either − appointees are still free to quit and both the President and Congress retain discretion over agency budgets − a fixed term would allow the growth of a spirit of independence and professionalism in OERI.

2. OERI's agenda setting should be guided by a 24-member policy-making board. At least one-third of the membership should be distinguished researchers who have done work on education issues, complemented by a balanced representation of practitioners, parents, employers, policy makers, and others who have made noteworthy contributions to excellence in education.

With OERI's history of controversy, constant charges of politicization, and fragmentation, bringing focus and stability to the agency is a bigger job than any one person is likely to manage. The board we propose is modeled closely on the National Science Board of the National Science Foundation. Most observers believe that this board has served its agency well. It would differ significantly from the boards of NIE. It would be larger and more diverse, helping to ensure that its members understand the views of the major groups concerned with education. It would be limited to people who have already proven their ability to make important contributions to research on education or to excellence in education, thus ensuring competence and some common understandings during its deliberations. In addition, the board would not set OERI's agenda on the basis of its members' own predilections, but rather would distill priorities from the needs and capabilities of the country after wide consultation with those concerned about education.

3. The OERI board should establish a process to develop priorities for OERI's agenda. The process should involve active participation of the various groups concerned with education. These priorities should

be set so as to maintain the continuity, stability, and flexibility needed to conduct high-quality research and to effect educational change.

OERI is currently required to publish proposed research priorities in the *Federal Register* every two years, resulting in the establishment of a new set of priorities. We propose long-term plans with a limited biennial update.

In addition, OERI's research agenda must reflect the priority needs of researchers, teachers, administrators, parents, students, employers, and policy makers; and the agenda-setting process must reflect the capabilities of the education R&D enterprise. Unrealistic objectives of quick fixes to complex problems or universal solutions to problems with multiple causes serve only to disappoint researchers and potential users of their work. Without the integration of needs and capabilities, the productivity, effectiveness, and applicability of the education R&D will suffer.

4. OERI should support a balanced portfolio of activities: basic research, applied research, statistics, development, evaluation, dissemination, and technical assistance; field-initiated and institutionally based R&D; and long-term sustained efforts and responses to newly identified needs and opportunities. To do so, OERI must substantially expand support for basic research, field-initiated research, and sustained R&D activities.

With an eye to leveraging the influence of the federal government in supporting widespread school reform, we made a large number of recommendations for reorganizing OERI, including the creation of a Reform Assistance Directorate, which would be the link between research and state and local reform efforts. More important, perhaps, than the specific design details is the spirit that informed our thinking.

The report calls upon OERI to provide leadership in developing learning communities. OERI should work with state agencies, local districts, teacher education institutions, and researchers to help practitioners and researchers create learning communities. Basing its conviction on collective knowledge and experience, the NAS committee concluded that widespread school reform will require partnerships between researchers and practitioners. Each has much to contribute. Researchers can provide breadth and depth of inquiry and rigor of investigation; they can elaborate new theories, conduct carefully controlled experiments, study programs and practices in multiple sites, and prepare national indicators of educational progress. Practitioners have an intimate and holistic understanding of the realities of schooling — that is, they accumulate craft wisdom from daily experiences. Among their ranks are exemplars of good practice and effectiveness whose "magic" needs to be understood and conveyed to others. Practitioners are also the ultimate implementers of most reform strategies.

OERI could encourage such partnerships in several ways. It could fund new approaches to conveying each group's needs to the other. It could support development of ways to better share the expertise of each group with the other. And it could support innovative collaborations where each group works with the other on their respective responsibilities.

OERI's efforts will have to be supported with leadership at the national, state, and local levels. For instance, school districts will have to provide released time for teachers; teacher education institutions will have to experiment with substantial changes in their programs; and policy makers and researchers will have to take the time to listen and communicate with practitioners much more effectively than they have in the past.

5. With regard to funding, a substantial increase in the budget and staffing of OERI is required if it is to play an important role in the nation's education reform efforts. The NAS report recommends increases in OERI's budget for more basic and applied research, more research-based development, laboratory staff with state liaison responsibilities, a minority fellowship program, more extensive refinement and evaluation of promising innovations, and consensus conferences to deal with findings about important and contested bodies of research and evaluation. If that increase is not forthcoming, the mission and activities of the agency should be significantly narrowed.

The committee recognizes that its funding recommendations would require a large expenditure. Some people will simply dismiss it as too expensive. We see it as a critical investment in the nation's future. Without the investment, and concomitant efforts at state and local levels, the country is not likely to come close to meeting the National Education Goals promulgated by the President and the National Governors' Association.

Over the first six years, our recommendations would cost the nation approximately $1.3 billion in additional expenditures. Over the same period, the nation will spend about $1,500 billion on elementary and secondary education in this country. It is clear that this added investment in R&D would be paid back many times over if it should improve the effectiveness or efficiency of our education system by even one percent. It also should be noted that even with full implementation of all our recommendations, federal investment in education R&D would still be significantly less than federal R&D investment in agriculture, transportation, or health.

References

Alexander, L. *America 2000: An Education Strategy.* Washington, D.C.: U.S. Department of Education, 1991.

Cuban, L. "Reforming Again, Again, and Again." *Educational Researcher* 19, no. 1 (1990): 3-13.

Elmore, R.F., and McLaughlin, M. *Steady Work: Policy, Practice and the Reform of American Education.* Santa Monica, Calif.: Rand Corporation, 1988.

Louis, K.S.; Dentler, R.A.; and Kell, D.G. *Putting Knowledge to Work: Issues in Educational Dissemination.* Boston: Abt Associates, Center for Survey Research, University of Massachusetts, 1984.

National Center for Education Statistics. *Trends in Academic Progress: Achievement of American Students in Science, 1970-90, Mathematics, 1973-90, Reading, 1971-90, and Writing, 1984-90.* Prepared by the Educational Testing Service. NCES 90-1294. Washington, D.C.: U.S. Department of Education, 1991.

National Education Goals Panel. *The National Education Goals Report: Building a Nation of Learners.* Washington, D.C.: National Education Goals Panel, 1991.

National Research Council. *Fundamental Research and the Process of Education.* Committee on Fundamental Research Relevant to Education, Assembly of Behavioral and Social Sciences, National Research Council. Washington, D.C.: National Academy Press, 1977.

National Science Foundation. *Federal Funds for Research and Development: Fiscal Years 1989, 1990, and 1991.* Vol. XXXIX, NSF 90-327. Washington, D.C.: National Science Foundation, 1991.

Porter, A.; Archbald, D.; and Tyree, A., Jr. "Reforming the Curriculum: Will Empowerment Policies Replace Control?" in *The Politics of Curriculum and Testing,* edited by S. Fuhrman. London: Taylor and Francis, 1991.

Sproull, L.; Weiner, S.; and Wolf, D. *Organizing an Anarchy: Belief, Bureaucracy, and Politics in the National Institute of Education.* Chicago: University of Chicago Press, 1978.

Timpane, M. "Federal Progress in Education Research." *Harvard Educational Review* 52, no. 4 (1982): 540-48.

U.S. General Accounting Office. *Changes in Funds and Priorities Have Affected Production and Quality.* GAO/PEMD-88-4. Washington, D.C.: U.S. Government Printing Office, 1987.

U.S. Office of Technology Assessment. *Power On! New Tools for Teaching and Learning.* OTA-SET-379. Washington, D.C.: U.S. Government Printing Office, 1988.

Commentary on Education Research

By John F. Jennings

The topic of education research is included in this volume because the legislative authority to fund such activity in the U.S. Department of Education had to be extended by Congress by 1992. Therefore, the Bush Administration and the education committees of the Congress grappled with that issue during the 102nd Congress (1991-1992).

Even if this legal authority had not been lapsing, however, education research would have been a good topic to choose for discussion. Education is a very labor-intensive enterprise; therefore, almost all of its funding is concentrated on paying for teachers and the buildings they require for classrooms. Very little money is discretionary — that is, available to be used in trying out new ideas or new approaches. Federal funding provided for the research, the demonstration, and the dissemination of new concepts has traditionally been an important source of funding for that purpose.

Research and demonstration ought to be the leavening agent to raise education to new levels. However, as the previous four papers have shown, the kitchen door has been slammed too many times in the last quarter-century, and therefore the loaf has fallen. Each paper tries to explain these failures to reach the promise of education research and demonstration, especially the most recent battles resulting in the defeat of the bill to extend the Office of Educational Research and Improvement during the 102nd Congress.

Diane Ravitch was the Bush Administration's Assistant Secretary for Research and Improvement in the U.S. Department of Education, and therefore the most important person in this field in the executive branch of the federal government. Congressman Major Owens (D-N.Y.) is chairman of the Select Education Subcommittee of the Committee on Education and Labor, the primary subcommittee having jurisdiction over education research in the U.S. House of Representatives. Gerald Sroufe represents in Washington the major organization for those working in the area of education research, the American Educational Research Association. Richard Atkinson and Andrew Porter served on the Committee on the Federal Role in Research of the National Academy of Sciences, which released its very influential report on the topic in 1992.

The four papers on this issue are excellent, but I would like to draw out some conclusions that they have only implied. These conclusions are important to keep in mind as the Clinton Administration and the new Congress in 1993 and 1994 again wrestle with the issue of how to improve education through research and demonstration.

First, the controversy over education research and development has been a heated debate going on for more than 25 years. The failure to pass an OERI bill in 1992 was just the latest phase of that debate. In other years the debate bubbled up in well-publicized congressional oversight, resulting in restrictions being placed on OERI and causing the agency to be very cautious. The Atkinson/Porter paper describes very well the long dispute over the federal role in education research.

What is new, though, is that the deadlock at the federal level has now resulted in the beginnings of a *privatization* of research and development. In 1991 the Bush Administration urged the creation of the New American Schools Development Corporation (NASDC), funded with private contributions from foundations and corporations. A major reason for creating this entity was to sidestep Congress, since the legislative branch could not demand accountability from a corporation relying on private and not federal dollars.

Only time will tell if that corporation can exist during a Clinton Administration that may not endorse such an effort begun under Bush. But another entity was created in 1992 that also focuses on education research and development, one which will be more impervious than the NASDC to the change of Administrations in Washington. Christopher Whittle began the Edison Project to find ways to "invent a new American school." That entity is solely reliant on Whittle's funds and on those he has raised in the private capital markets.

In 1992 NASDC had about $50 million pledged from corporations and foundations to support its work. Whittle has said he will spend $60 million on the development stage of his effort to create profit-making private schools. Then he expects to spend $2.5 billion to establish and operate these schools. Compare these amounts to the $58 million now spent on national research and development in the U.S. Department of Education — almost all of it obligated to continue the ongoing system of federal research centers and laboratories.

Critics of NASDC and of Whittle's drive to create profit-making schools ought to direct their energies to breaking the federal deadlock over research and development. There is such interest in the country in improving schools that private means may be found to do this if public funds are not available.

Much may be learned from such private efforts, but the topics on which these entities focus will be of their own choosing and not of any elected representatives accountable to the public. In the past, liberals and conservatives all agreed that the federal government had as its duty funding education research; but lack of agreement on the means to accomplish this has led to a federal deadlock and a subsequent opening for private entrepreneurs.

The second point begins with recognition that federal dollars for research are indeed very limited — only $58 million in a $30 billion budget for the U.S. Department of Education; but they are very important dollars to any Secretary of Education because, even with all the restrictions placed on them by Congress, they are much freer than the funds in the remainder of the budget. Therefore, Secretaries of Education go to them to carry out their priorities. Then the political controversies arise, usually from the opposition party.

These funds are looser because almost all of the Education Department's budget is composed of "formula-grant" programs or student assistance programs over which a Secretary of Education has little discretion. A formula-grant program allocates by law certain amounts of funds to each state or county for particular purposes. Examples are the Chapter 1 program, the Individuals with Disabilities Education Act, and the Perkins Vocational Education Act. Student assistance programs by law entitle qualified postsecondary students to certain amounts of grants and loans. Examples are the Stafford Loan Program and the Pell Grant Program.

Diane Ravitch gave a good example of how a Secretary of Education used these research and demonstration funds to carry out his ideas. Secretary Alexander earmarked several million dollars for the development of national standards in education, even though he did not have explicit authority in the law or from Congress for that purpose. He was able to do this even during a time when such funds were very limited and when intense partisan bickering was going on between a Democratic Congress and a Republican Administration.

It is important to recognize that a Secretary will always try to find funds to carry out his or her ideas, and also that a two-party system of government leads to members of the party different from the Secretary's party being suspicious of his or her motivations. Therefore, to get out of this muddle, some nonpartisan, objective body has to give guidance on the overall purposes for education research and development.

Each of the four authors agreed on that objective; they disagreed on the particulars of the constitution and powers of this body. A good chance to resolve this dispute was lost in 1992 by a Republican President and a Democratic Congress who could not agree. The executive branch and the legislative branch are both in the Democrats' hands in 1993 and 1994, and they may not want an objective board limiting their uses of discretionary dollars. Then it will be the Republicans' turn to complain about the uses of these funds.

Thus a quarter-century dispute gradually grows into a three-decade-long argument. Both Democrats and Republicans must recognize that they must give up their chance every few years to control the agenda if there is to be a long-term commitment to achieving national goals through use of education research and development.

Besides these two points about the beginnings of privatization of research and of the need for compromise to break the deadlock that now exists, a number of other observations can be made about the defeat of the OERI bill in 1992. Small bills such as this are sometimes sidetracked while larger bills, such as the Neighborhood Schools Act and the Higher Education Act, go through the legislative process. Therefore, the best chances for passage of smaller bills sometimes come from being attached to larger ones, as OERI was in the past added to reauthorizations of the Higher Education Act.

Also, timing is critical with legislation. If either the House or the Senate had passed an OERI bill in 1991, the first year of the two-year Congress, final passage would have been more likely, since the bill would have had a better chance to escape the last-day vagaries of Congress.

Another lesson about policy making is supposed to be that a President proposes legislation but it is actually Congress that disposes. That is true, but a President can intervene with Congress to help push or stop a bill. As noted by Congressman Owens, the Republicans in the House followed the Bush Administration's pleadings and held up final passage of the OERI bill until late in the legislative session, and thereby endangered its final passage.

Another lesson is that a program does not always stop when the legislation reauthorizing it is defeated. The research functions of the Education Department continued in 1993 after the defeat of the OERI bill because the appropriations bill included money for them, which results in de facto reauthorization. The drawbacks, though, are that such appropriations are only for one year at a time, and the appropriations committees are reluctant to increase funds for a program not reauthorized in the usual way; for example, OERI was given the same funding as the previous year.

More is learned in defeat than in victory, or so the sages say. But the failure at the federal level to resolve the dispute over education research is frustrating a sincere effort to achieve the National Education Goals. All parties involved ought to give in a little to reach a long-term solution, if for no other reason than to retain some public accountability over funds used for research and development.

PART IV.
EDUCATION FUNDING

Investing in Education: The Bush Record

By Thomas A. Scully

Thomas A. Scully is a partner with the Washington law firm of Patton, Boggs, and Blow. During his four years in the Bush Administration, he served in the White House as a deputy assistant to the President and as the associate director of the Office of Management and Budget for Human Resources, Veterans, and Labor. Among other responsibilities at OMB, he oversaw the development of the Department of Education's 1990-93 budgets. He also was active in the development of Administration policy on school choice, higher education, and elementary and secondary education issues.

At the end of George Bush's term, the media furthered the impression that the record of the "Education President" was heavy on rhetoric but a little light on substance and accomplishments. In reality, the opposite was probably true. The Bush Administration had some difficulty focusing its education accomplishments and packaging them in a way that had general appeal to the press and therefore to the voters. But that should not diminish what was a record of real accomplishment — a record of expanding access to education and social services for millions of low- and middle-income students. That record included substantial increases in education funding across the board, but more importantly encompassed the beginning of a movement to change the way we educate our kids and the way local communities organize their school systems.

The substantive differences between the Bush Administration and the Democratic Congress were relatively minor in many areas. The primary philosophical difference was in the area of school choice, but that battle was significant enough to slow legislative reform in other areas. President Bush consistently pushed for private school choice. He believes that the most important changes in education must be made at the local level — restructuring schools and reinventing the way we teach our children. That is why the "GI Bill for Kids" and other Administration initiatives promoted private and public school choice for low- and middle-income students. The goal was not to hurt the public school system. On the contrary, it was to stimulate change, growth, and healthy competition. By allowing the constituents of our public schools — parents and children — to have options for quality education and the power to change their schools, we can drive energy back into what often have become lethargic and bureaucratic local school systems. George Bush believes in the importance of maintaining a strong public school system. But in doing so we should not shy away from shaking up the system if that is what is needed to ensure that it remains vibrant. A public school system that is not capable of competing with private schools is a system that cannot educate students to compete in the highly competitive world economy.

These philosophical battles overshadowed the fact that President Bush requested a 41% increase in education funding over four years. He also proposed, and pushed through the enactment of, the first major child-care program. At the same time, the Head Start program was more than doubled in size to serve more than 720,000 children. President Bush also pushed for major management reforms to remedy abuses in the student loan program and expanded both the Guaranteed Student Loan (GSL) Program and the Pell Grant Program — providing affordable access to postsecondary education and training for millions of low- and middle-income students.

Yes, the education community thought that even more funding was needed; and certainly some were disappointed that philosophical differences over school choice slowed progress on standards and testing. But in the tight fiscal environment of the Bush years, education was a true priority and President Bush delivered real progress in many programs. Upon reflection, I believe historians will find that President Bush's unprecedented increase in education funding and his focus on school reform indeed fulfilled his promise to be the Education President.

The Bush Funding Record

The Education Department. During the Bush Administration, federal appropriations for the Education Department increased by $7.6 billion — 33%. Had Congress enacted the funding levels that President Bush requested, the department's funding would have increased by 37%. See Table 1.

Table 1
Education Department and Head Start Funding Grew 38%, 1989 to 1993
(Budget authority; dollar amounts in millions)

Education Department	1989 Actual	1993 Request	1993 Enacted	Dollar Change 1989 to 1993	Percent Change 1989 to 1993*
Educational excellence	$ 0	$ 768	$ 0	---	---
Compensatory education	4,579	6,828	6,709	+$2,130	+ 47
Federal Pell grants	4,484	6,641	6,001	+ 1,517	+ 34
Guaranteed student loans (mandatory)	4,285	6,046	5,125	+ 840	+ 20
Education for the disabled	1,961	2,943	2,966	+ 1,005	+ 51
Vocational rehabilitation (mandatory)	1,889	2,138	2,183	+ 294	+ 16
Vocational education	918	1,151	1,177	+ 259	+ 28
State and campus-based student aid	1,330	1,052	1,458	+ 128	+ 10
Drug-free schools and communities	355	654	598	+ 243	+ 68
Impact aid	733	532	750	+ 17	+ 2
Disadvantaged student support services	227	417	392	+ 165	+ 73
Adult education	162	304	305	+ 143	+ 88
Mathematics and science education	137	316	275	+ 138	+101
Research, statistics, and assessment	78	243	152	+ 74	+ 95
Historically black colleges	84	122	112	+ 28	+ 33
Other programs and activities	1,734	2,183	2,311	+ 577	+ 33
Total, Education Department	$22,956	$32,338	$30,512	+$7,556	+ 33
Head Start	1,235	2,802	2,776	+ 1,544	+125
Total, Education and Head Start	$24,191	$35,141	$33,288	+$9,097	+ 38

*Average annual increase, 1989-1993, applied to 1993 enacted, except for educational excellence, which is the same as proposed for 1993; Head Start, which is a 25% increase over 1993; and mandatory programs, which equal current services.

The increases reflected the President's focus on education. The Education Department's increases were the largest of any federal agency in the area of domestic discretionary funding (nonentitlement spending). The increases included a 47% increase in Chapter 1 funding, from $4.6 to $6.7 billion. There were some philosophical disagreements in the compensatory education area; the Administration wanted to permit low-income students to continue to benefit from Chapter 2 if they were in an area with a local choice program and elected to take their grants to private or parochial schools. But the overall funding levels clearly demonstrate the consistent theme of all education funding in the Bush years: focused funding increases for low- and lower-middle-income students.

In four years, funding for disadvantaged-student support services grew by 73% and education for the disabled rose by 51%. Likewise, adult education programs grew from $162 million a year to $305 million, an 88% increase. I was unable to find any other periods of comparable growth in the histories of these programs.

Another major area of emphasis was math and science education. The President created an interagency group to identify the most effective strategies to raise math/science achievement and the appropriate funding levels. As a result, funding more than doubled (101%) and focused on the programs that should prove to be most effective.

Early Childhood Development. Consistent with the test of his agenda to promote aid for low- and middle-income children and families, President Bush focused resources on child care and early childhood development.

Head Start probably received the most public attention; the President increased the program from $1.2 billion in 1989 to $2.8 billion in 1993 — a whopping 125%. There has been lots of talk about making Head Start an "entitlement," and the Clinton Administration may try to do so. But few programs have ever grown at the rate that Head Start expanded between 1989 to 1993. The program now covers all eligible four-year-olds who want to participate. It is hard to find anyone who does not support Head Start, but massive expansions mean finding the funds to pay for them. The decision to increase Head Start by 25% in 1993 was not reached lightly; the $600 million had to be found from other programs under the domestic funding cap that was in place. With a $250 billion to $300 billion deficit, an expansion of Head Start to the $4 billion to $5 billion level that some anticipate will be tough to finance. It is also possible that some other programs may be more ef-

Table 2
Major Programs for Early Childhood Development
Increased 58%, 1989 to 1993
(Except where noted, budget authority; dollar amounts in millions)

	1989 Actual	1992 Actual	1993 Enacted	Dollar Change, 1989 to 1993	Percent Change, 1989 to 1993
Head Start	$ 1,235	$ 2,802	$ 2,776	$ 1,541	125
WIC	1,929	2,840	2,860	931	48
Earned income tax credit: refunded credits (outlays) (mandatory)	4,002	7,894	8,396	4,394	110
Dependent care tax credit: outlay equivalent (mandatory)	4,875	3,805	3,385	(1,490)	-31
Child care and development block grant	--	850	893	893	N/A
Child nutrition (mandatory)	4,591	6,480	6,827	2,236	49
Disabled infants and preschool programs	317	501	539	222	70
Maternal and child health	554	674	665	111	20
AFDC Jobs day care (mandatory)	17	371	371*	354	2082
AFDC at-risk day care (mandatory)	--	300	300*	300	N/A
AFDC transitional day care (mandatory)	--	75	75*	75	N/A
Health earned income credit (outlays) (mandatory)	--	610	513	513	N/A
Healthy Start	--	143	79	79	N/A
Community and migrant health centers	180	265	197	17	9
Even Start	15	90	89	74	493
Total	$17,715	$27,700	$27,965	$10,250	58

*Midsession review estimate

fective at delivering marginal new dollars for educational and social services to needy children and families. See Table 2.

In addition to his rapid expansion of Head Start, President Bush funnelled enormous new funding into the Even Start Program, which promotes intergenerational literacy. That program grew from $15 million in 1989 to $89 million in 1993 (a 493% increase). President and Mrs. Bush were very focused on improving adult literacy and the family learning activities that the Even Start Program fostered. It is no surprise that this program was a continual funding priority.

One of the President's proudest accomplishments was passage of family child-care legislation that brought new assistance to low-income families. President Bush first proposed a tax credit and voucher-based child-care program during the 1988 campaign. Over the course of the next two years, he worked hard to get it enacted. That program includes an expansion of the Earned Income Tax Credit (EITC) discussed below and the new Child Care Development Block Grant (CCBG). CCBG requires states to offer child-care vouchers to the families of low-income children and allows those families to choose where the funds are used — from public or private centers to home-based care or religious providers. It not only provides almost $1 billion a year in new funding for child care for needy families, but also provides a model for providing educational assistance to low-income families through vouchers. The Pell Grant Program effectively allows low-income students to choose public or private higher education — and it has not undercut the public system. If child-care vouchers provide the same choice, without undercutting public child-care facilities, it will provide a push for efforts to provide private school choice for low-income families in elementary and secondary education.

Other Assistance to Meet National Education Goal One: Getting Children Ready to Learn

In addition to creating a new child-care program and expanding Head Start, President Bush fostered the largest expansion of direct aid to low-income families since the advent of the Great Society. The President proposed an expansion of the EITC as part of his child-care package, and a broad expansion of this program to aid the working poor who have children was included in the 1990 Budget Reconciliation Act. Spending on the EITC was expanded from $4 billion in 1989 to $8.4 billion in 1993 — a 110 % increase. The program is the purest form of direct assistance to low-income children and families and constitutes a significant positive movement in welfare reform. Effectively a negative income tax for low-pay workers, it provides positive work incentives for low-income parents and reduces many of the financial disincentives or "welfare cliffs" that discourage parents from taking low-wage jobs that may be less attractive than Aid for Dependent Children (AFDC) or welfare benefits.

The Women, Infants, and Children (WIC) program ensures that millions of low-income mothers receive nutritional help to give their children a healthy start. The President increased WIC funding from $1.9 billion to $2.9 billion, nearly a 50% increase. The President further proposed a $143 million per year "Healthy Start" program to target new infant mortality funding for particularly low-income areas. Congress funded the program at only $79 million for 1993.

Programs for disabled infants and preschool children also enjoyed substantial increases. Funding grew from $317 million in 1989 to $539 million in 1993 − a 70% increase.

Elementary and Secondary Education: Support for the National Goals

In September 1989 President Bush convened the National Education Summit with the nation's governors. The President and the governors agreed to establish National Education Goals and to work on strategies to achieve the goals and on ways to measure progress toward achieving them. As Table 3 demonstrates, the President focused substantial resources on attaining these goals; but funding was never the primary focus of the national goals. Change, restructuring, and reform were the targets; and the President, with the aggressive help of Secretary Lamar Alexander, a bipartisan group of governors, and thousands of communities across the country, made great strides in changing the education agenda of the nation. Outside the beltway, where real reform must take hold, the America 2000 reform strategy was adopted by 44 states and in more than 2,700 communities.

While increased federal funding was not the focus of America 2000, the resources committed were substantial. Funding targeted to programs advancing preschool development more than doubled, from $9.3 billion in 1989 to more than $20 billion in 1993. Math and science education funding, which was the focus of an intensive interagency review, increased by 76%, to more than $2.2 billion for 1993.

223

Table 3
Federal Program Resources in Support of the National Education Goals Increased 42%, 1989 to 1993
(dollar amount in millions)

	1989 Actual	1993 Proposed	1993 Enacted	Dollar Change, 1989 to 1993	Percent Change, 1989 to 1993
By Age Category					
Preschool years	$ 9,260	$20,297	$20,813	$11,553	125
School years	15,783	21,996	21,001	5,218	33
Post-high school	30,112	37,487	36,635	6,523	22
Not age specific	1,242	1,521	1,623	381	31
Total	$56,397	$81,302	$80,072	$23,675	42
By Department/Agency					
Education	$22,421	$31,821	$30,843	$ 8,422	38
Health and Human Services	7,950	17,830	18,203	10,253	129
Defense	12,823	13,756	13,239	416	3
Agriculture	7,354	10,632	10,225	2,871	39
Labor	3,776	4,153	4,435	659	17
Veterans	892	1,164	1,147	255	29
Other	1,180	1,946	1,980	800	68
Total	$56,397	$81,302	$80,072	$23,675	42

Reform of Higher Education

The broad base of public support for higher education programs has been threatened in recent years by highly publicized abuses in the Guaranteed Student Loan (GSL) program and in the corollary abuse of Pell Grants in some institutions. Although many for-profit trade schools (so-called "proprietary schools") provide high-quality training, there is a pattern of abuse among many institutions that demands reform. The GSL default rates among proprietary schools has approached 50% in recent years.

President Bush proposed substantial increases in both the GSL and Pell programs, but the increases were tied to tough reforms targeted at abusing schools. The argument was simple, and it remains compelling today: Loan or grant dollars are wasted by funding the attendance of unwary students at abusing schools; and those dollars are not available to fund high-quality training for needy students at effective postsecondary institutions. Higher education resources are finite; we have to ensure that they are used to provide high-quality education and training. No social goal is met by giving an 18-year-old student a loan to attend a bogus trade school and then drop out after two weeks. This is particularly true when the school keeps the money and the government chases the delinquent student for years for loan repayment. Yet this is a frequent scenario today. These schools must be policed; and President Bush, with bipartisan support in Congress (Senator Sam Nunn in particular), set out to crack down on abuses in the GSL and Pell programs. In the reauthorization of the Higher Education Act, completed in July 1992, Congress did adopt some of the reforms needed but did not go nearly far enough. A direct-loan program will not solve the problem. In fact, by giving individual proprietary schools more unfettered access to federal funds, it is likely to magnify abuses – a true case of the fox guarding the chicken coop.

Despite these problems, assistance for higher education was substantially increased across the board. President Bush proposed increasing Pell Grants for students at all income levels with the largest increases focused on those most in need. Overall, Pell levels were raised by 34% – to more than $6 billion. And the President had proposed even greater increases than Congress enacted. Eligibility for the student loan program was expanded in the 1992 reauthorization, and hundreds of thousands of new students are receiving aid from Pell, GSL, and other federal aid programs. See Table 4.

Table 4
Administration Pell Grant Proposals Called for 22% Increase in Funding over 1992, a 48% Increase over 1989

	1992 Enacted (as of 2/92)	1993 Proposed	Dollar Change, 1992 to 1993	Percent Change, 1992 to 1993
Pell grants in total				
Budget authority (in millions of dollars)	5,463	6,641*	+1,178	+22
Maximum award (in dollars)	2,400	3,700	+1,300	+54
Average award per student (in dollars)	1,452	1,846	+394	+27
Funding by family income category (in millions of dollars)				
Under $10,000	3,398	3,697	+299	+9
$10,000 to $20,000	1,355	1,601	+246	+18
$20,000 to $30,000	616	712	+95	+15
$30,000 to $40,000	165	221	+57	+34
$40,000 to $50,000	38	47	+9	+24
$50,000 and above	10	10	---	---
Average award by income category (in dollars)				
Under $10,000	1,635	2,137	+502	+31
$10,000 to $20,000	1,466	1,921	+455	+31
$20,000 to $30,000	1,100	1,305	+205	+19
$30,000 to $40,000	809	999	+190	+23
$40,000 to $50,000	649	764	+115	+18
$50,000 and above	552	752	+200	+36
Presidential Achievement Scholarships				
Budget authority (in millions of dollars)	---	170	+170	---
Scholarship awards per recipient (in dollars)	---	500	+500	---

*Includes shortfall funding

Outlook for the New President

It is impossible to find an advocacy group that ever thinks its programs are sufficiently funded. The Bush years were years of high deficits, restrained federal spending, and tough funding decisions. Yet they included unprecedented increases in funding for children's programs — from Head Start and WIC to elementary and secondary education programs. There was *no issue area* in the Bush Administration that was a higher priority for funding, and the facts bear that out.

Many of the important gains in education reform — and the increases in education funding — were drowned out in the public debate by the high-profile battle over school choice. But by any objective standard, President Bush made great gains for children and for education reform. Given the large deficits and difficult fiscal problems the nation faces, President-elect Clinton will be hard pressed to deliver the same level of funding increases. And he will face the same tough decisions — raising taxes or cutting other programs — to sustain the current growth of these programs.

Investment in Education: A Key to Restoring America's Future

By Leon E. Panetta

Leon E. Panetta (D-Calif.) was chairman of the House Budget Committee in the 102nd Congress. He has since been appointed by President Clinton and confirmed by the Senate to serve as director of the Office of Management and Budget.

Three years into the 1990s, what most Americans believe must be a decade of enormous change for our country has so far been one of wasted opportunity. As Bill Clinton takes office, our nation stands at the most important crossroads we have faced in many decades. Until his election it seemed that we were motionless, frozen into inaction. That is no longer the case, but we must seize this rare opportunity or it will surely be lost.

Renewed investment in our children's education is one of the most obvious needs of the post-Cold War era and, until now, one of the most obvious examples of missed opportunity.

The American people understood the need for taking stock and making some real changes long before Washington did. Americans of every generation have left a better life for their children. That's the American Dream. One of the ways we have done that is by providing the next generation with the best possible education. But the public understands that changes in the nation's and the world's economy are making future gains in prosperity ever less likely. And they understand that it will be impossible without educational gains.

What's incredible is that so little has been done. Whatever the reason — politics, fear, inertia — the President and the Congress have mostly been sleepwalking through the early 1990s, leaving our country, our people, and our children at great risk for the future. It's no wonder that the American people are frustrated.

During the last half of 1991 the House Budget Committee devoted enormous effort to exploring the issues facing our country in the 1990s and into the 21st century. We held 26 hearings and briefings and 14 bipartisan caucuses, reviewing the state of the economy and long-term problems in our society, including education.

In December we issued an extensive report, titled *Restoring America's Future: Preparing the Nation for the 21st Century*. In it we laid out the problems as we saw them and offered a three-part prescription for Congress and the President to follow over the next decade as we seek to address the nation's economic and social problems.

A broad national consensus is forming around the ideas we expressed in that document. One could see them reflected in the plans offered by both presidential candidates, particularly Governor Clinton. It is my hope that they also will be reflected in the course of action we pursue next year.

The problems we focused on have grown even more urgent in the year since we issued the report. Among them:

1. The nation's economy is as fragile as it has been at any time since World War II. It suffers not only from unemployment and other problems associated with the recent recession but also from serious long-term dislocations that threaten the economic well-being of this and future generations.
2. While the 1990 budget agreement is reducing deficits from what they would otherwise have been, deficits are still too high and are projected to resume growing at an alarming rate during the latter half of the decade.
3. The nation faces serious challenges in many facets of society, especially education, health care, housing, and infrastructure. These problems, too, threaten the nation's ability to achieve economic growth and a better life for our children and grandchildren.
4. The American people's confidence in the ability of the executive and legislative branches to serve the public and address the nation's long-term problems has been badly shaken. There should be significant changes in the way government functions.
5. Finally, in the demise of the Warsaw Pact, the disintegration of the Soviet Union, and the end of the Cold War, we have more of a challenge than a problem. We have been handed a rare, historic opportunity to establish new priorities and begin a decade of rebuilding and change. But, again, we already may be squandering that opportunity.

Our recommendations for actions over this decade flow naturally from our reading of the problems. They are:

1. The federal government needs to be streamlined and better managed so that it is more effective and more cost-efficient.
2. Budget deficits are the nation's most serious long-term economic problem; and a comprehensive, long-term deficit-reduction plan is absolutely critical to growth.
3. The nation faces a number of social crises with a direct impact on our future strength, and we should invest our limited resources in response to three in particular: education, health care, and job creation.

Government Streamlining. Neither budget control nor effective investments can be achieved without better management within the executive and legislative branches. Also, improved delivery of services is essential to increased public confidence in government.

The management function of the Office of Management and Budget has suffered because of an emphasis on the agency's budgetary and regulatory responsibilities. Management must be given higher priority within the agency. In addition, administrative costs of programs must be controlled and, where possible, the size of bureaucracies must be reduced.

Deficit Reduction. Deficits are bleeding the country's financial resources dry. Our ability to have a growing economy and address our country's serious problems, including education, depends to a great extent on our willingness to make tough choices to cut spending and raise taxes in order to close the deficit gap. We must reduce the deficit by half over the next four years and even further in the future.

There are four areas that must be addressed: defense spending, domestic discretionary spending, entitlement spending, and revenues. My own view is that we can bring defense spending down more than the Bush Administration was planning. In terms of domestic discretionary spending, there are non-priority areas that should be either reduced or frozen. Education is clearly not one of those areas.

Entitlement spending and taxes are the areas with the greatest potential for deficit reduction. They are fraught with political peril; at least many elected leaders think so. But the relative success this year of Paul Tsongas and Ross Perot tells me that the American people are more ready than ever to hear the bad news.

In terms of entitlements, here are some simple facts: They make up about half of the budget; about half of that is for retirement programs, mostly Social Security; nearly a third is for the health entitlements — Medicare and Medicaid — and they are the primary source of the projected growth in the deficit in the future. If we are serious about reducing the deficit, health-care reform, with meaningful cost controls, obviously will be critical. And we will need to look at other means of reducing entitlement costs as well.

Revenues also have to be part of the package. An income tax increase for the wealthy is certainly one possibility, but others also will need to be considered.

Targeted Investments. Finally, the long-term health of our economy and well-being of our people are dependent on investing in ways that will promote greater growth and security within our society.

With limited resources, we must focus on the areas that need the most attention, we must target proven programs as well as innovative new ones, and we must commit to pay for any investments we make.

I have noted that two of the key areas for investment are health care, job training, and job creation. Providing insurance for those who lack health care and investing in proven programs such as WIC and other nutrition programs, as well as childhood immunization, are essential. So is investment in the Job Corps and other training programs. Investment in our deteriorating infrastructure, in environmental clean-up, and in health, scientific, and energy research can provide critical job dividends.

Education, the third key investment, is at least as important as the other two. It is a direct investment in the productivity of our children and a critical factor in determining not only their individual standard of living but the standard of living of theirs and future generations.

Now is the time for the federal government to make a stronger commitment to education. Our current education system is not preparing our children for the 21st century, so we must make new investments to achieve the goals the nation already has set for the next decade.

Although the federal government has always made a smaller contribution to overall education funding than have state and local sources, its share has declined significantly over the past 12 years and was down to 8.3% in 1992. For elementary and secondary education, the federal contribution has decreased from 9.1% to 5.6%.

This decrease in the federal commitment to education is reflected in other trends. As a share of Gross Domestic Product, federal education spending peaked in 1981 and declined over the next decade. At 0.45% of GDP, it is now only slightly higher than its 1968 level. When adjusted for inflation and population size, federal education spending also reached its peak in 1981 at $123 per capita, after which it experienced a sharp decline. In 1991 spending was down to $100 per capita.

Clearly, it is time to make up for these losses by funding programs that are consistent with the federal government's primary role of ensuring access to a quality education for all its citizens. One measure of access is our children's readiness to learn once they start school. In that regard, we should increase our commitment to fully fund Head Start, a program that is a model for the one-stop shopping concept of providing health, nutrition, and education services at a single preschool site. It is a concept that ought to be pursued.

Head Start has a proven record of success in preparing disadvantaged children for school; but because of funding constraints, it currently serves only one in three eligible children. Similarly, Chapter 1 compensatory education funding, which continues the enrichment process for disadvantaged children in the elementary grades, currently reaches fewer than two-thirds of all eligible children. Full funding for this program should be a primary goal of our federal education strategy.

We also must support growth in vocational and adult education programs as we focus on making today's labor force more productive in an increasingly competitive global economy. The U.S. currently has more than 20 million adults who are functionally illiterate and up to 83 million who have inadequate reading skills. The literacy and basic education needs of these adults must be addressed with strong federal leadership aimed at enhancing our economic security with a well-educated work force.

From education to streamlining of government, from deficit reduction to health care, this is an ambitious agenda. But our nation faces daunting challenges. Our new President and the new Congress are confronted with the same problems we confronted in the budget committee a year ago. If they can forge the kind of leadership the American people deserve, we can reach our goals and create for our children a bright future, one of hope and possibility, one that keeps the American Dream alive for yet another generation.

Education Funding and the Budget Enforcement Act

By Jim Sasser

Serving his third term in the U.S. Senate, Jim Sasser (D-Tenn.) is an ardent defender of domestic investment in America. As chairman of the Senate Budget Committee, he is the first Tennessee senator to chair a major committee in nearly 40 years. Senator Sasser is also a member of the Appropriations, Banking, Housing and Urban Affairs, and Governmental Affairs Committees.

During the 1992 presidential campaign, the *Wall Street Journal/* NBC News poll asked voters to choose the best way to spend a hypothetical 25 billion federal dollars. A clear majority, 56%, said "invest" in education, training, and infrastructure; "reduce the deficit" came in second at 31%. One might wonder, with such public support for "investment," with the constant hue and cry about the "financial crises facing the nation's schools," why hasn't federal funding for education increased significantly?

I was asked by the Institute for Educational Leadership and Phi Delta Kappa, the professional fraternity in education, to present my point of view on education funding as it has been debated before the U.S. Congress. I believe this request came to me because I have firsthand knowledge of the budget process; I have been chairman of the Senate Budget Committee since 1989. IEL and PDK wanted an account of the key role the Budget Enforcement Act plays in the federal education funding debate.

Fortunately, the other essays in this book will provide a complementary context and appropriate background. Susan Frost, executive director of the Committee for Education Funding, will address the need for education funding as well as funding levels for specific education programs.

And my former House counterpart, Budget Committee Chairman Leon Panetta, provides his perspective on education funding in relation to larger budget planning and overall deficit reduction efforts.

Therefore, the bulk of this essay focuses on the congressional budget process, specifically the Budget Enforcement Act's influence on education funding during the 102nd Congress. My intent is to explain and emphasize the power of budgeting to future education policy makers. At the end of the essay I will briefly cover a few topics that have a national as opposed to federal effect on education funding.

The Congressional Budget Process

Before the appropriations committees determine the exact funding level for every federal program, Congress struggles through an elaborate budget process. The annual debate over our nation's priorities culminates in a budget resolution. While this resolution is not signed into law by the President, it does impose binding constraints on Congress. It provides the broad outlines of a spending plan that the appropriations committees must follow and fill in with details.

It wasn't until 1967 that the federal government adopted a unified budget. And it wasn't until 1974 that the Congressional Budget and Impoundment Control Act established the House and Senate Budget Committees and what has come to be known as the congressional budget process. Three times since then, in 1985, 1987, and 1990, that process has been revised.

The Budget Enforcement Act (BEA) of 1990 created "caps" or discretionary spending limits and built "firewalls" between the monies available for defense and domestic spending. The BEA also established the pay-as-you-go procedure, which requires that changes in the tax code or mandatory spending not increase the deficit. The reach of the budget process was increased by the BEA; both appropriating and authorizing legislation must conform to the rules and restrictions of the budget process.

Influence of the BEA on Education Funding

During the 102nd Congress, education funding was greatly affected by the Budget Enforcement Act. On two occasions the firewalls prevented Congress from shifting savings in defense spending to investment in education and other domestic programs. And twice the pay-as-you-go requirement thwarted the efforts of education advocates to insure full funding for two highly successful programs. In the pages that follow, the story of these four battles and their unhappy endings will be explained.

At the Committee for Education Funding's awards dinner in September, a lobbyist summed up the goal of the education community's efforts to bring down the firewalls by changing the name of the popular movie to "Honey, I Blew Up the BEA." Everybody laughed, even though the walls and the BEA were still the law of the land.

The purpose for BEA's firewalls was to prevent the wholesale shifting of dollars from one category of federal spending to another. In the early Eighties, domestic spending had been hacked down while the defense budget was boosted. Following 1985, as defense spending began to decline after the longest peacetime military buildup in America's history, proponents of defense sought procedural ways to protect the Pentagon. During the general give and take of the 1990 Budget Summit, the Bush Administration acceded to continued defense cuts in exchange for an artificial division between defense and domestic accounts. The walls were meant to protect priorities, but ultimately they stifled congressional ability to react to changing world circumstances. Against all common sense, the budget firewalls managed to outlast the Berlin Wall.

With the end of the Cold War, Washington and the nation began to speak of a "peace dividend." These buzz words captured the notion that our country would see a financial windfall from no longer having to invest billions in armaments for protection from our enemies. Many observers said it was time to invest that dividend at home — in our people, our cities, and our infrastructure. Others wanted to apply the dividend to our national debt. Thus the debate over national priorities, and the Budget Enforcement Act, was engaged.

The Appropriations Category Reform Act of 1992, which I introduced on February 25, 1992, would have allowed rational choice between defense and discretionary spending. It would have taken down the firewalls while retaining the overall caps on spending that hold down the deficit. And since the firewalls were scheduled to be phased out in fiscal year 1994, my bill would have started that process only a year early.

During impassioned floor statements in both houses of Congress on this important legislation, just two lines of argument were heard. Opponents wanted to uphold the "budget agreement" fashioned by Congress and the President in the fall of 1990, no matter how much the world had changed since then. And supporters wanted to reap the peace dividend of our success in ending the Cold War.

The Committee for Education Funding was right to call the vote on S.2399 one of the most important education votes of the 102nd Congress. After a compelling floor debate and valiant lobbying efforts, the vote on March 26 was on cutting off the debate on the motion to proceed to actual debate on S.2399. We needed 60 votes to overcome this procedural hurdle; unfortunately, the vote was 50 yeas and 48 nays. I was proud to have lead the fight and am thankful to those who supported our efforts.

The Harkin Transfer Amendment. Since the walls and the caps were still in place as the House and Senate Budget Committees worked on the FY 1993 Budget Resolution, there was little latitude to provide greater funding to education or other domestic priorities. Therefore, the Appropriations Committees had to work under very tight constraints. Rather than accept these restrictions, the chairman of the Labor, Health, and Education Appropriations Subcommittee decided to attack the firewalls one more time.

In September it was the BEA that prevented advocates of health, education, and training programs from transferring $4.1 billion from the Department of Defense to pay for Senator Harkin's "Strategic Children's Initiative." When the Harkin Transfer Amendment was offered to the FY 1993 appropriations bill for the Departments of Labor, Health and Human Services, and Education, it was defeated on a procedural vote to "waive" the Budget Enforcement Act. Again, the BEA prevailed; the vote was 36 yeas and 62 nays.

Pell Grants and Pay-as-You-Go. The other provision of the Budget Enforcement Act that put a damper on education funding during the 102nd Congress was the "pay-as-you-go" requirement. Under BEA, legislative proposals to change the tax code or entitlement programs cannot increase the deficit. To meet "pay-go," a "revenue offset" must be included in the legislation to counterbalance any increases in mandatory spending or loss of revenue.

After years of insufficient appropriations, frustrated advocates of the college financial-need, formula-driven Pell Grant Program sought to insure full funding by making the program an entitlement. The 1992 Reauthorization of the Higher Education Act was their legislative vehicle. The Senate and House took slightly different approaches.

The Senate Labor and Human Resources Committee originally proposed to make the Pell Grant Program an entitlement in 1997. Since cost estimates of bills are done for the first five years, the committee proposal seemed to have no costs attached. By delaying implementation, the proposed entitlement provision would not trigger the pay-as-you-go requirement. But the provision violated another rule of the Budget

238

Enforcement Act, Section 303(a), by authorizing legislation in a year not covered by the budget resolution.

Since Senate advocates knew they could not garner the 60 votes needed to waive pay-go but thought that they could muster the simple majority of those voting needed to waive Section 303(a) of the BEA, they included the delayed implementation of a Pell entitlement in their bill, S.1150.

As the day for Senate floor consideration drew nearer, the advocates became less certain they would have the votes. They faced a quandary: If they could not muster a majority to waive Section 303(a), the bill in its entirety would fail, not just the Pell entitlement provision. It was too great a gamble, so the provision was eliminated just prior to consideration of the bill on Senate floor.

The House Education and Labor Committee originally proposed to make the Pell Grant Program an entitlement in 1993 at a cost of $12.6 billion over five years. Since the House bill, H.R.3553, did not include an "offset," the House Budget Committee chairman and others were opposed to the provision. Again, rather than risk defeat of the entire bill by losing a motion to waive the pay-as-you-go requirement, the Pell entitlement provision was struck from the bill before it reached the House floor.

Head Start Entitlement: Held at the Desk. When the School Readiness Act of 1991, S.911, reached the Senate floor, it was "held at the desk" and never brought up for consideration by the full Senate. This bill to make the Head Start early childhood education program an entitlement died with the end of the 102nd Congress. The cost of making this well-regarded program an entitlement was more than $20 billion over five years. Since S.911 did not include any offset, the bill's sponsors needed 60 votes to waive the pay-go requirement. They knew the Budget Agreement would prevail, just as it had on so many occasions (not only those mentioned herein), so no vote of certain defeat was sought.

The Budget Enforcement Act in the 103rd Congress

The BEA will continue to play an integral role in the 103rd Congress. The overall spending caps will still be in place; they will be a significant restraint on FY 1994 planning. But the firewalls between domestic and defense spending will no longer restrict the Congress or our new President from placing a greater priority on investing in people.

In the first few months of the 103rd Congress, the nation's debt ceiling will have to be raised. The current statutory limit on how much debt the U.S. can incur is $4,145 billion. The last three times the debt ceiling was raised, Congress also passed major legislation to review the budget process. Thus budgetary imaginations are working overtime on Capitol Hill these days. We could see anything from "investment-based budgeting" to "enhanced rescission" to re-emergence of a Balanced Budget Amendment to the Constitution. Any of these structures would have a profound impact on the federal government's future role in education funding.

Federal Education Funding vs. National School Finance Issues

It is important to step back for a minute and remember that federal education funding is only 6% of spending on elementary and secondary education in this country. While the Department of Education was allocated more than $12 billion for K-12 education, state and local governments funnelled nearly $200 billion to our public education system. Since the state share of total funding is 48% and the local share is 46%, the pivotal decisions about education funding are not made on Capitol Hill. Three national, not federal, education funding debates are mentioned below to alert future education policy makers.

Equity in School Funding Law Suits

When great disparity in per-pupil funding between school districts has been ignored or exacerbated by state legislatures, activists and concerned parents have sought redress in the courts. In the last five years more than half the states have tried cases or have had cases pending where the school finance system is being challenged. Many of these suits have come on the heels of the May 1988 ruling by Kentucky Judge Ray Corn that lead to the declaration of that state's system of education as unconstitutional and brought a court-imposed overhaul of K-12 education. (In Tennessee, the *Small School System* v. *McWherter* case is awaiting a decision from the State Supreme Court.) The outcome of these suits can have a huge effect on education funding by directing state legislatures to raise and fairly distribute revenue.

Interaction Between Education Reform and School Finance Reform

The links between education reform and improvements in school finance are becoming more clearly defined. During the 102nd Congress

240

"school delivery standards" were debated for the first time. Advocates of such standards understand that greater accountability may lead to increased funding. Outgoing Secretary of Education Lamar Alexander believes that accountability in the form of school choice will be demanded by the public before the schools see any significant increase in funding. And school finance expert Allan Odden reminds education reform advocates that restructuring will not take root unless schools tackle finance with a private-sector level of discipline.

Public Opinion on the Education Crisis

Public opinion polls* have found a "reality gap" between the opinions held by employers, educators, and policy makers as opposed to those of students, parents, and the general public on what needs to be done to improve our schools. The public seems to yearn for the 19th century, little red schoolhouse model, while the "experts" are pushing for 21st century schools. To tackle this mismatch, a public awareness campaign, called "Keep the Promise," recently has been launched by the Business Roundtable, the National Governors' Association, and the American Federation of Teachers. This ad campaign could have a significant influence on education reform and funding at every level — federal, state, and local.

Words to Remember

Jonathan Kozol explains in his 1991 book, *Savage Inequalities*, that "if excellence must be distributed in equitable ways, it seems Americans may be disposed to vote for mediocrity." His words remind me of the warning in *A Nation At Risk* that "the educational foundations of our society are being eroded by a rising tide of mediocrity that threatens our very future as a nation and a people. . . . Excellence costs, but in the long run mediocrity costs far more." It is the responsibility of the general public as well as policy makers at the local, state, and federal levels to recognize the need to correct our "education deficit."

---

*Public Agenda Foundation, *Cross Talk* (Washington, D.C., February 1991); and Louis Harris Education Research Center, *An Assessment of American Education* (New York, September 1991).

Closing the Education Investment Gap: Lessons from the 1980s

By Susan Frost

Susan Frost is executive director of the Committee for Education Funding (CEF), a coalition of major education associations whose members represent elementary, secondary, and postsecondary education interests. She has served as the coalition's director since 1983 and is considered an expert on the federal budget process and its effect on education policy. During her tenure at CEF, the committee has coordinated and produced the annual Education Budget Alert, *an authoritative resource on federal education programs and their funding. CEF's most recent publication,* Blueprint for a Better Tomorrow: A Plan for Federal Investment in Education, *outlines the education community's agenda for the 1990s and calls on the President and the 103rd Congress to close the education investment gap.*

If America is to assume a leadership role in the new global economy, we must provide every child, youth, and adult with the opportunity to reach his or her full potential. The economic productivity and social well-being of all Americans depend on an educated work force. We can no longer ignore the federal responsibility in meeting this national imperative.

Today, only 2% of the total federal budget is invested in the education of our nation's students. (See Figure 1.) Over the last 12 years, the federal share of elementary and secondary spending has been cut drastically — from 9.1% to 5.6%. Among advanced industrialized countries, the United States ranks 11th in public school spending (see Figure 2). Federal investment in elementary, secondary, and vocational education as a percent of the Gross Domestic Product has plunged

Figure 1
Estimated FY92 Actuals vs. FY81 Actuals

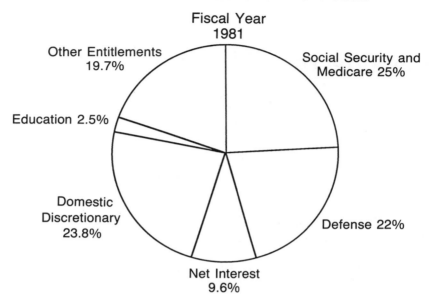

Fiscal Year
1981

Other Entitlements
19.7%

Social Security and
Medicare 25%

Education 2.5%

Domestic
Discretionary
23.8%

Defense 22%

Net Interest
9.6%

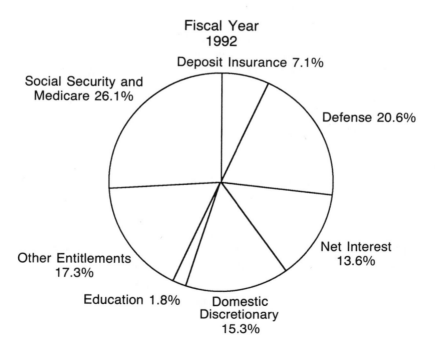

Fiscal Year
1992

Deposit Insurance 7.1%

Social Security and
Medicare 26.1%

Defense 20.6%

Net Interest
13.6%

Other Entitlements
17.3%

Education 1.8%

Domestic
Discretionary
15.3%

Source: Committee for Education Funding.

Figure 2
Public Spending on Education as a Percent of Gross Domestic Product (Current Expenditures)

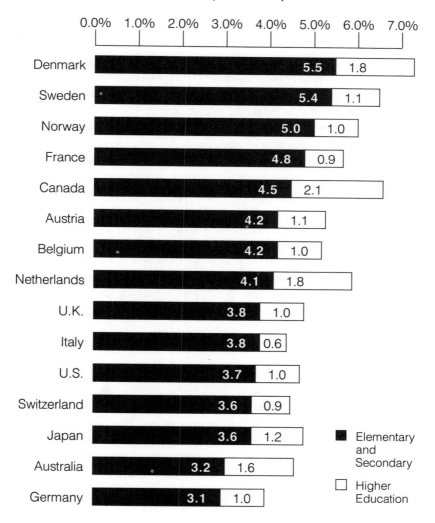

Source: American Federation of Teachers.

downward since the early 1970s. The share invested in higher education peaked in 1981 and has fallen ever since. Most state and local governments responded to this federal disinvestment by dedicating a larger share of state tax dollars to education. Although some of this funding paid for school reform initiatives, the bulk of new state resources went to services for children with disabilities — a federal mandate that the states have borne without the promised commitment of adequate federal funding.

In the 1990s nearly two-thirds of the 50 states are coping with operating deficits that already have resulted in severe cutbacks in education programs. The resulting decline in available funds has turned back many educational improvements. Reduced state and local resources are forcing school districts to cut school budgets drastically, resulting in increased class sizes and limited services to students with special needs. Campuses, faced with state budget cuts, are increasing tuition, reducing faculty, and limiting outreach and support services for low-income students.

Most of the funds for elementary and secondary education will continue to come from state and local governments. But national leaders must address the "savage inequality" of demanding academic excellence from every child while denying our most disadvantaged students the resources to meet those demands. Only when the federal government has met this fundamental responsibility can new initiatives built on this foundation succeed.

The State of Education Today

Contrary to the rhetoric of the 1980s, an informed examination of the American education system suggests that it is not in a state of decline. Gerald Bracey reminds us in an article, "The Big Lie About U.S. Education" (1991), that what many adults remember as the "golden age" of American education was actually far from the democratic ideal. "This enlightened epoch actually turns out to be a time when fewer than 50% of a class graduated, when minorities were invisible, and when 'special education' meant keeping both physically and mentally disabled students out of sight" (p. 106). Although we have clearly made great strides over the last 40 years, the challenges of the 21st century demand a new commitment to the education of our children. The schools of the 1980s cannot meet the demands of the global economy in the year 2000 and beyond. The profound changes facing the nation demand higher standards in education and the workplace.

246

Most children come from healthy and secure families, have the benefit of a preschool education, and arrive at school ready to learn. Most children spend 12 years in neighborhood schools that are supported by parents and serve the diverse needs of the community. Most children are taught by competent, experienced, and caring teachers and learn the skills needed to graduate from high school and seek employment. Many students have the opportunity, due to family circumstances and commitment, to go on to college and postgraduate education and become our nation's core of leaders in business, law, medicine, science, and the humanities.

But one out of five children lives in poverty and, unlike his or her more advantaged peers, comes from a family that cannot afford to meet basic health, nutrition, and education needs. Most of these children attend schools in poor areas, whether urban or rural, where citizens struggle to pay higher taxes for fewer services. Many of these children attend dilapidated schools with libraries that have no books, science labs with no equipment, and classes of 30 to 40 students with no permanent instructor. A high-skill/high-wage job is beyond the realm of possibility; a college education is someone else's dream. High school dropout rates reflect the students' hopelessness.

Today, millions of these children are denied access to essential aid and services because proven federal programs remain significantly underfunded. Seventy percent of preschool children eligible for Head Start go unserved. More than four million eligible disadvantaged children currently are denied Chapter 1 reading and math instruction. Without the support services that Chapter 1 provides — smaller classes, extra hours of instruction, specially trained teachers — these four million children are at risk of failure. A recent report by an independent commission on Chapter 1 states that poor and minority children have gained considerable ground during the past 25 years, primarily through Chapter 1, but that the rules of the game have changed. "Basic skills no longer count for as much as they once did. If Chapter 1 is to help children in poverty to attain both basic and high-level knowledge and skills, it must become a vehicle for improving whole schools serving concentrations of poor children. . . . We know how to teach all students successfully; there can be no excuses anymore for continued failure to do so" (Commission on Chapter 1, 1992, pp. 5-6).

Federal funding for the excess costs of educating the 4.8 million disabled children in America's schools has fallen to 8% — far below the commitment in law to support 40% of these costs. At the same time, a rising number of children with emotional and behavioral problems, who require special education due to factors ranging from poor prenatal care to profound language deficiencies, are entering our classrooms.

Across the country, school buildings are unsafe and in disrepair; and aging labs and libraries are ill equipped to meet the demands of today's technological society. Due to insufficient budgets, school districts educating high percentages of military children and children overcoming language, social, and economic barriers are struggling. The education infrastructure that serves our citizens from the very young to the very old is at risk, as public libraries across the country are cutting personnel, limiting hours of service, and even closing their doors.

The child who receives Head Start and Chapter 1 services often becomes the young adult who must depend on federal grant aid to go to college. But the value of the Pell Grant, the foundation of federal student aid, has fallen from 46% to 23% of average tuition costs, accompanied by a marked decline in minority enrollment. Despite the promises to reverse this trend made in the sweeping 1992 reauthorization of the Higher Education Act, the maximum Pell Grant for the poorest students was cut this year by $100. At the same time, the number of students eligible to receive a Pell Grant has increased dramatically as a result of the weak economy. This growth encompasses students pursuing a baccalaureate education with drastically reduced parental or personal resources and workers seeking to acquire or upgrade their job skills through technical training.

Students increasingly have been forced to rely on loans to finance their education and training. With average annual loan awards above $2,700, many students leave school with accumulated debts between $10,000 and $20,000. Low-income students, faced with the need to take on overwhelming debt to finance their education, often give up their hope of advanced training or a college degree.

Why have we failed to invest in the successful federal programs and services that we know are necessary to improve the education of all children and to give them the opportunity to participate fully in a productive economy? The answer is simple: To do so costs money. An examination of the political and fiscal climate of the 1980s and a review of the arguments made against increasing funds for federal education programs makes it clear that educators still face some of the same obstacles in making the case for public investment in our nation's students that we have faced over the last 10 years.

A Decade of Disinvestment

A decade ago, the release of *A Nation At Risk* by the U.S. Department of Education shocked the American public with its warning that we are committing "an act of unthinking, unilateral educational disarmament." The report marked the beginning of a national debate on the future of American education and provided a new, larger agenda of education reform. It clearly outlined the federal government's responsibility for ensuring that the commitment to educational excellence not be made at the expense of equitable treatment of our diverse population of students, but it fell short of calling for a greatly expanded federal investment in education.

> The federal government, in cooperation with states and localities, should help meet the needs of key groups of students such as the gifted and talented, the socioeconomically disadvantaged, minority and language minority students, and the handicapped. In combination, these groups include both the national resources and the nation's youth who are most at risk. (National Commission on Excellence in Education 1983, p. 32)

This key recommendation on the federal role in education was virtually ignored. The Reagan Administration, caught off guard by the attention the report generated, declared that the findings reinforced its position that education was a state and local responsibility and that increasing funds for education would have no effect on educational outcomes.

The National Education Goals, adopted by the nation's governors and the President in 1989, once again provided a framework for action. Ambitious educational improvement targets were set forth for all Americans, from early childhood through adulthood, to be reached by the year 2000. A National Goals Panel was created to report on the nation's progress in achieving these targets and to develop new standards and methods of assessing the educational achievement of all students. But partisan politics thwarted attempts to address the need for resources to meet the goals, and the Bush Administration was adamantly opposed to calling for increased funds. As a result, teachers, administrators, parents, and students were once again told to do more with less.

In Jonathan Kozol's poignant book, *Savage Inequalities: Children in America's Schools* (1992), a high school principal describes the tenor of the 1980s in starkly human terms:

> If they first had given Head Start to our children *and* prekindergarten, *and* materials *and* classes of 15 or 18 children in the elemen-

tary grades, *and* computers *and* attractive buildings *and* enough books and supplies *and* teacher salaries sufficient to compete with the suburban schools, and then come in a few years later with their tests and test-demands, it might have been fair play. Instead, they leave us as we are, separate and unequal, underfunded, with large classes, and virtually no Head Start, and they think that they can test our children into a mechanical proficiency. (p. 143)

Education and the Federal Budget Deficit

The 1980s was also a period of remarkable changes in federal budget policy. Annual spending outpaced revenues by an average of 22% per year. The gap between spending and revenues caused the federal debt to quadruple and yearly interest on the debt to reach nearly $200 billion — seven times the total amount spent each year on education at the federal level. As annual deficits skyrocketed, Congress and the Administration turned to changing the federal budget process as a way to force difficult political decisions on budget priorities. In 1986 the Gramm-Rudman-Hollings Deficit Control Act was signed into law and an immediate "sequester" or across-the-board cut was applied to all appropriated programs. Ironically, proponents of the new budget law agreed to include all education programs in the sequestered pot at the same time that they argued that we could no longer mortgage our children's future to finance the debt.

Efforts over the last several years to force hard fiscal choices by legislating enforcement mechanisms to reduce the deficit have continued to place a disproportionate strain on federal investment. A second version of Gramm-Rudman-Hollings and budget summit agreements in 1988 and 1990 have failed to produce the promised results and have failed to address the relative value of investment versus consumption spending. While school-age children and college-bound youth have been told repeatedly that budget agreements and rules prevent a significant investment in their education, billions of dollars have been added to the federal deficit to pay for uncontrolled health-care costs and such "off-budget" items as the savings and loan bailout. Over the same period, across-the-board spending cuts that included education increasingly took the place of decisions based on sound economic policy. Although the appropriators on the Labor, Health and Human Services, Education Subcommittee were able to make marginal investments in education and children, real strides were thwarted by the restrictions of the 1990 Budget Act. By focusing only on balancing total receipts against total expenditures for a given year, our leaders failed to allow for long-term invest-ment in America's future. As a result, critical investments in the edu-cation of our students and families were not made. (See Figure 3).

Despite the end of the Cold War and a public outcry for a domestic agenda financed by a peace dividend, the FY 1993 Budget Resolution and subsequent appropriations bills were rigidly held to the separate defense and domestic spending ceilings set in the 1990 Budget Act. Senator Jim Sasser (D-Tenn.), chairman of the Senate Budget Com-mittee, and Representative John Conyers (D-Mich.), chairman of the House Committee on Government Operations, sponsored legislation to "break down the walls" and allow defense savings to be used for domestic investment. The failure of Congress to pass this legislation, which the Bush Administration strongly opposed, reinforced the status quo and the political gridlock that prevailed in Washington. Education and chil-dren's health programs were once again forced to compete for the same limited resources, while the business community and others who rhe-torically supported investing in children called for defense savings to be used exclusively for deficit reduction.

Changing Our National Priorities

It is in the allocation of our national resources — not in our promises, but in our spending decisions — that we demonstrate our national pri-orities. America must invest in the education of its citizens. At the same time, we must reduce the federal deficit. Both actions are necessary to ensure the nation's long-term economic growth, and both will re-quire more than short-term and short-sighted budgetary decisions.

Over a year ago, Leon Panetta (D-Calif.), chairman of the House Budget Committee, held several committee hearings as background for a proposal, released in December of 1991, to balance the budget within 10 years. The report was not formally approved by the Budget Com-mittee. (Ranking Republican William Gradison included "additional views," and other members were cautious about putting their name on a report that proposed politically difficult spending decisions in an elec-tion year.) In place of real deficit reduction, investments in the future, and hard fiscal choices, a majority of Congress opted to join the Administration in promising action in the future by supporting a balanced budget amendment.

The Panetta plan balanced the federal budget by 2001 by reducing spending for defense and low-priority domestic programs, entitlement savings, and reductions in administrative expenses by streamlining

Figure 3
President vs. Congress: Education Funding Increases
($ in billions)

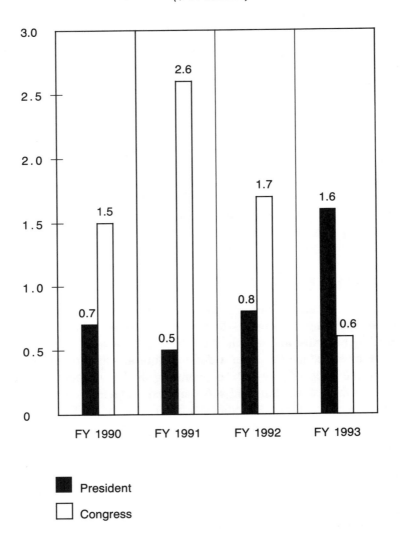

Source: Committee for Education Funding.

government. The plan called for a cumulative $300 billion to $370 billion investment in areas critical to rebuilding America, including education, preventive health programs, work force training, technology, and infrastructure. A total of $100 billion to $120 billion over 10 years would be targeted to Head Start; Even Start; Chapter 1; Education for Children with Disabilities; Math/Science Education; creating, expanding, and improving apprenticeships, cooperative education, Tech Prep, and other vocational programs; and providing financial aid to higher education students. Although the Panetta recommendation gained little momentum, it was one of the first proposals to combine investment in human capital with balancing the federal budget.

Shortly after the Panetta proposal was released, the Center for Strategic and International Studies created a Commission for Strengthening America to develop an action plan to put the U.S. house in order. Senators Sam Nunn (D-Ga.) and Pete Domenici (R-N.M.) co-chaired the bipartisan commission, which was made up of 17 business and labor leaders, members of academia, congressional members, and state and local government officials. The composition of the group was similar to the National Economic Commission (NEC) that failed to reach consensus when the political forces of the 1988 election split the group along partisan lines.

The Commission's report was released in October of 1992 and, like Panetta's plan, called for balancing the budget over 10 years and at the same time investing in children, education, research and development, technology, and infrastructure. The report made several education policy recommendations and proposed a federal investment of $87 billion over 10 years for the Chapter 1 reading and math program.

The Committee on Economic Development (CED), a progressive group of 200 top business executives, issued a report, *Children in Need*, almost nine years ago that called for a new partnership between business and education. The report argued that improving the prospects for disadvantaged children is not an expense but an excellent investment that can be postponed only at a much greater cost to society. CED's most recent report, *Restoring Prosperity: Budget Choices for Economic Growth*, was released in December 1992 and focuses on reducing the deficit and investing in long-term economic growth. "CED strongly believes that inadequate saving and investment, and corresponding excessive consumption, is undermining our prospects for long-term economic growth, rising standards of living, and international economic competitiveness and leadership. Meeting the fundamental economic goals of our society will be impossible if we cannot muster the political will to slow the growth of consumption and shift these resources to investment" (p. 6). These reports show a marked departure from most of the reports in the 1980s. Instead of a conspiracy of silence on the need to tie federal resources to improving our education system, investment in the education of our future work force to promote our long-term prosperity is now considered a top budget priority.

The Future

President Clinton and the 103rd Congress have a historic opportunity to build the foundation for the nation's economic health and growth. The American people are ready for a new direction, forged by new leaders who are willing to face the challenges ahead. President Clinton's national economic strategy, *Putting People First*, called for closing the investment gap by allocating $50 billion each year over the next four years to programs that are aimed at economic growth, while at the same time cutting the budget deficit in half. Clinton's proposal "recognizes that the only way to lay the foundation for renewed American prosperity is to spur both public and private investment. To reclaim the future, we must strive to close both the budget deficit and the investment gap."

One proposal to ensure the implementation of this strategy is to develop the federal budget into an investment budget and a consumption budget. The creation of a developmental investment budget would provide a framework for displaying and analyzing the information needed for policy makers to consider the investment effects of budget decisions. Human capital investment, such as education, work force retraining, and research and development, would be included in the budget for the future so that explicit decisions on the funding levels for each of the categories could be made.

But reordering our nation's priorities and investment in education and other programs that have long-term payoff requires not only leadership from the President and a framework for action, but the political will in Congress to make these difficult choices. It will be essential for students, parents, teachers, and educators of all stripes to send a strong and unified message to Washington that they are ready to work with the President and the Congress to restore our proud tradition of educational opportunity for all Americans.

References

Bracey, Gerald W. "The Big Lie About U.S. Education." *Phi Delta Kappan* 73 (October 1991): 104-17.

Center for Strategic and International Studies. *The CSIS Strengthening of America Commission First Report.* 1992.

Commission on Chapter 1. *Making Schools Work for Children in Poverty: A New Framework.* 10 December 1992.

Committee for Economic Development. *Children in Need: Investment Strategies for the Educationally Disadvantaged.* 1987.

Committee for Economic Development. *Restoring Prosperity: Budget Choices for Economic Growth.* 1992.

Kozol, Jonathan. *Savage Inequalities: Children In America's Schools.* New York: Harper Perennial, 1992.

National Commission on Excellence in Education. *A Nation At Risk: The Imperative for Educational Reform.* Washington, D.C., April 1983.

Commentary on Education Funding

By John F. Jennings

The topic of education funding is important because dollars undergird policy. In other words, it is difficult to carry out any policy unless sufficient funding is provided. As the ancient Romans said, money makes the world go round.

The federal government has never been the principal source of funding for education in the United States. Local school districts, colleges and universities, states, and private sources have always provided the bulk of the funding for both elementary and secondary and postsecondary education.

Federal funding has been significant, though, in showing the priorities the nation places on certain activities in the schools. For instance, the National Defense Education Act of 1958 funded the improvement of mathematics and science education and of foreign language instruction during the late 1950s and early 1960s because the country had become concerned that America had lost its lead over the Soviet Union when the U.S.S.R. launched Sputnik.

Today, the federal government concentrates its funds on improving education for disabled and disadvantaged students in elementary and secondary education and on providing loans and grants for students to pursue postsecondary education and training. Other activities receive attention also, such as improving mathematics and science education; but the bulk of the dollars are spent on the first two priorities.

The four persons writing in this section on the issue of education funding focused on the trends during the Bush Administration, with some discussion of the previous Reagan Administration. Thomas Scully was President Bush's chief advisor on matters affecting education and labor. Congressman Leon Panetta (D-Calif.) was chair of the Budget Committee in the U.S. House of Representatives in the late Eighties and early Nineties and now serves as President Clinton's director of the budget. Senator Jim Sasser (D-Tenn.) is chair of the Senate Budget Committee. And Susan Frost is executive director of the Committee for Education Funding, an umbrella group representing all the major national education organizations.

The topic they discussed is better understood if one is familiar with procedures the federal government uses to determine whether and to what degree an activity ought to be funded. The first point to know is that there is a big difference between authorizing a program at the federal level and actually funding it. The authorization process and the appropriation process are two entirely separate procedures.

A program is authorized when Congress passes a law and the President signs it, thereby creating an activity, such as a program to help gifted students. But that program, although authorized, does not become operational until it receives an appropriation in another law passed by Congress and signed by the President. Dozens of programs are authorized by federal law but never go into operation because they did not receive funding.

The authorization and appropriations processes are handled separately in the Congress. The authorizing committees for most education programs are the Education and Labor Committee in the U.S. House of Representatives and the Labor and Human Resources Committee in the U.S. Senate. Appropriations committees in each body of Congress deal with the funding for these programs.

Programs are usually authorized by Congress for terms of five years, so that any legislated changes can take effect before the law is up for review. Congress also has established three separate cycles for most elementary and secondary education, postsecondary education, and vocational and adult education programs. These laws have been written so that each cycle expires in a separate Congress, so that a full two years can be spent reviewing each area.

Thus in a six-year period each one of the broad areas of education is debated and changes in the laws are enacted. That general scheme has been followed for nearly two decades, although exceptions have occurred. In 1993 Congress will depart from these cycles to reopen the Higher Education Act for a review of President Clinton's ideas on community service. The Higher Education Act was supposed to be closed for amendment after the changes enacted in 1992, and the 103rd Congress was scheduled to focus exclusively on elementary and secondary education.

With regard to the appropriations process, no such five-year cyclical procedure can be followed, because appropriations for all federal programs are decided on an annual basis. That means that every year each federal education program must be reviewed — to some extent — by the House and Senate appropriations committees, and a determination is made on how much funding to provide. The appropriations committees are supposed to determine only whether to fund a program and the appropriate level of funding, not to change the rules in any program. Amending laws is the function of the authorizing committees.

Besides being pressured to make decisions every year on every program, the appropriations process is further complicated by the overlay of the congressional budgetary system. Before the appropriations committees can write their bills, Congress must enact a concurrent resolution setting out in broad terms the amount of revenue to be raised and the allocation of this revenue over broad areas of federal activity, such as defense, agriculture, etc. This resolution is binding only on Congress; it does not go to the President for his signature.

Timing of the appropriations process is as follows: The President submits his budget in January or February. The House and Senate Budget Committees write their budget resolutions, which are then considered by each chamber and then reconciled. Usually this process is not completed until June or July. Only after that can the 13 appropriations bills be written by the committees, enacted by the separate houses, and reconciled. This process usually takes until late September or October. Thus the whole year, each year, is filled with debate and decisions on funding federal programs. And for an individual education program to receive an appropriation, it must jump many hurdles during this year-long process.

To improve the chances of funding, a program should be included in the President's budget, preferably at a high level. The budget resolution should have a large enough amount for the general area of education to accommodate the appropriation for the program. And last, the appropriations bill must include the actual amount for the program. These are three high hurdles to jump to secure funding.

This funding procedure has become even more complicated since 1990, when the Budget Enforcement Act (BEA) became law. That statute contains a five-year budget agreement made by President Bush and the Congress in order to help reduce the deficit.

The BEA raises revenues and places ceilings on federal expenditures. It also separated — for the first three years — the funds to be spent for defense and those for domestic programs, including education. So-called "walls" were placed around these amounts so that no funds could be shifted from defense to domestic programs, and vice versa. Further-more, the third year of the agreement required domestic spending to be reduced from the levels needed to maintain programs. In other words, cutbacks in spending on domestic programs, such as education, had to occur.

Senator Sasser and Congressman John Conyers (D-Mich.) tried in 1992 to remove these "walls" so that funds could be shifted to domestic programs from defense. Their legislation lost in the House by a vote of 187 to 238 and in the Senate by a vote of 50 to 48 (due to a proce-dural rule, 60 yea votes were needed in the Senate).

The appropriations bill that then followed contained the lowest in-crease for education in many years. The second hurdle of the budget resolution was not cleared when the Sasser and Conyers' bills went down to defeat, and so the total amount available for the third hurdle − edu-cation appropriations − was low.

In the battle over the "walls" bill, President Bush fought to kill the bill since he wanted to retain as high an amount as he could for de-fense. In the Senate, 40 Republicans voted against the bill and only three for, 47 Democratic senators voted for the Sasser legislation and only eight against. The partisan breakdown in the House was as sharp as in the Senate. All 162 Republicans voted against Sasser − the Conyers bill; 186 Democrats voted for it and 76 against. One independent member voted for the bill.

These votes highlight a common pattern. Democrats usually are more inclined than Republicans to support higher spending on domestic pro-grams, including education. Republicans frequently will say that bet-ter uses ought to be made of current funds and that the answer does not rest in seeking additional appropriations.

President Clinton campaigned on investing more in education and training, and the Democrats control both the House and Senate in 1993 and 1994. Consequently, it would seem that the budget battles should turn in education's favor in the next few years.

Clinton also promised during this campaign to reduce the annual budget deficit. In his economic message to the Congress, delivered early in 1993, he explained how he wanted to achieve both objectives: invest-ment in education and training and deficit reduction. He emphasized that both objectives had to be achieved to restore the country to eco-nomic and social well-being.

The President and the Congress are now making these decisions; and in the area of education, what they decide will be influenced heavily by the debate of the last few years, as described by the various contributors to this publication. When policy is made, the past truly is prologue.